The U.S. Payment System:
Efficiency, Risk and the Role of
the Federal Reserve

The U.S. Payment System: Efficiency, Risk and the Role of the Federal Reserve

Proceedings of a Symposium on the U.S. Payment System sponsored by the Federal Reserve Bank of Richmond.

edited by
David B. Humphrey
The Federal Reserve Bank of Richmond

Kluwer Academic Publishers
Boston/Dordrecht/London

Distributors for North America:
Kluwer Academic Publishers
101 Philip Drive
Assinippi Park
Norwell, Massachusetts 02061, USA

Distributors for all other countries:
Kluwer Academic Publishers Group
Distribution Centre
Post Office Box 322
3300 AH Dordrecht, THE NETHERLANDS

Library of Congress Cataloging-in-Publication Data

The U.S. payment system: efficiency, risk, and the role of the Federal
    Reserve: proceedings of a symposium on the payment system /
    sponsored by the Federal Reserve Bank of Richmond, May 25–26,
    1988, held at Williamsburg, Virginia; edited by David B. Humphrey.
        p.   cm.
    Bibliography: p.
    Includes index.
    ISBN 0-7923-9020-2
    1. Check collection systems—United States—
Congresses.   2. Payment—United States—
Congresses.   3. Electronic funds transfers—United
States—Congresses.   4. Clearinghouse—United States—
Congresses.   I. Humphrey, David B.   II. Federal Reserve
Bank of Richmond.
HG1692.U18   1989
332.1' 13—dc20   88–8119
                                                               CIP

Printed in the United States of America

Contents

Contributing Authors

Mohsen Anvari
Professor of Finance
Faculty of Commerce and Administration
Concordia University
1445 de Maisonneuve Blvd West
Montreal, Quebec H3G 1M8, Canada

Allen N. Berger
Senior Economist
Board of Governors of the Federal Reserve System
20th St. and Constitution Ave., N.W.
Washington, DC 20551

E. Gerald Corrigan
President
Federal Reserve Bank of New York
33 Liberty St.
New York, NY 10045

James F. Dingle
Securities Advisor, Bank of Canada
Deputy Chairman, Canadian Payments Association
Bank of Canada
234 Wellington St.
Ottawa, Ontario K1A 0G9, Canada

Robert W. Eisenmenger
First Vioo President and
Chief Operating Officer
Federal Reserve Bank of Boston
600 Atlantic Ave.
Boston, MA 02106

Gerald R. Faulhaber
Professor of Public Policy and Finance
The Wharton School
University of Pennsylvania
Philadelphia, PA 19104

Marvin S. Goodfriend
Vice President and Economist
Federal Reserve Bank of Richmond
P.O.B. 27622
Richmond, VA 23261

Donald R. Hollis
Executive Vice President and Corporate Partner
The First National Bank of Chicago
One First National Plaza, Ste 0026
Chicago, IL 60670

David B. Humphrey
Vice President and Payment System Advisor
Federal Reserve Bank of Richmond
P.O.B. 27622
Richmond, VA 23261

Manuel H. Johnson
Vice Chairman
Board of Governors of the Federal Reserve System
20th St. and Constitution Ave., N.W.
Washington, DC 20551

Robert J. Listfield
Principal
Golembe Associates, Inc.
303 Congress St.
Boston, MA 02110

Robert E. Litan
Senior Fellow and Director of the Center for Economic Progress
The Brookings Institution
1775 Massachusetts Ave., N.W.
Washington, DC 20551

David L. Mengle
Research Officer
Federal Reserve Bank of Richmond
P.O.B. 27622
Richmond, VA 23261

Almarin Phillips
John C. Hower Professor of Public Policy and Professor of Law and Economics
The Wharton School
University of Pennsylvania
Philadelphia, PA 19104

Anthony M. Santomero
R. K. Mellon Professor of Finance
The Wharton School
University of Pennsylvania
Philadelphia, PA 19104

Hal S. Scott
Professor of Law
Harvard University Law School
Cambridge, MA 02138

Clifford W. Smith, Jr.
Professor of Finance and Economics
William E. Simon Graduate School of Business Administration
University of Rochester
Rochester, NY 14627

Bernell K. Stone
Harold F. Silver Professor of Finance
School of Management
Brigham Young University
672 Tanner Building
Provo, UT 84602

Donald P. Tucker
Chief Economist
Commerce, Consumer, and Monetary Affairs Subcommittee of the Committee on
   Government Operations
U.S. House of Representatives
Washington, DC 20515

Michael Urkowitz
Executive Vice President
Service Products Sector
The Chase Manhattan Bank
One Chase Manhattan Plaza
New York, NY 10081

Preface

The U.S. payment system is in the midst of a significant transition. Some of the changes to our payment system, involving its efficiency, the risks inherent in the payment process, and the role of the private and public sectors in the payment mechanism, are the subject of considerable debate and controversy.

In recent years, the Federal Reserve Bank of Richmond has played an active part in the development and implementation of policies to improve the payment process. The Bank's operations staff has represented the Federal Reserve System in work with the banking industry to help shape and implement programs to increase efficiency and reduce payment risk. Further, our Research Department has made payment system research an important part of its agenda. The mix of practical experience and research has resulted in a unique perspective on payment system issues that led us to organize a symposium on the U.S. payment system, held on May 25–26, 1988, in Williamsburg, Virginia.

Reflecting our belief in the importance of combining both practical experience and theory in addressing payment issues, we invited practitioners, scholars, and policymakers to share their ideas. The symposium provided an opportunity for those researchers who are studying payment issues to present their ideas and to have these ideas evaluated by experienced practitioners.

The symposium led to the production of a number of high-quality papers and critical commentaries that we believe are of enduring value and broad interest to those with an interest in payment matters. We greatly appreciate the contribution of time and creative energy extended by all those who participated in the program. Special thanks are due to Bruce J. Summers, Senior Vice President of the Bank, who helped plan the symposium, and David B. Humphrey, Vice President of the Bank, who edited this compendium. The resulting book is a fitting tribute to all those who made the symposium possible.

Robert P. Black, President
Jimmie R. Monhollon, First Vice President
The Federal Reserve Bank of Richmond

The U.S. Payment System: Efficiency, Risk and the Role of the Federal Reserve

CONFERENCE OVERVIEW: PROGRESS IN BRINGING ABOUT A MORE EFFICIENT AND SAFER PAYMENT SYSTEM

Robert W. Eisenmenger

Developing a payment system in any country is an interesting interdisciplinary effort requiring the skills of economists, lawyers, engineers, and politicians. The chapters that follow make it abundantly clear that the U.S. payment system is immensely complex and can evolve only with the active cooperation of all those who make, receive, and process payments. The 25,000 U.S. depository institutions that now handle transaction balances have difficulty enough agreeing among themselves on new technology, new formats, and new pricing arrangements. It is even more challenging to gain acceptance from the large number of user groups: individuals, different types of businesses, and a variety of government entities. Thus, many improvements to our payment system simply cannot be made unless all the major participants in the system benefit in roughly equal fashion, or unless some entity—such as the Federal Reserve— plays a leadership role or mandates change for the good of the whole even though the distribution of benefits is unequal.

For example, for years many experts have argued that electronics would soon usher in a checkless society. Instead, the check continues to be the preferred method of payment for 85 percent of all small-dollar payments

1

other than cash payments. Checks are preferred because they enable the writers to make payments at the time of their choosing, for variable amounts, at any location, and with paper record of payment.

Another reason checks are preferred is that the writers gain valuable float because of the inevitable delays in processing checks. Thus, even though the real resource cost for our entire society would be significantly reduced if major users agreed to make payments using the automated clearinghouse (ACH), most check writers would not gain from the change. Thus, they continue to write checks. Unless changes can be made that benefit check writers or offset their lost float benefits, most people will be writing checks 20 years from now.

Despite this and other problems, however, most of the authors of these chapters suggest that we can make good progress in reducing payment system costs and risk over the long run. In their chapter, David Humphrey and Allen Berger have demonstrated that the payment system as it now exists costs almost $60 billion annually. Any improvements that can chip away at this large total are welcome. I am optimistic that improvements can be made, for several reasons:

1. We can make many productivity improvements that do not require a totally revamped system or that can be obtained with modest regulatory changes.
2. The Electronic Data Interchange (EDI) revolution now underway could dramatically reduce costs for all corporate participants. Once corporations choose EDI, they may be induced to use electronic payments even though they lose check float.
3. The Federal Reserve System has begun to set uniform standards for check collection and electronic payments. Standards should encourage further technological improvements and bring cost reductions to the payment system.
4. Superregional banking and interstate banking will bring substantial increases in productivity. In fact, one of the major driving forces in bank mergers is the potential for payment-related operational improvements that result from consolidation.

Following are some examples of these four broad categories—productivity improvements, the EDI revolution, the role of the Federal Reserve in setting standards, and the increasing importance of interstate and superregional banking. I conclude with a brief comment about daylight overdraft risk.

Productivity Initiatives Are Still Possible Apart from Major Payment System Changes

The entire payment system has enjoyed major productivity gains in both check and electronic payment processing in recent years. In the Federal Reserve Banks, the average annual gain in labor productivity has been 2.3 percent for check processing, 17.9 percent for wire transfers, and 10.6 percent for automated clearinghouse operations during the ten-year period 1977–1986. These productivity improvements were generally accomplished with a series of incremental improvements in automation. I am sure that similar increases in productivity have occurred in the private banking sector.

Productivity gains through automation will almost certainly continue. For example, in 1987 the Federal Reserve completed a laboratory analysis of the use of digitized image technology to capture pictures of checks in a high-speed sorting environment. The resulting pictures can be manipulated on the display screen of a personal computer to increase productivity by eliminating further handling of the checks themselves while continuing to allow the extraction of any information on them. The initial results were promising, and the Federal Reserve is now doing additional applied research with IBM and Unisys. As a result of this Federal Reserve initiative, several large banks are now conducting their own R&D programs on high-speed digitized image technology in the belief that this new technology will provide an important means for increasing check-processing productivity in the coming decade.

Humphrey and Berger suggest that digitized image technology be used to take pictures of the front and back of all large-dollar checks—for example, all those over $25,000—and that collecting banks receive payment from payer banks on the basis of transmitted pictures of checks. This might permit same-day collection of most large business checks, which now take one or two days to be collected. This would dramatically reduce the float wedge incentive that now encourages corporations to use checks rather than electronic payments. To make this possible, new collection rules for large-dollar checks would be needed to permit the submission of a picture of a check for collection rather than the original check itself. The point is that this productivity improvement could be made if check collection rules were changed by regulation.

Admittedly, economics would limit the use of digitized images if this technique were applied only to the collection of large checks, which constitute a relatively small fraction of the total number of checks. The logical question is, Are there means for electronic handling of the billions of smaller consumer checks?

One interesting experiment was considered two years ago by the City National Bank in Los Angeles. At that time, it proposed the use of a retail point-of-sale (POS) terminal that would accept checks as well as debit and credit cards. The equipment would have read the MICR encoding at the bottom of the check. When the clerk punched the TOTAL button on the cash register, that information would have created an ACH message to be sent to the customer's bank. The clerk then would have simply stamped the check PAID and handed it back to the customer. The check in this case would have been used only to provide information to the terminal and a receipt record for the customer. All other parts of the transaction would have been handled electronically.

In this concept, of course, the check writer loses float, and for this and other reasons, this interesting idea was not implemented by City National Bank. To make this type of concept more acceptable, Vons Supermarket in California installed POS terminals that accept checks, debit cards, or any other identifying card. When the check or card is put through the terminal, the magnetic stripe on MICR code information is read to identify the customer. Then the supermarket debits the customer's account with an ACH entry with—and this is important—a 48-hour lag. Furthermore, there is no customer transaction charge for this service. In this case, Vons Supermarket obtains the advantage of a quick checkout procedure and an inexpensive payment system, and the customer continues to enjoy float.

In his chapter, Bernell Stone suggests that POS payments have an untapped potential of 60 billion items' annually replacing checks and cash transactions. If the Vons Supermarket set up becomes widely adopted, that potential could become reality.

The Electronic Business Data Interchange Revolution Could Be of Major Importance

Modern manufacturing and product distribution techniques—for instance, the just-in-time parts delivery strategy—require that suppliers and their customers communicate with each other in a fully automated way to gain the necessary speed and accuracy in their business relationships. The Electronic Data Interchange addresses every aspect of a business relationship. In a fully developed system, a manufacturer scans a supplier's parts catalog, queries the availability of a desired part, transmits an order, settles on a price, places a purchase order, queries the delivery status, acknowledges receipt, notifies on rejected shipments, and submits payment—all by electronic communication.

This approach can dramatically reduce costs for salaries, paper handling, postage, and most importantly, inventory. To give one example, General Motors is establishing EDI, including electronic payments, with all its 20,000 suppliers. When this process has been completed, 4.8 million payments annually, totaling $48 billion, will be automated. General Motors estimates that its annual savings from EDI will amount to $1.3 billion, or $200 per car. Because EDI savings are so all-encompassing, it is likely that corporations will be encouraged to substitute electronic payment for check payments even though they may lose some check float.

At this time, however, payment processing has not been incorporated effectively into the EDI process. Although Stone suggests that the payment message should be handled in a separate flow from corporate trade payment information, I think it is clear that the payment flows should accommodate end-to-end automation. That is, the payment message should flow from the originating corporation to the sending bank, to the receiving bank, and finally to the receiving corporation. Both the trade and payment flows should also use compatible formats so that trade information could easily be reconciled with related payment data, thereby promoting the efficiency of both commerce and banking. Thus, the issue of the banking industry's role in EDI as well as the development of compatible format architectures between electronic payments and EDI should be addressed soon. This brings up the topic of standard setting by the Federal Reserve.

Standard Setting by the Federal Reserve Should Bring Further Payment System Improvements

As mentioned earlier, 25,000 depository institutions in the United States offer check-writing privileges. In addition, hundreds of thousands of merchants and businesses endorse checks with the names and routing numbers of their banks. Thus, the check collection system is badly fragmented. The problem is not so much the size of the typical participant. After all, small businesses in agriculture and the fast-food industry have made remarkable gains in productivity during the last 20 years. Rather, it is the necessity for having all or almost all participants use standardized procedures and technology so that they can effectively interact.

For these reasons, the check business has always needed a referee and leader. In the 1950s and 1960s, when MICR coding was introduced, the Federal Reserve, the American Bankers Association, (ABA) and data-processing equipment vendors played the integrating role. More recently, the Society for Worldwide Financial Telecommunications (SWIFT) set standards for international financial transactions. And the Federal Reserve has been playing a very active role lately as a result of new regulatory power given by Congress:

1. The Federal Reserve, working with an industry advisory committee from the ABA, the Independent Bankers Association of America (IBAA), the Bank Administration Institute (BAI), and the thrift and credit union industries, has tested and established standardized procedures and time limits for handling returned checks. The new standards will significantly reduce the risks of loss for banks of first deposit and their customers.
2. The Federal Reserve, working with the same advisory group and also with the American National Standards Institute (ANSI), has established endorsement standards for banks of first deposit and subsequent endorsers. Within a year, these new standards should significantly speed up the flow of returns and simultaneously reduce processing costs.
3. The Federal Reserve is exploring a machine-readable endorsement standard, using bar code or another technology, that may enable paying banks and intermediaries to automate the reading of the bank of first deposit endorsement. Such a development could significantly increase the efficiency of the return process.
4. The Federal Reserve also hopes to take a leading role in establishing banking industry standards for digitized image processing. It is working on standards for legibility as well as technical standards for the interchange of digitized electronic information. With such standards, images created by one bank processor using vendor A's digitized image equipment could be transmitted to and received by another bank using vendor B's equipment.
5. The Federal Reserve has just established an electronic payment format advisory committee. The goal is to develop format architecture standards that would enable depository institutions to exchange different types of electronic payment information with all other depositories as well as with their own customers in a fully automated fashion. This should encourage the development of EDI and the increased use of electronic payments.

Thus, the Federal Reserve is working to increase the efficiency of the dominant check system and simultaneously to advance the cause of electronic payments.

Superregional Banking and Interstate Banking Will Bring Increased Productivity and Increased Competition

Humphrey and Berger have demonstrated that mergers of individual banks into superregional entities and mergers of institutions located in different regions will significantly reduce the float wedge and bring about large real-cost savings.

Such mergers will also increase the ability of large depository institutions to compete with the Federal Reserve in the check business. As more checks become "on us" items and as more checks are directly exchanged between collecting and paying banks, the Federal Reserve Banks will process an ever-smaller fraction of the aggregate total of all checks. Moreover, they will be handling the payments directed to the lower-volume, more remote, higher-cost end points. This will make it increasingly difficult for the Federal Reserve to match costs and revenues and simultaneously maintain a universal nationwide payment system. In his chapter, Don Tucker suggests that the Federal Reserve has a substantial amount of market power and should be more generous in its treatment of private correspondent banks. However, we must also remember that the inevitable result of banking consolidation in the United States will be a relatively less important processing role for the Federal Reserve Banks.

I would now like to make a few optimistic comments about controlling payment system risk. For years the Federal Reserve Banks, and some large commercial banks have provided large amounts of intraday overdraft credit to their customers, free of charge. Generally, the financial risk associated with any particular credit is very small, but the total exposure is huge. Recent publications by Board of Governors staff, a recent speech by Roland Bullard, and the chapter by Serald Faulhaber, Almarin Phillips, and Anthony Santomero all suggest that this problem can best be solved with pricing or clearing balances rather than rationing devices. The daylight overdraft problem has baffled the banking industry for the past ten years. Fortunately, we now seem to be reaching a consensus about direction, even though implementation will undoubtedly raise many thorny issues.

I PAYMENT MARKET EFFICIENCY

Part I focuses on payment efficiency and why apparently cheaper electronic payment methods have not replaced paper checks, as has been widely expected since the 1960s. Robert Eisenmenger, in the preceding conference overview chapter, addressed efficiency issues in the U.S. payment system, a system that costs almost $60 billion annually. His concern was how this cost may be reduced through policies that stimulate the substitution of electronic payments for paper checks. For corporate users of the payment system, he suggested, potential gains from the implementation of electronic data interchange (EDI) will be great enough to offset the loss of check float if electronic methods are used. The major cost savings would be from making invoice and accounting information electronic along with the payment. Eisenmenger also touched on several other future developments in the payment market that can lower costs and increase productivity. For example, bar code technology (as is currently used in supermarkets) could speed the processing of check return items, and digitizing the check image would make check collection electronic even though consumers would continue to write checks.

The next two chapters should read together, for they are complements. Bernell Stone presents a concise yet broadly based summary of the many, essentially nonquantifiable, reasons why electronic payments have not readily replaced checks. Stone documents the various institutional barriers, market requirements, and user uncertainties that always attend the development of a new product. In the case of electronic payments, such practical considerations drive a wedge between the new technology and its ultimate acceptance in the marketplace. In addition, Stone closely examines a number of important areas where electronic payments have been or could be applied, such as controlled disbursement, cash concentration, bill payment, and point-of-sale. These examples are used to outline the main reasons why electronic payment applications have met or failed to meet expectations.

One generalization to be drawn from Stone's analysis is that each potential application of electronic payments is unique in some important way, while the electronic product being developed has not been tailored sufficiently to meet important user and application needs. Also, the fact that electronic payment is a multiparty decision is often ignored because of the difficulty of dealing with it. Banks and other financial institutions are the main suppliers of electronic payments, but the net gain to them can be minimal because such payments undercut their output and their revenue from providing check services. Thus, consumers who wish to use electronic payments often find that their banks are unenthusiastic suppliers. Even if some banks supply the service, other banks or retailers, especially at the point-of-sale, are not set up to receive payments electronically. Stone ends on an optimistic note by outlining three areas where electronic payments could be most profitably applied and discussing the market requirements for successful realization of these applications.

Commentary on the Stone chapter is provided by Michael Urkowitz, who supports many of the reasons given for the currently slow substitution of electronic for check payments. But he is optimistic that many of the barriers, particularly for EDI, will be lessened or removed in the near future. While Urkowitz agrees with

Stone's approach of segmenting the market for electronic payments by product categories, he suggests a further segmentation: banks and other suppliers could identify differences among end users for the same electronic application.

As mentioned, the Stone chapter should be read along with the next chapter, by David Humphrey and Allen Berger. While Stone deals with essentially nonquantifiable reasons why electronic payments have not lived up to expectations, Humphrey and Berger discuss one of the few quantifiable aspects. This concerns the importance of giving up check float when electronic payments are adopted. Viewed from the perspective of society as a whole, electronic payments are shown to be considerably cheaper than checks. But when the distributional benefits accruing to individual users are factored in, the situation is reversed. The distributional benefits reflect float transfer payments that, for society as a whole, net to zero and involve low real resource costs. But to individual users, receiving float benefits makes checks, on average, the cheaper way to pay. The result is a "market failure" in the payment market, because check costs to individual users do not well reflect the real costs involved and resources are misallocated, with too few electronic payments being used.

Humphrey and Berger quantify float and real resource costs for nine different payment instruments, including such nonelectronic payment instruments as cash, checks, credit cards, travelers checks, and money orders. The electronic instruments are also broadly based and include automated clearing house (ACH), point-of-sale (POS), automatic teller machine (ATM) bill payment, and wire transfers. Costs are also broken out, for the first time, by major user groups (consumers, business, and government). Since business checks are written for the largest dollar amounts and often take the longest time to collect, they represent the area where monetary disincentives to use electronic payments are greatest. Several policy recommendations are offered that could reduce the market failure brought about by check float.

Commentary on the Humphrey-Berger chapter is provided by Donald Hollis. He takes strong issue with parts of the authors' analyses, specifically the suggestion that the Federal Reserve reconsider an earlier proposal to use electronic presentment for large-dollar checks. While this would be one way to reduce the float benefit to check writers and thereby provide less disincentive for using electronic payments, Hollis considers such market intervention to be inappropriate.

The last chapter in part I, on the Canadian payment system, is by Mohsen Anvari. Like the United States, and unlike Europe, Canada relies heavily on the use of checks. Check users in Canada, however, obtain no (free) float. Further, the system in Canada is arguably more efficient than in the United States because the more concentrated nature of Canadian banking reduces the number of times an item requires handling before being collected. Payment market failure is not a problem in Canada; float benefits are zero, and individual check user costs thus reflect real social costs. Even so, electronic payments have not made great inroads into areas where checks are typically used. Anvari ascribes part of the problem to the fact that check payments in Canada are very efficient. Thus, the real-cost differential between checks and electronic payments in Canada is lower than in the United States and thereby provides smaller marginal efficiency gains to users of electronics. But mostly the reason likely lies in the many practical barriers to electronic payment use, described by Stone and also by Anvari in the Canadian context. Still, opportunities for cooperation in shifting to lower-cost electronic payments may be greater in Canada, for two reasons. First, Canada has a concentrated banking system, making interbank cooperation easier. Second, a noncompetitive relationship exists between the Bank of Canada and commerical banks, since the central bank, unlike the Federal Reserve, does not supply payment services.

Commentary on the Anvari paper is provided by James Dingle. He supports the view that expanded use of electronic payments in Canada is largely driven by diverse cultural and institutional factors along with the cost of labor (used intensively in checks) relative to the cost of data communication and computation (used intensively in electronics). Examining the diverse rates of acceptance of electronic payments in the United States, Canada, and a number of European countries, he finds a similar dual explanation of institutional factors and relative input costs rather than a dominance of one or the other.

1 THE ELECTRONIC PAYMENT INDUSTRY: CHANGE BARRIERS AND SUCCESS REQUIREMENTS FROM A MARKET SEGMENTS PERSPECTIVE

Bernell K. Stone

This chapter treats electronic payments as an issue of technology displacement. Thus, the concerns are product design and development and the creation of a production-sales-support infrastructure. Rather than viewing the automated clearing house (ACH) as an alternative to checks and other contemporary payment mechanisms, we focus on technology displacement for several important segments of the payment market. This chapter considers two broad classes of use: successes, and opportunities yet to be realized, the latter being payment uses, such as corporate trade payments, where there is currently very little transaction volume.

A major thesis of this chapter is that those usage categories with the greatest potential volume and also with the greatest potential for economic and societal benefit are the areas (1) having the most complex product design-development problems; (2) requiring production-sales-support capabilities that transcend existing payment service organizations; and (3) involving significant noneconomic barriers to displacement.

We first discuss technology displacement, then briefly review barriers to ACH progress, assess recent progress in advancing electronic payments, identify major usage segments, discuss the product requirements and the

13

barriers to be overcome, assess implications for ACH system features, and conclude by considering the major issues to be resolved

Technology Assimilation and Deplacement

Technology assimilation refers to the conversion of a technical capability into an accpeted, widely used product. Figure 1–1 depicts the three stages in most technology assimilation situations: gestation, rapid growth, and saturation and mature growth.

Gestation is the period during which the product is defined, refined, and tested on the market. This is a period of market research, user education, and product testing and development. During the gestation phase, market awareness grows. Capabilities for producing, selling, distributing, and supporting the product are developed. Organizations are created to provide this support.

Rapid growth is the second stage of technology assimilation, during which volume grows significantly and customer awareness of the product becomes widespread. In its early phase, rapid growth is often constrained by limits on production capacity and support but in the later portion of this stage, there is adequate or even surplus production capacity. Thus, prices often decline over the course of the rapid growth stage, providing further incentives for accelerated volume growth.

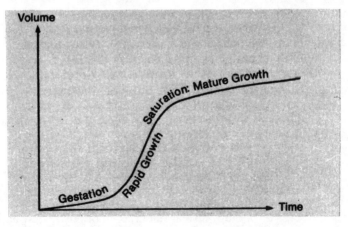

Figure 1–1.   Typical growth stages for a new technology-based product. Source: Stone (1986c)

Saturation and mature growth occur when virtually all potential users have adopted the new product. Sales growth then depends on replacement, upgrading to new models, and growth in the population.

Gestation Attributes

It is useful to break the gestation stage itself into components. *Early gestation* is characterized by market research, by efforts at converting a technical ability into products, or at least product concepts. It is a time of considerable research and development. Often refinement and extension of the basic technical capability are required.

Middle gestation involves fairly well-defined product concepts, although product development and refinements are still very much in process. There are usually conferences on the product opportunity. Often newsletters are started. A technical and popular literature may emerge, including books, if the technology and product opportunity are both economically important and complex. Trade associations may be formed if there are many potential product-service providers. When pertinent, standards efforts are usually started in the middle gestation stage.

Late gestation is characterized by product announcements, pilot-tests, and many new entrants. There are often false starts—the pilot-tests indicate problems, and the product must be refined or redesigned. There are usually many product variations competing in parallel for acceptance by the early adopters. Many products cater to niche needs. There may be customization for important users as competitors seek to test their products and gain market credibility. Finally, the early adopters begin using some of the products. Volume begins to grow. Awareness among potential users increases.

Custom production evolves into organized, standardized production. The focus shifts from production to selling. Distribution-selling-support organizations are built. There is considerable training.

The Importance of Market Segmentation

It is common to say that gestation is over when 5–10 percent of saturation volume is reached, especially if volume growth is accelerating explosively. The two criteria of 5–10 percent volume and accelerating growth suggest that the ACH is still in gestation. In terms of check displacement, current

ACH volume is less than 2 percent of the total check-draft-ACH volume. Moreover, the fairly stable growth rate of the 1980s does not suggest the explosive, accelerating growth characteristic of the rapid growth phase in most technology displacement situations. Thus, from the perspective of the overall check displacement market, the ACH seems still to be in the gestation stage.

For anyone familiar with the ACH, classifying its current stage of gestation as early, middle, or late would seem difficult. It seems to have at least some of the characteristics of each gestation stage. For instance, corporate trade payments seem still to be in middle gestation, with several formats (CTP, CTX, CCDX) being efforts at product definition. Payroll and insurance debits seem beyond gestation, in steady, if not rapid, growth. Variable-amount bill payment is probably in early gestation.

It seems that different usage segments of the ACH are in very different stages of technology displacement. A major theme of this chapter is that meaningful analysis of, and forecasting for, ACH growth requires detailed segmentation of the payment market by usage categories and possibly other differentiating attributes. Broad generalizations about the overall electronic payment market as a presumably homogeneous technology displacement opportunity have been, in this author's opinion, a major reason for a long history of overly optimistic forecasts for rapid growth of electronic payment volume. Moreover, meaningful product design and development as well as good network planning and good product distribution-sales-support planning require detailed evaluation and understanding of segment characteristics.

Viewing the check-draft-ACH market as an undifferentiated payment service is very misleading. Some payment usage segments are out of gestation and into rapid growth. Others are still in early gestation: for instance, variable-amount bill payments, nonrecurring bill payments, trade payments, and point-of-sale are still in gestation and seemingly still working on product definition, design, and development.

In the government sector, social security, other retirement-pension benefits, and payroll are clearly out of gestation and into rapid growth. For instance, the ACH has 30–40 percent of the social security market.

In the commercial sector, total volume is still under 1 percent of the total commercial check-draft volume. But payroll, pension-retirement payments, preauthorized insurance debits, and cash concentration seem to be out of gestation and into rapid growth. Interestingly, cash concentration, with over 90 percent of the retail deposit concentration now in ACH transfers, seems to have already completed rapid growth and entered the saturation and mature growth stage of technology displacement.

Key Segment Questions

We may ask some questions about differences in usage segment penetration:

1. Why have some segments emerged from gestation while most, especially those with the greatest volume potential, have not yet done so?
2. Why has cash concentration of retail deposits been so successful? What differentiates it from other corporate payments?
3. What key attributes make a segment a good candidate for rapid growth?
4. What attributes make a segment a bad candidate for rapid growth?
5. What barriers or obstacles impede ACH volume growth, and to what extent are these barriers segment-specific?

Clearly, the ability to answer these questions and to assess accurately the potential market for pertinent segments are central to planning both overall ACH system evolution and the ACH strategy and product focus for depository institutions. In fact, gaining the understanding to answer these questions well and to do meaningful market analysis and planning is part of the infrastructure building that typically characterizes gestation activites.

The Speed of Rapid Growth

Characterizing the second stage of technology displacement as rapid growth can be misleading in that the term *rapid* might suggest that product adoption takes place over just a few years. Figure 1–2 summarizes the time to go from 10 percent to 50 percent market penetration for a variety of household technologies. Only black-and-white and color television took less than 10 years, although both were in gestation for more than 30 years. VCRs, the next fastest technology, took slightly more than 10 years to peretrate the market, though VCR adoption is commonly cited in the popular press and the professional literature as an example of ultrarapid adoption time.

The personal computer is another product often cited as an instance of very fast adoption. Yet PCs required almost 12 years to go from 10 percent of the estimated mature market penetration to the currently estimated penetration of roughly 50 percent. And microcomputer use in business has yet to reach even 25 percent of most industry estimates of mature volume.

PCs and household products represent much easier technology assimila-

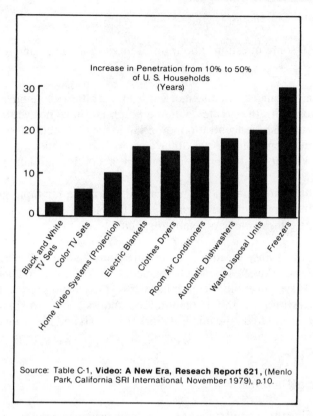

Figure 1–2.   Speed of diffusion of major consumer products. Reproduced from
Displacing the Check, (1983).

tion situations than most payment market segments, at least from the
viewpoint of both the adoption decision and the requirements for production, distribution, sales, and product support. Thus, 10 years for going
from 10 percent to 50 percent of saturation penetration should be viewed
as a relatively fast case of rapid growth. It is reasonable to expect most
usage segments of the payment market to have rapid growth periods of
10 years.

Industry Structure

Figure 1–3 depicts the structure of the electronic payment industry. The
term *industry* is an attempt to focus attention on the production and dis-

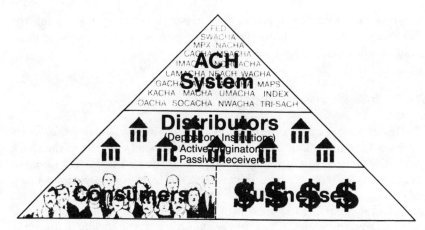

Figure 1–3.   The industrial structure of ACH payment services. Source: Stone (1986c)

tribution structure in a framework analogous to product manufacture, sales, and support. Such a structure is appropriate for the automotive industry, where there are a limited number of manufacturers and many distributors. It is common in banking to talk about services and service products. In this chapter, the term *product* is used interchangeably with *service product*. *Payment product* means an organized, structured servicing capability for meeting customers' payment and payment-related needs.

Particular payment usage categories (such as point-of-sale or consumer bill payment) will require different payment products. Again, to draw analogy with the automotive industry, there are differences between needs for large trucks, small trucks, utility vehicles, and automobiles, and these are reflected in product differences.

In talking about payment products, it is important to understand that a product is much more than merely "the means to transfer funds between bank accounts," although fund transfer is a component of most electronic payment products.

To understand this point, it is useful to look at check-based payment products. We consider two examples: controlled disbursing and cash concentration.

The Controlled Disbursement Product

Controlled dispersing is the ability to write checks on a control account so that once checks are presented to the drawee bank, they are processed quickly with a same-day report to the company. The company informs the cash manager of the daily funding requirement so that the manager can avoid an overdraft without having an excess balance.

The Cash Concentration Product

The check-based cash concentration product involves an elaborate infrastructure of information support and processing in addition to the check itself. The company, a bank agent, but more often a third-party information support service, receives deposit reports from company retail units, accumulates the deposit data, executes a variety of control tests (such as units not reporting or departures from normal deposit amounts), and generally reports control data to the company. At a specified time, the third-party information service transfers the deposit data to the company's concentration bank. Then the concentration bank, acting as an agent for the company, creates depository transfer checks (DTCs) for the appropriate amount from blank-check stock by encoding the MICR line appropriate to each drawee bank and depository accout used by the company's retail units and enters the completed depository transfer checks into the check-processing system. The company is given information on deposit activity, generally via the concentration bank's balance reporting system so that the cash manager at corporate headquarters knows the availability schedule at the concentration bank from eacy day's concentrated deposits.

In this check-based concentration product, the DTC is a small part of the total information control and transfer service. It is also a small part of the total cost per concentrated deposit. The DTC clearing and settlement is a product building block for the concentration service, just as a motor and wheels are components of the automobile. The concentration product is the overall capability to gather deposit information, perform control tests, report on control violations to the company, transfer data to the concentration bank, create MICR-encoded checks in an automated way, report immediately on the cash concentration activity via balance reporting system, and then report in detail later, generally via both the analysis report and an electronic bank statement.

In terms of payment function, the ACH ability to transfer dollars between accounts is the functional analogue of the depository transfer check. Thus, the ACH transfer ability is a product building block in the same sense as the DTC. In fact, the structure of the ACH debit makes it possible to substitute an ACH debit for a DTC without significant change in the rest of the concentration product. Therefore, it is logical to expect the ACH debit to displace the depository transfer check in cash concentration, since it is less costly to create than the DTC and since the network cost for ACH clearing and settlement is comparable to the network charge for check clearing and settlement.

Cash concentration is used not only to illustrate the difference in a payment-based product and the clearing-settlement component of that product. It is one of the few payment usage categories where simple substitution of ACH transactions for checks (drafts) is viable. Thus, we shall return to this example to analyze ACH successes vis-à-vis areas where the ACH has yet to realize significant volume.

Industry Complexity

To continue the analogy with automobile manufacture, it is useful to think of payment clearing and settlement as analogous to a motor—a crucial component necessary for every car and truck but only part of the total from the viewpoint of the final purchaser.

It is here that the complexity of the payment business complicates industrial structure considerations. In check-based payment products, banks use clearing-settlement services as part of particular payment products, such as controlled disbursement or cash concentration.

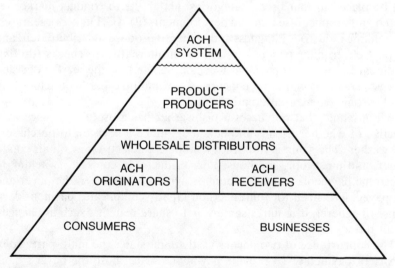

Figure 1–4.   The industrial structure of electronic payments: a more complex but complete picture.

The payment product creation is analogous to a car assembly plant, where motor, body, and other parts are combined in the final product. In car production, there is a vertically integrated manufacturer who provides dealers with a ready-to-sell product. Thus, when clearing and settlement are viewed as a product component for either check-based or ACH-based payment products, the product creation and final assembly are shifted to banks and other depository institutions, who are the nominal distributors.

With regard to checks, we can think of major banks that provide correspondent services as final manufacturers and wholesale distributors who resell to the final dealers. Figure 1–4 depicts this more complex structure.

While such a structure has emerged in check-based services, the role of the correspondent as product assembler and wholesale distributor is still evolving in electronic payments. However, there is some evidence of banks providing ACH processing as a correspondent service and, in the GM system, of banks reselling access to a customized electronic payment service to other banks as a correspondent service.

Displacement Barriers

In Stone (1986a; 1986b; 1986c) and Stone and White (1986a; 1986b), barriers to ACH progress were noted and discussed extensively. These barriers can be placed in four broad categories: (1) ability to conduct market research and product research and development, (2) ACH network features, (3) banking industry willingness and ability to produce, distribute, sell, and support electronic payment services as an alternative to checks (drafts), credit cards, and other payment mechanisms, and (4) the market decision process, generally requiring concurrence of multiple parties to change to an electronic payment alternative.

A household that purchases a dishwasher has a useful appliance irrespective of whether friends and neighbors make a decision to purchase a dishwasher. The same is true for a hammer, an electric saw, in air conditioner, and most tools and household products. In contrast, switching to electronic payments generally requires agreement between the payer and the payee. The need for joint decision greatly complicates payment decisions. In general, it requires some way to share benefits, such as changed credit terms.

The concurrence of two parties vastly understates the multi-party complexity of payments. To provide payment service, both the payer's bank and the payee's bank must participate. Moreover, in many usage segments, such as trade payments, an active receiving institution is crucial to benefit realization.

A critical economic distinction between electronic payments and checks is that electronic payments involve a relatively high fixed cost with very low variable cost. For a business to justify investment in new systems and conversion to electronic payments, it requires volume. For a bank to justify investment in a higher fixed-cost payment service, it must consider not only the issue of adequate volume but also the potential loss of existing check-based business. Viewed across the entire banking industry, the problem is more than just volume. To the extent that individual banks would have to invest in relatively high fixed-cost delivery-support systems, the logical long-run industry structure is a few low-cost service providers. Hence, banks, anticipating an erosion of profitable check and other nonelectronic payment services and a long-run loss of business, are reluctant to invest in electronic payment services. This reluctance is reflected today in the small number of active ACH originators and the even smaller number of active receivers, especially in markets like trade payments.

Current industry organization suffers from the high number of passive ACH banks and other depository institutions. A majority of banks in the regional associations are not inclined to invest in ACH improvements. In contrast to an organization like SWIFT, the National Automated Clearing House Association (NACHA), an association of regional associations, lacks membership commitment in terms of resources for ACH development.

As a bank's bank, the Fed is primarily a provider of network, processing, and settlement services. Moreover, it is limited by the 1980 Monetary Control Act to cost markup pricing. Thus, its total investment in research and development is constrained by ACH volume and logically invested in its own service delivery network rather than in bank products, software, and service capabilities.

To summarize, ACH volume involves a complex interaction of multiparty decisions. There is a chicken-and-egg dilemma. To view electronic payments favorably, various parties must be convinced that there is profitable volume for them. But volume grows only when there is investment in ACH service capabilities, in distribution-sales-support activities, and adoption decisions by pioneer users. As with the early stages of telephone and television, complex multiparty interdependence can mean very long gestation periods.

Progress in Infrastructure Creation: 1980–1988

The 1980s have been a decade of progress in building infrastructure for electronic payments. The most significant progress has occurred in the

ACH system per se rather than in the crucial areas of (1) defining, designing, and developing products and (2) creating necessary infrastructure for producing, distributing, selling, and supporting the products. This section highlights the progress in infrastructure creation. Subsequent sections deal with product design and development and production-sales-support in the context of particular payment usage segments.

Fed Product Orientation

A major structural change that occurred in the early 1980s was the Federal Reserve's approach to the ACH. With service pricing mandated by the 1980 Monetary Control Act, the Federal Reserve became more product-service-oriented and focused on efficiency and the need to be competitive with private-sector service alternatives. For the ACH, this change was particularly dramatic. First, the Federal Reserve changed its view of itself as a service provider. After 1981 the Federal Reserve viewed itself as an integrated provider rather than as a contractor providing services to NACHA and the regional ACH associations. Second, the Federal Reserve appointed a product director and product manager for electronic payments and thereby began a much stronger service and customer orientation.

Much of the progress summarized in the rest of this section is attributable to the Federal Reserve's increased orientation towards service and cost.

Processing Efficiency: Cost Enhancements

One of the most important areas of progress in the ACH is the cost per item. This improvement is a combination of volume growth and significant efficiency improvements in Federal Reserve processing. In 1981 the price of a standard ACH interregional transaction involved an 80 percent subsidy. Thus, the effective cost per item at the time pricing was implemented in 1981 was roughly 24 cents per electronic funds transfer (EFT) transaction. The unsubsidized cost for an interregional transaction today is roughly one-tenth this amount. Figure 1–5 portrays this cost trend, providing a conservative estimate of future values for the interregional cost of the basic transactions of prearranged payment and deposit (PPD) and cash concentration and disbursement (CCD).

The improvement in the transaction cost per item is attributable to three factors: volume growth, pricing structure, and efficiency improvements. Volume growth provides more transactions to cover fixed costs and thus

COST OF BATCH EFT AT CENTRAL SWITCH

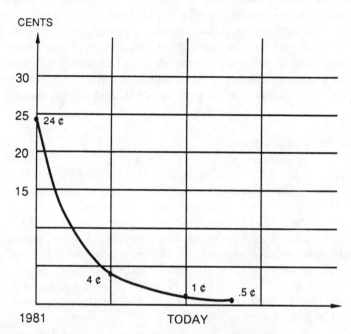

Figure 1–5.   Estimates of ACH cost per item since 1981.

lowers the average cost per item. The pricing structure now charges explicitly for previously unpriced services such as tape mounting and storage and for return items. To the extent that ACH revenue arises from previously unpriced activities, the cost trend in figure 1–5 will overstate the cost per item benefits from volume growth and efficiency improvements. However, the point of figure 1–5 is not the precise numerical improvement in ACH prices but rather the trend and ACH clearing and settlement prices vis-à-vis comparable check charges. The ACH is clearly cost-competitive with checks today, and the future will strengthen this advantage. One of the major barriers to ACH viability, cost relative to checks, has clearly been overcome.

The third cost improvement factor is efficiency enhancement carried out by the Federal Reserve and non-Fed regional processors. Both the Federal Reserve and the other regional processors have improved processing efficiency substantially. Some of this improvement probably results from experience gained in ACH processing. However, much of it is attributable to specific cost reduction activities, namely: (1) standardization of Federal Reserve processing that involved a reduction of the number of different computer operating systems in the various districts from three to one, (2) a reduction in the number of regional processing centers from 34 to 26, (3) refinements in software and operating efficiency, and (4) improvements in communication efficiencies as the Federal Reserve Communication System FRCS80 was phased in. Trends in communication costs and functionality promise even more dramatic improvement as FRCS90 is implemented.

Interface to Service Providers

A major defect in the ACH system has been a reliance on magnetic tape and diskettes as the major data interface mechanisms. Like checks, these mechanisms depend on physical delivery and thus on some form of transportation. Therefore, ACH transactions face the same weather and other transportation-related delays as checks. Moreover, the ACH must provide for adequate time both for physical delivery from originating institutions and for physical delivery to remote receiving locations.

Transactions received and delivered by direct telecommunications are not increasing, but computer-to-computer communications are, using PC software and bulk data software.

PC Software. The PC software gives a low-volume originator or receiver an efficient interface to the Federal Reserve compared to magnetic tape and diskette. Moreover, compatibility of this software with the Federal Reserve's wire transfer software for PCs means a very low cost to use the PC software.

Bulk Data Software. This software enables the high-volume processor to transmit computer-to-computer directly into the ACH or to receive computer-to-computer transmissions from the ACH directly in a format that is compatible with the transmissions between regional ACH processing centers.

Electronic Functionality

With the implementation of pricing that reflects the cost of tape and diskette handling and with the comparative economic advantages of direct communication, it is just a matter of time until virtually all interface with the ACH is electronic. The computer-to-computer communication interface has significant implications for cost and service functionality.

When it becomes independent of physical location to ensure reasonable delivery times, the ACH can have fewer processing points. Therefore, the fixed cost of ACH processing will decrease further. For instance, moving from 26 processing centers to 12 centers could cut the fixed cost per item by more than 50 percent.

Tape handling and storage are major components of the variable cost of ACH processing today. Elimination of these components provides additional efficiencies and the ability to reduce transaction costs still futher. The long-run trend in long-distance communications is a dramatic reduction in costs compared to the gradually increasing cost of long-distance transportation, labor (involved in tape and diskette handling), and physical space (for tape equipment and storage). With the implementation of Federal Reserve's communication system FRCS90, the communication efficiency enhancements will further contribute to cost reductions.

In addition to allowing significant cost improvements, moving to direct data communication as the primary data receipt and delivery mechanism is critical for realizing the service functionality benefits of automated payments in terms of greater speed, security, and reliability. As long as the ACH is dependent on the physical movement of tapes and diskettes, it is virtually impossible to differentiate the ACH from checks, since both are subject to comparable time delays.

Pricing and software for a direct interface are inplace, but it will take several years to accomplish the transformation in the primary interface mechanism.

Returns

ACH return items processing was a major headache in the early 1980s. One bank reported that its average time to receive returns was 11 days. Moreover, most returns involved creation of paper documents with their inherent costs and incompatibility with an automatic electronic system. Happily, return item processing is a much smaller problem today. A mechanism for electronic returns and appropriate pricing of paper return instruments have greatly improved return times and costs. Nevertheless, more can clearly be done. Returns processing is an area where a direct communication interface can effect a dramatic improvement. With direct links, automated returns can be back to the originating institution on the next processing cycle A one business-day return time is clearly an area where the ACH can and should dominate checks.

Reliability

Reliability refers to the certainty that an ACH item correctly entered into the system will be delivered first to the receiving institution and then to the transaction receiver's account correct and on time. While reliability is greatly enhanced today compared with the early 1980s, the ACH still has room for considerable progress. As noted by Richard Oliver at the NACHA conference in Dallas in March 1988, ACH reliability is still inferior to that of checks.

System reliability should be enhanced by a direct communications link between the ACH network and the originating and receiving institutions and by attention to operating procedures. Reliability, however, depends critically on the operations of the originating and receiving institutions. While an electronic system not dependent on physical transportation should theoretically dominate checks, time and effort are required to realize this potential.

New Service Capabilities

The creation of the night cycle processing option in 1979 is an important service enhancement. Moreover, delivery cutoff times have been made progressively later. These later times have been passed on to cutomers by depository institutions, especially those banks servicing the cash concentration market. Later delivery deadlines were the crucial factor in making the ACH viable for cash concentration.

The night cycle has been complemented by the Sunday delivery option, again an especially attractive feature for cash concentration.

The other major area of capability innovation is addendum information transactions. This effort has focused especially on facilitating trade payments, which generally require remittance advice information. Three formats (CTP, CTX, and CCDX) have been introduced. The CTP format was pilot-tested in 1983 and pronounced a success with much fanfare. However, very little volume developed. Experience has shown that the CTP format has many problems, some of which are noted by Stone and White (1986a), White (1985a), and Woo (1985).

The CTP capability is typical of the gestation stage of technology displacement, namely false starts from which more refined products emerge. Thus, the CTP effort should be viewed as part of the market learning that must take place in introducing new technology-based products.

The CTX and CCDX information addenda are two new transactions that take complementary approaches to remittance advice. The CTX transaction supports the ANSI X12.4 remittance advice standard and allows for variable-length information records in contrast to the fixed records of the CTP transaction. These two transactions are discussed further in the context of products for serving the trade payment usage segment.

Progress: Synthesis and Critique

This review of ACH enhancements indicates that much has been done in building infrastructure. However, most of the progress lies in refining the basic network capability of transferring electronic payment records between depository institutions. Even the night cycle and the Sunday delivery window are expansions in basic payment record processing. The only significant effort at new functional capabilities is the addition of the new transactions for including addenda records, namely CTP, CTX, and CCDX. But these transactions have not yet generated significant volume. Their viability as a volume-generating enhancement is yet to be proved in the marketplace.

If the ACH network is viewed as a product building block, then it is clear that product designers have a less costly and better tool for transferring funds between accounts at different depository institutions. Extrapolation of the current improvement trends implies that the ACH should be a dramatically better tool by the early 1990s. Moreover, communication costs and functionality likely for FRCS90 suggest that the current favorable trends in cost, quality, and reliability should even be surpassed.

In contrast to the very favorable improvement record for the basic network tool, there seems to be much less progress in converting the tool into viable products and building the production, sales, and support infrastructure. Since commercial banks and other depository institutions are the designated distributors, this failure must be viewed as a problem of distribution infrastructure.

The following sections evaluate ACH successes and failures for particular usage segments and then return to the issue of the production-sales-support infrastructure and the ability of the banking industry to improve it.

Market Segments

In many discussions of electronic payments and their failure to displace checks, drafts, and other contemporary payment mechanisms, it is common to treat payment as a homogeneous capability without regard for the many different types of payments. This undifferentiated view of payment is reflected in the design and organization of the ACH system in two ways.

Value Transfer. The essence of an ACH transaction is the use of computer communication technology to process an electronic check image. More precisely, the two basic ACH transactions (PPD and CCD) provide the ability to move dollars between accounts of two different depository institutions. The PPD (CCD) credit transaction is the equivalent of a check or draft written by the payer and deposited into the payee's account. The PPD (CCD) debit transaction is the equivalent of a preauthorized check or draft created by the payee (or payee's agent) and deposited directly into the payee's account.

Required Transactions. As noted in Table 1–1, the ACH has a number of transactions in addition to the standard PPD and CCD transactions. However, the only mandatory transactions that all ACH members must be able to receive and process are the PPD and CCD transactions. All others are discretionary at this time and are supported by only a few depository institutions. The discretionary transactions currently constitute a very small proportion of ACH volume. Thus, for all practical purposes, it is fair to say that the ACH today is an electronic mechanism for transferring value between accounts at depository institutions, embellished by some optional, but relatively unused, discretionary capabilities for information support of particular payment transactions.

Information Control Requirements

As noted, the PPD and CCD transactions are the electronic equivalents of checks (drafts). Given a dollar amount and the account numbers and institution identifiers of the payer and payee, value transfer can take place. Therefore, one can argue that *the necessary requirement* for the ACH to displace checks has been met. It can even be argued that since the PPD and CCD records include the payment amount and account numbers and institutional identifiers of *both* payer and payee, these ACH records are superior to the check MICR line, which initially has only the payer's

Table 1-1. Summary of ACH Transaction Formats

Consumer Transactions		Mandatory[a]	Record
PPD	Prearranged Payment & Deposit	Yes	94 char.
MTE	Machine Transaction Entry	No	94 char.
CIE	Customer Initiated Entry	No	94 char.
POS	Point-of-Sale	No	94 char.
SHR	Shared Network Transaction	No	94 char.
Corporate Transactions[b]		Mandatory	Record
CCD	Cash Concentration and Disbursement	Yes	94 char.
CCDX	CCD Plus	No	94 char. + one addendum
CTP	Corporate Trade Payments	No	94 char. +16 to 4990 addendum
CTX	Corporate Trade Exchange	No	94 char. + variable = length addendum

[a] *Mandatory* means that an institution belonging to the ACH must be able to receive and properly process this transaction.

[b] CCDX addendum is in ANSI X12 standard with a maximum length of 94 characters; CTX is ANSI X12 standard with greater length, essentially the character capacity of CTP.

account number and institution and which requires encoding to add the payment amount to the MICR line so that it is machine processible.

The problem with the above logic is the assertion that the data in the PPD and CCD records constitute *the* necessary requirement for most classes of payments. When viewed as a payment product, the check (draft) per se is only part of a generally complex information control structure that requires additional capabilities beyond the value exchange data of the standard PPD and CCD transaction records.

The information control requirements vary across various types of payment transactions, for example payroll, point-of-sale payments, and corporate vendor-supplier payments. Moreover, the information control requirements also vary across payers and payees for a given payment category. For instance, the information requirements for trade payments to suppliers can vary. The fact that the ACH now has three types of information addenda records (CTP, CTX, and CCDX) is evidence of these differences. The fact that a corporate buyer-supplier pair needing remittance advice information in any data content standard other than

ANSI X12.4 (such as the UCS standard or any of the many industry-specific standards) cannot be served easily by any of these three addendum types indicates further the variation in information control requirements within a payment usage category, in this case the category of vendor-supplier payments.

Payment Product Segments

A payment product consists of the ability to transfer value plus the necessary information control capabilities to support the needs of a class of payers and payees. In general, each major payment usage category will require at least one electronic payment product. However, variation in information control requirements among payers or payees can mean the need for multiple products to service fully a usage category.

In check payments, the information control capabilities are usually not part of the check (the payment mechanism per se) but rather involve information exchange in addition to the check. Most common is the remittance advice (payment advice) that often accompanies a check payment.

Check features such as certification or check-processing attributes such as stop payment can be important control tools. Much of control arises from event sequencing, especially not releasing payment until invoice validity is established. Another example in preauthorized payments is advance notice from payee to payer of the amount and timing of a pre-authorized payment, for instance, the notice of an insurance debit mailed well *before* the debit date so that the payer can object or stop payment.

The PPD and CCD transactions are intended to provide additional capabilities beyond pure value exchange. The multiplicity of ACH transaction types constitutes implicit, and in some cases such as CTP, CTX, and CCDX transactions, explicit recognition that (1) value transfer pre se is not a sufficient electronic capability to displace checks, (2) additional information or control capabilities are necessary and vary by usage category, and (3) information control features vary within a major usage category, as evidenced by three different ways of handing addendum information for trade payments.

The paradox of the current evolution of the electronic payment capabilities is that the ACH has many transaction types in the sense of multiple information structures to process, whereas the check (draft) has a single standard record, namely, the MICR line. The various information needs and control features such as certification are handled outside of the value exchange record processing. Because of the multiple transaction types,

ACH record processing is relatively more complex than check processing. Moreover, the discretionary acceptance of transactions other than PPD and CCD means that these transactions must still be viewed as product components rather than as complete payment products.

A Necessary Displacement Condition

For the ACH to displace checks within a payment usage category, it is necessary to create products that at least provide comparable information control features. Comparable does not mean identical. It is not necessary to automate the check information control features per se. Rather, it is possible to use computer communication technology to modify or even enhance the information control capabilities. Clearly, ACH displacement of checks and other payment alternatives would be enhanced if ACH-based products were to have superior information control capabilities.

ACH Successes

The ACH successes to date have occurred in those usage categories where PPD or CCD transactions have substituted for checks or drafts as value exchange instruments with the information control features of the paper-based payment system left intact. Table 1–2 summarizes these usage categories.

Table 1–2.   Payment Segments Successfully Using the ACH

Consumer Payments	Business Payments
Social security	Cash concentration[a]
Pension and retirement payments	Dealer/distributor payments[b]
Payroll	Dividend payments
Insurance debits	
Loan payments, recurring fixed payments[c]	

[a] Cash concentration is not a value exchange between two parties but rather a transfer of funds between two business accounts at different banks. Thus, the payer and the payee are the same legal entity. Therefore, the usual problems of payer and payee concurrence is not a barrier to progress in this usage segment.

[b] Dealer/distributor payments are a many-to-one situation where the manufacturer usually has the ability to influence the dealers/distributors and the economics that justify a customized information control system. Most of the payments are CCD transactions.

[c] Recurring fixed-amount loans have only very limited volume but are included here, since there is a complete product and evidence of some growth acceleration.

Cash concentration is an excellent case example. More than 90 percent of retail deposit transfers now use the ACH. The depository transfer check has been effectively displaced by the ACH for concentrating retail deposits. The ACH is, moreover, the dominant transfer mechanism for most other concentrating transfers.

ACH success in the usage categories summarized in Table 1-2 supports the view that the ACH can serve as a check displacement vehicle within the existing infrastructure simply by using the ACH instead of a check. The problem is that most other payment categories do not fit the instrument substitution model, especially those usage categories with significant volume potential, such as corporate trade payments or point-of-sale payments.

Unrealized Opportunities

Table 1-3 summarizes actual and potential volumes for three major payment categories—corporate trade payments, variable-amount recurring bill payments, and point-of-sale payments. These areas constitute a majority of the noncurrency payments. Point-of-sale involves not only check (draft) displacement but also credit card and currency transactions. The volume potential here exceeds that of all other check payments.

The rest of this chapter focuses on success requirements for ACH-based

Table 1-3.   Unrealized Opportunities: Current and Potential Volume

Usage Category	Current Volume	Potential Volume
Trade payments	500,000[a]	9-10 billion/year
Variable-amount bill payments	Negligible[b]	18-22 billion/year
Point-of-sale	n/a	50 billion/year[c]

n/a = not available.

[a] This figure is predominantly dealer/distributor/franchise payments using CCD transactions rounded upward to reflect volume in trade payments. This excludes cash concentration transactions, which are within-company and therefore not trade payments but a separate corporate usage category.

[b] Most variable-amount bill payments today are telephone bill payments and very limited use of budget payment plans (level payments based on an estimate of the annual bill with an annual adjusting payment/refund). This author's survey-in-process suggests that serious use of the ACH for varying-amount bill payments is very limited.

[c] This figure is ad hoc and consists of the roughly 10 billion point-of-sale checks now written annually, automation of 25-30 billion of the total credit card and bank card transactions, and displacement of up to 15 billion plus of the 100 million plus currency transactions at point-of-sale.

products from an industrial organization viewpoint. Issues treated are product design, sales-distribution-support structure, and noneconomic barriers to providing the products an product support infrastructure.

Product Hypotheses

Since product development in each market is still in process, it is impossible to say conclusively what the successful electronic payment products will be. Nevertheless, much can be said about product and market attributes: there are dramatic differences in these markets in terms of geography, communication requirements, cost-benefit structure, and so on. Table 1–4 summarizes these attributes. Before we contrast the markets, we summarize each briefly.

Market Description

Corporate trade payments are business-to-business payments for supplies and services. Virtually all trade payments today are checks sent with a remittance advice, generally in response to an invoice. The process is expensive, and the potential savings from electronic data interchange (EDI) are large, with electronic payments being a small part of the total. In fact, for financial EDI (invoicing, payment, remittance advice, and related information transactions), payment is a small part of the total. As part of an interdependent system, business-to-business electronic payments depend very much on growth in overall EDI.

The main issue in trade payments is how redesign of information and payment flows will occur. In today's check-based trade payments, the payment and remittance information are transmitted together to the payee. Formats such as CTP and CTX assume that electronic payment and remittance advice will be processed together, as in today's check-based payments. CCDX could handle a separate electronic invoice. While startup costs and infrastructure support are greater with a separation of payment and remittance, a mainframe-based version of such a system appears to be the low-cost, more flexible, better overall, long-run solution.

Variable-amount recurring bill payments have very limited ACH volume. Relative to trade payments and point-of-sale payments, this seems like a neglected area. However, the technical delivery requirements for a consolidated bill (advance notification with scheduled future debit date and amount unless stopped by the consumer) seem relatively easier than

Table 1-4. Contrasting Attributes of Three High-Potential Markets for Electronic Payment Services

	Trade	Bill	Point-of-sale
Geographic distribution	National	Local	Local with limited national requirements (like ATM servicing)
Logical service banks	1. Major cash management banks 2. Top 200–400 banks in size	All depository institutions	Depository institutions issuing bank cards
Benefits and costs	1. Trade payment automation $0.20–$1.00 saving 2. Remittance processing $0.50–$1.00 for simple advices $3–$6 for typical advices 3. Very large for complex multi-invoice advices	1. Bill mailing 2. Remittance mailing 3. Remittance processing: document-electronic 4. Dunning-collection 5. Consumer time, problems	Uncertain: High cost for in-store terminals and real-time communications.
Costs	High: variance in corporate startup costs.	*Startup* Change in billing system Change in bank statements *Operation* Exception-cancellation processing	1. Terminals in retail unit 2. Real-time communication 3. Credit validation 4. Credit status file 5. Audit trial 6. Error processing 7. Fraud prevention, access security
Benefit-cost ratio	High: once significant proportion of trade transactions are in electronic data exchange system.	High: Moderate benefit to biller and consumer with relatively low development and operating costs.	Uncertain: Service value constrained by cost of currency, check, and credit card as alternative point-of-sale payment methods.

those for either trade payments or point-of-sale. The main structural barrier is the need for virtually all the depository institutions in a bill area to cooperate in a standard master billing and processing system. The economics (saving five to eight mailings per month per household, several cents per bill processed, and fewer overdue, dunned accounts) are favorable.

Point-of-sale is an area of active use for gasoline retailess and one being actively evaluated by most other retailers. As noted by Stone (1984) and White (1985a), many efforts have been real-time-focused. Here costs are high. This author believes direct transaction cost to the retailer must fall below 5 cents per transaction for a viable system . The real-time pilot-tests have not met this requirement and have generally indicated a need for further product development.

Market Contrasts

Trade payments are national in scope, with most of the corporate check business concentrated in at most 40 banks. Variable-amount recurring bills are mostly local and are widely distributed toay over the entire population of depository institutions.

Trade payments logically involve direct computer-to-computer communication between businesses and banks and also between banks and the ACH. One, or at most two, central processing points is the low-cost, logical processing configuration for trade payments. Variable-amount recurring bills are primarily drawn on in-area institutions. Mailed printed documents are the logical interface to the consumer, with a voice telephone or push-button-keyed telephone being a reporting mechanism for exceptions and other overrides of the scheduled debits. Tapes would do for company-bank communication, since delivery is local. Processing would be batch-oriented. Processing could be sent to a central mainframe but would most likely to local, possibly a bank-owed consortium or a lead bank serving as the main processor for all depository institutions in an area. Settlement could even be via correspondent accounts. There would be very little out-of-region volume.

Trade payments and variable-amount recurring bills are clear opposites in geography, communication, and processing requirements. Point-of-sale is both local and national, including some need for real-time verification and validation. It probably has a local versus out-of-region mix comparable to the mix on automatic teller machines.

In benefits, the trade payments category ranks very high, although much of the benefit is in automated low-error remittance advice processing rather than in payment per se. Bill payments are next in benefit-cost rank, with moderate benefits but very low delivery cost. Point-of-sale is the least certain, with moderate benefits but potentially high costs, especially if there is a high proportion of real-time, on-line transactions.

The implications of the other contrasts in Table 1–4 are equally striking. Each involves differences in geography, logical service banks, network requirements, customer interface, and benefit-cost ratio. Each usage segment involves very different service products. The differences seem more striking than the common attribute of being payment-based.

Conclusions

A market segment view of products indicates very different requirements for those major uses where there is currently great volume potential but very little actual volume. The immediate needs are more for payment product creation and bank production, distribution, sales, and support than for network innovation. However, the network, ACH features, and communication requirements are very different. Rather than a single ACH system, it may be that several different systems are needed. Even though these ACH systems would be functionally distinct, they could share processing and communication reasources.

References

Arthur D. Little, Inc. 1980. *Electronic Data Interchange for the Gorcery Industry: Feasibility Report*. Cambridge, Mass.

Bequai, August. 1981. *The Cashless Society: EFT at the Crossroads*. New York: Wiley.

Bright, James R. 1964. *Research Development and Technological Forecasting*. Homewood, Ill.: Richard D. Irwin.

Carey, Kristen E., and Kevin Carr, 1982, "ACH Transaction Processing: An Overview of Information Flows and Controls." *Journal of Cash Management* 2 (3): 32–47.

Cohen, Allen M. 1983. "Treasury Terminal Systems and Cash Management Information Support." *Journal of Cash Management* 3 (4): 9–18.

Corrigan, E. Gerald. 1981. "The Payments Mechanism System: Emerging Changes and Challenges." In *The Future of the U.S. Payment System*. Conference Proceedings (June 23–25). Federal Reserve Bank of Atlanta.

———. 1982. "Federal Reserve System Pricing: An Overview." *Journal of Cash Management* 2 (3): 48–56.

Displacing the Check, 1983. Special Issue of *Economic Review* 68 (August). Federal Reserve Bank of Atlanta.

Federal Reserve Bank of Atlanta. 1981. *The Future of the U.S. Payments System.* Conference Proceedings (June 23–25).

———. 1984. *Payments in the Financial Services Industry of the 1980s.* Conference Proceedings (September 22–23, 1983). Westport, Conn.: Quorum Books.

Frisbee, Pamela. 1986. "History of the ACH." *Economic Review* 71 (March): 4–8. Federal Reserve Bank of Atlanta.

Gambs, Carl M. 1972. "The Economics of an Automated Payment System." Ph.D. Dissertation, Yale University.

Hill, Ned C., and Daniel M. Ferguson, 1985. "Cash Flow Timeline Management: The Next Frontier of Cash Management." *Journal of Cash Management* 5 (3): 12–22.

Hill, Ned C., and Robert A. Wood. 1983. "I'm O.K., You're O.K.: The Electronic Win-Win Deal." *Canadian Cash Management Review* 4 (6): 3–5.

Keenan, Gerald L. 1986. "ACH Return Items." *Economic Review* 71 (March): 19. Federal Reserve Bank of Atlanta.

Kelly, Patrick, et al. 1978. *Technological Innovation: A Critical Review of Current Knowledge.* San Francisco: San Francisco Press.

Kutler, Jeffery. 1981. "Fed of Atlanta's Check Study: Monumental and Maligned." *Transition* 11 (1): 13–16.

Lee, John F. 1983. "CHIPS: More Than Just Another Clearing System." *Transition* 11 (1): 14–20.

Monhollon. J. R., and Bruce J. Summers. 1987. "The Role of the Federal Reserve in the Electronic Payments Evolution." *Journal of Cash Management* 7 (2): 23–26.

National Automated Clearing House Association. 1983. *NACHA Corporate Trade Payments Notebook.* Washington, D.C.

Rawlings, Brown R. 1981. "Future of the Check System." In *The Future of the U.S. Payment System.* Conference Proceedings (June 23–25). Federal Reserve Bank of Anlanta.

Smith, Samuel D. 1980. "An Assessment of Electronic Funds Transfer Systems to Meet the Needs of the Corporate Treasurer." Thesis, Stonier Graduate School of Banking, Rutgers University.

———. 1982. "The Current Status of Corporate EFT." *Journal of Cash Management* 2 (2): 28–40.

Stone, Bernell K. 1983. "Cash Cycle Management and the ANSI X12 Committee." *Journal of Cash Management* 3 (4): 37–38.

———. 1984. "Corporate Perspectives on Cash Management." In *Payments in the Financial Services Industry of the 1980s.* Conference Proceedings (September 22–23, 1983). Federal Reserve Bank of Atlanta. Westport, Conn.: Quorum Books.

———. 1986a. "Desiderata for a Viable ACH." *Economic Review* 71 (3): 34–43. Federal Reserve Bank of Atlanta.

———. 1986b. "Electronic Payment Basics." *Economic Review* 71 (3): 9–18. Federal Reserve Bank of Atlanta.

———. 1986c. "Electronic Payments at the Crossroads." *Economic Review* 71 (3): 20–33. Federal Reserve Bank of Atlanta.

Stone, Bernell K., and George C. White. 1986a. "Corporate Trade Payments: Hard Lessons in Product Design." *Economic Review* 71 (4): 9–12. Federal Reserve Bank of Atlanta.

———. 1986b. "Scenarios for the Future of the ACH." *Economic Review* 71 (4): 29–49. Federal Reserve Bank of Atlanta.

Summers. Bruce J. 1986a. "Dr. Frankenstein and the ACH." *Economic Review* 71 (4): 4–8. Federal Reserve Bank of Atlanta.

———. 1986b. "Federal Reserve ACH Services: Past and Future." *Economic Review* 71 (4): 40–41. Federal Reserve Bank of Atlanta.

Tarpley, Fred A., Jr. 1984. "Technological Diffusion." In *Payments in the Financial Services Industry of the 1980s.* Conference Proceedings (September 22–23, 1983). Federal Reserve Bank of Atlanta. Westport, Conn.: Quorum Books.

White, George C. 1979. "Electronic Banking and Its Impact on the Future." *Magazine of Bank Administration* 55 (December): 39–42.

———. 1982. "EFT Opportunities for the Innovative Corporation." *Journal of Cash Management* 2 (2): 42–48.

———. 1985a. "CCD or CTP or CTX—Which Corporate Format to Use." *Journal of Cash Management* 5 (4): 55–58.

———. 1985b. "Which Electronic Point-of-Sale Direct Debit Option to Consider—ACH or On-Line?" *Journal of Cash Management* 5 (2): 28–32.

Woo, B. K. 1985. "Why Corporate America Has Not Embraced Electronic Corporate Trade Payments." *Journal of Cash Management* 5 (4): 41–44.

COMMENTARY

Michael Urkowitz

Bernell Stone's chapter provides an outstanding analysis of the automated clearing house, one component of the United States electronic payment industry. The chapter's major contribution is its ability to create a framework for assessing the current status of this industry and thereby enabling one to better define issues that shape our future.

My intention is to add to Mr. Stone's framework; I have no material disagreement with the chapter's principal points.

The chapter segments the ACH payment market by usage category. It then concludes that the segments with the greatest volume potential are still in the gestation period. Therefore, these segments

1. Have the most complex product design and development problems
2. Require production-sales-support capabilities that transcend existing payment service organizations
3. Involve significant noneconomic barriers to displacement.

The Chase experience would emphasize the second and third points. The greatest barriers to growth are indeed noneconomic and require effective, nontraditional support systems if they are to be overcome. In particular, we believe the principal challenge is a marketing challenge and must be addressed as such.

Mr. Stone catalogs the virtues of segmenting the market by product categories. We feel that segmentation should be carried one step further—into categories that represent end users. It is the end user, after all, who will ultimately create product volume.

To attract the end user, depository institutions must identify the direct and indirect value that ACH will provide. For example, consumers are classified as the greatest source for potential ACH volume. Yet banking institutions, acting as wholesalers, have traditionally channeled their resources into selling the payment mechanism to the corporations that distribute the product to the universe of end users.

This is where I feel we have been shortsighted. As bankers, we must generate the incentive for both the distributor and end user to displace paper payments for electronic payments. A comprehensive marketing effort must be implemented to target two different constituents: our customers and our customers' customers.

In our work in approaching the end user, we are encouraged at the progress made to date. Although overall ACH volume has continued to grow, the numbers climb dramatically in the niche segments where the economic and societal benefits associated with electronic payments have been positioned, packaged, and promoted by the corporation. At this time, these success stories are represented by small segments, such as selected supermarket point-of-sale programs, the insurance industry's direct-debit programs, and direct deposit of payroll. We know from experience that proper segmentation of the end user market will result in the same degree of success in other applications.

Although Mr. Stone does not identify the corporate-to-corporate category as a volume growth segment, we find in it another illustration of relevance of end user segmentation. In selling corporate-to-corporate ACH services, we again require marketing strategies and tactics to motivate two levels of users: our corporate customers and our corporate customers' trading partners. A depository institution must approach the latter with the same degree of marketing sophistication and savvy it would expend on its corporate customers.

Mr. Stone's chapter evaluates the many issues associated with the product life cycle. In its comparisons with consumer durable goods, I feel that his thesis understimates the psychological aspects associated with acceptance of service products. Durable goods, such as freezers and VCRs, are tangible, single-decision products. Electronic payments, both consumer and corporate, are intangible products, which require a change in attitude and, more significantly, in behavior patterns. Behavioral patterning produces a longer product life cycle, as evidenced by the credit card, which remained in gestation for over 15 years. For this reason alone, I feel that it is imperative for banks to work cooperatively with the distributor to compress product acceptance time lines.

The role of the ACH as an information system is another provocative topic discussed in Mr. Stone's paper. Information has become a vital commodity to every corporation and institution. It ties departments, branches, and subsidiaries together. It increases productivity in the nation's back offices. It enables executives, not only CFOs but employees in purchasing, operations, marketing, sales and other areas, to manage, to react, and to take action. Electronic information, coupled with payments, represents ultimate value. And banks, with their access to the ACH, have a powerful tool for influencing decisions on how and to what extent this commodity reaches corporate America.

In his chapter Mr. Stone makes reference to ACH as potentially displacing checks, "if ACH-based products were to have superior information control capabilities." I'd like to take this concept one step further. In addition to paper payments, the ACH maintains the ability to displace a host of internal corporate MIS systems, and the U.S. Mail, which today distributes the bulk of payments and information.

Currently, the industry identifies the greatest barrier of corporate-to-corporate payments as the inability of the ACH to link with the numerous corporate information systems established. If the lack of an industry standard were indeed the sole barrier, it would be easily overcome with technology. Just as significant, however, is the nontangible barrier that all products in gestation face. This includes cognizant acceptance and operational assimilation of electronic information.

For example, the large corporate market has been viewed by depository institutions as one common entity or segment. All members of this segment are viewed as maintaining uniformity in technical capability and information requirements. When we examine the large corporate market more closely, we in fact find a heterogeneous mix of users, representing different phases of evolution in their willingness and ability to fully integrate electronic information.

One dilemma—what we refer to as the EDI dilemma—is, whether corporate information should move with the payments, or should payments move independently, without detailed information?

We believe it is premature to conclude which way corporate America will assimilate EDI. However, bankers can and should maintain the fexibility to respond to the situation, work with leading-edge companies to understand EDI's implications, and influence the ultimate decisions. We should recognize that if ACH is relegated to providing solely the value transfer service, our long-term opportunities will be limited.

In closing, I applaud Mr. Stone's chapter for its comprehensive and well-organized review of the electronic payment system—a subject that is complex, intricate, and at times, frustrating. But to overcome all barriers in marketing the ACH, banks must take the initiative to work with all constituencies to realize its rewards and benefits.

2 MARKET FAILURE AND RESOURCE USE: ECONOMIC INCENTIVES TO USE DIFFERENT PAYMENT INSTRUMENTS

David B. Humphrey and Allen N. Berger

Market failure occurs when there is a divergence between a product's *private cost*, the price faced by a purchaser, and its *social cost*, the value of real resources that are consumed when the product is produced. This holds even if private costs reflect efficient or minimum cost production. For institutional and legal reasons rooted in history, there is a substantial degree of market failure in the U.S. payment system. The use of some important payment instruments are in effect subsidized or taxed because of the divergence between their private and social costs. While there can be situations where such a divergence is in the public interest, this is not the case for the U.S. payment system. Here the subsidies and taxes distort incentives and misallocate resources, so that from a social viewpoint some payment

The opinions expressed are those of the authors alone and do not necessarily reflect those of the Board of Governors, the Reserve Banks, or their staffs. Eugene Snyder assisted us in generating many of the data estimates used in this chapter. Comments by Jim Dingle, Ed Ettin, Grady Foster, Don Hollis, Ed Kane, Elliott McEntee, and Neil Murphy are acknowledged and appreciated.

45

instruments are underused and others are overused. The market failure in
the U.S. payment system is the central focus of this chapter.

The two main components of payments market failure are float and
large-dollar payment risk. Float is comprehensively discussed in this chapter. Risk is discussed in the chapter by Faulhaber, Phillips, and Santomero.
In what follows, we estimate the value of the wedge between private and
social costs created by float for several types of payment instruments,
focusing especially on check float. This analysis is further refined by esti-
mating the value of the float wedge by type of check user: consumer,
business, and government. Knowledge of this divergence enables us to
estimate the existing incentives to overuse checks and to approximate the
value of resources that may be saved if the float wedge were removed and
instruments with lower real resource costs were instead chosen. Removal
of the float wedge requires that the float costs associated with the various
payment instruments be allocated to the decision maker, who typically
chooses which instrument to use, rather than be borne by others who do
not make that choice.

Several methods for facilitating the removal of the float wedge are analyzed. One conclusion is that, except for government payments, the shift
from checks to electronic payment methods is likely to remain slow unless
certain public policy actions are taken to address check float. Even then,
only business users are likely to be strongly influenced, with consumer
users only moderately affected. Another possibility is that the float wedge
will be partly reduced exogenously by payments suppliers. Interstate banking may significantly speed up the collection of checks between banks by
increasing the proportion of banks in which the payor and payee both have
their accounts, by reducing the number of institutions through which a
check is passed before being presented for payment, or by encouraging
a shift to electronic methods. While this chapter deals with an important
quantifiable inducement to overuse checks and underuse electronic payments, other important but essentially nonquantifiable influences operate
here as well. The chapter by Stone outlines and discusses these noneconomic influences which, along with measured check float, contribute to the
slow growth of electronic payments.

Market Failures and How They Can Be Corrected

Decisions made in a market setting reflect only the private costs faced by
market participants. If there is a significant divergence between private
and social costs, resource allocation may be improved if private costs can
be adjusted up or down to reflect better the full social costs of market

actions.[1] Simply put, one cannot expect market participants to make decisions that best reflect resource use for society as a whole unless the prices observed in the market reflect the full social (instead of private) cost impact of products or services being sold or produced. When market failure is significant, it has in the past been addressed through at least three different means: negotiation by market participants, government regulation, and direct taxes and subsidies.

Negotiation by Market Participants

Voluntary negotiation or action by market participants themselves occured, for example, in the health insurance industry when it became clear that certain users had an incentive to overuse insured health services and confer negative externalities (higher future insurance costs) on all participants. The negotiated solution was to adopt user copayment provisions and larger deductibles so that users would face more of the costs of using medical services and thereby constrain demand.

An example of negotiation in the payments area has occurred in Canada. The Canadian banking industry, working with the central bank, voluntarily removed much of the float wedge for check payments. Customer account crediting and debiting conventions and interbank settlement procedures were adopted whereby check writers face more closely the full cost of their actions; much of the market failure was corrected. This example is discussed more completely later.

Government Regulation

A second and more commonly used method to address market failure is direct government intervention or regulation. One recent example is that states are adopting statutes requiring firms that own, buy, or sell industrial property to clean up toxic waste on their property. In the past, firms have sold or abandoned industrial sites that later were determined to have produced negative externalities (health risks) for neighboring communities. Clean-up costs often had to be assumed by the states rather than by the producers of the wastes or by those consumers who purchased the products whose production created the problem. In either case, users (producers or consumers) did not incur the full costs of their actions but instead shifted some of those costs to others not involved in the production/consumption decision.

Another example, similar to the payments problem, concerns the historical precedent set by the Post Office in charging for the delivery of first-class mail. It is not well known, but prior to 1855 letter writers faced no charges for the letters they sent in the United States. Instead, the receiver of the letter paid the fee. This practice had evolved earlier in England and Continental Europe. Since the user of the mails did not bear the cost, this pricing arrangement increasingly led to abuses. Specifically, travelers often sent letters to indicate to family and friends that they had arrived at their destinations safely. Once the letter arrived, the outside handwriting would be recognized and the letter refused, since the essential message—safe arrival—would be self-evident (Scheele 1970, 32–33). Also, more users entered the market and sent advertisements and solicitations, which receivers often refused to accept (U.S. Postal Service 1986, 6–7, 14–15).[2] This created a negative externality in that the Post Office had provided a service for which it was not paid. The market failure was corrected in the 1840s in England and in 1855 in the United States through the passage of legislation requiring payment by letter senders through newly issued postal stamps rather than continuing to charge receivers.

Direct Taxes and Subsidies to Alter Behavior

A third method for correcting market failure involves the use of taxes or subsidies to induce behavioral changes through the price system. An example here is that consumers in a number of states are assessed a small deposit fee on purchases of beverage cans and bottles. Because this deposit is refunded when these items are returned to any store, an incentive is created for the purchaser not to litter or, if littering occurs, for others to clean it up.

Better known are the federal and state government subsidies to users of public education services, lowering their private costs. Because positive externalities are thought to be conferred on the rest of society when individuals attend school, the net social costs of education are less than the private costs that otherwise would be faced. The subsidy reduces the private costs of education decisions and brings them closer to net social costs.

The Social and Private Costs of Different Payment Instruments

Composition of Payment Transactions

This chapter examines the difference between social and private costs for nine different payment instruments. Nonelectronic instruments include, in rank order of use, cash, checks, credit cards, travelers checks, and money orders. Electronic instruments, also in rank order of use, include automated clearinghouse (ACH), wire transfer of funds, point-of-sale (POS), and automated teller machine (ATM) bill payments. The estimated payments volume composition for each instrument is shown in table 2–1. Electronic payments account for less than 1 percent of all transactions, while cash and checks together comprise 97 percent. Looking at noncash transactions only, checks comprise 85 percent, while the use of all electronic instruments rises to 2 percent. This situation is quite different if the dollar value of payments associated with each instrument is examined. Here electronic payments are very important, with wire transfers accounting for 82 percent of total payment value. The value of check payments are only 16 percent of the total, while all other electronic and nonelectronic payment instruments make up the remaining 2 percent.

Social or Real Resource Costs

The unit social costs in table 2–1 reflect the real resource costs estimated for the production of each physical instrument and the processing cost associated with tendering and collecting each instrument in 1987.[3] Processing costs include accounting and mailing costs incurred by payors, processing and accounting costs incurred by payees who receive the instrument, and processing and transportation costs incurred in collecting the items by the banking system and the Federal Reserve.[4] From society's point of view, use of cash would be cheapest, at $0.04 per transaction, and indeed it is the most utilized (column 1).[5] Next cheapest would be ACH ($0.29), followed by two other electronic payment methods (POS at $0.47 and ATM bill payment at $0.66).[6] While checks rank as the fifth cheapest payment method ($0.79), they are the second most heavily used. Finally, credit cards, travelers checks, money orders, and wire transfers are the payment instruments most expensive to use.

A rough measure of the correspondence between payment instrument use (column 1) and the social cost of each instrument (column 2) is obtained by computing the Spearman rank correlation coefficient. This measure correlates the ranking of use with social cost and is $r_s = 0.22$. The positive correlation shows that instruments with lower social costs are generally used more intensively, although the strength of this relation is not as high as it could be (namely 1.00). A higher value would indicate a stronger positive ranking between use and social cost and might represent a more efficient allocation of resources. Of course, other factors that are difficult to quantify, such as convenience and acceptability, are also important and may have affected this correlation.

Table 2–1. Estimated Social and Private Costs of Different Payment Instruments

Type of Payment Instrument	Volume Composition	Unit Social Cost	Float Transfer Payment (+ for Cost, – for Benefit)	Unit Private Cost
	(1)	(2)	(3)	(2) + (3) = (4)
Nonelectronic				
Cash	83.42%	$0.04	$0.05	$0.09
Checks	14.07	0.79	–0.83	–0.04
Credit cards	1.53	0.88	–0.44	0.44
Travelers checks	0.40	1.18	0.00	1.18
Money orders	0.24	1.79	0.00	1.79
	99.66%			
Electronic				
ACH	0.28%	$0.29	–$0.00	$0.29
Wire transfers	0.03	7.33	–0.02	7.31
POS	0.02	0.47	0.00	0.47
ATM bill payment	0.01	0.66	0.03	0.69
	0.34%			

Source: Appendix tables 2–A1 and 2–A2.

Float Transfer Payments

A major cost or benefit excluded from the social cost estimates is float (column 3). These costs or benefits, however, affect the unit private cost, or the effective price faced by payment users (column 4). Float is the time period between when a payment is tendered and when investible funds are made available to the payee.[7] Strictly speaking, float generates a transfer payment of the interest earned on these funds from one part of society to another and does not itself use real resources. However, the procedures used to generate or reduce float by those segments of society touched by its distributional effects are included in the estimated social cost. Thus, if float were zero, not only would social costs equal private costs (neglecting the existence of market failure for large-dollar payment risk) but the social costs of some instruments would be reduced as well.

Float costs for the two most used payment instruments—cash and checks—are quite large. For both of these instruments, float costs are estimated to exceed real resource costs. The value of float associated with the use of cash is 1.18 times its real resource cost, while for checks it is 1.05. The important difference is that cash users *pay* this float transfer payment to the government, while check users *receive* it as a benefit from payees. In both cases, there is a substantial wedge between the private and social costs of a payment transaction with these two instruments. These wedges lead to market failure and encourage overuse of checks and underuse of cash.[8]

Users of credit cards also receive an important, although considerably smaller, float benefit if balances are promptly paid, since a month or more elapses before bills must be paid. This applies to about half of all credit card users. Because of float, the user cost of a credit card is estimated to be only one-half its social cost, providing some incentive to overuse this instrument as well. Users of travelers checks and money orders incur relatively small float costs. However, both these instruments are offered in competitive markets, so float costs are viewed as merely another way to recoup production and processing costs rather than reflecting a transfer payment. Finally, electronic payments generate virtually no float and are rarely used except for large-dollar business payments.

Private Costs of Payment Instruments

The unit private costs faced by payment users (column 4) are the unit social costs (column 2) plus the float transfer payment (column 3). Checks have the largest float benefit, which dominates social cost, giving a *negative* unit private cost of −$0.04. While electronic payments have relatively low social costs, their private costs are higher than that for checks because they lack a float benefit to the user. As a result, electronic payments are underused from a social viewpoint: the relative user price favors checks, while the relative social costs favor electronics. A difficulty in encouraging users to switch to electronics is that no amount of cost reduction for electronic instruments can match the negative private costs of checks.

It should be noted that the figures used here include only financial or out-of-pocket costs. Other important cost factors, such as speed, security, availability, and acceptability, could in principle be included, but these are difficult to quantify accurately. Payment decisions are also affected by user preferences for familiar payment instruments or by habit persistence.

The importance of relative prices faced by users (private costs) in determining actual use can be inferred from the rank order relation between estimated unit private costs and actual use. As would be expected, the Spearman rank correlation coefficient between private cost and use (r_s = 0.65) is stronger than that for social cost and use (r_s = 0.22). This value is still less than 1.00 and, as such, likely illustrates the degree to which we are unable to fully capture or accurately quantify the true social and private costs of each payment instrument.[9]

Costs Of Checks by Major User Groups

While the average unit private cost of a check is estimated to be negative for the average check user (−$0.04 in table 2–1), a different picture emerges when three major user groups are examined separately. These three groups, who together wrote an estimated 47 billion checks in 1987, are composed of consumers (accounting for 55 percent of all check written), business (40 percent of all checks), and government (5 percent of all checks). This breakdown is shown in table 2–2. The unit social or real resource cost of each check written was assumed to be the same for all groups, at $0.79 an item, although there is probably some slight variation among them in practice.

Why Check Float Benefits Differ

The total interest earned on check float in 1987 is estimated to be $39.1 billion, but this is not distributed uniformly across groups of check writers.[10]

While consumers write the most checks, their estimated float benefit is lowest (table 2–2, column 3). There are two reasons for this result. First, the average dollar values of checks written by the three groups are quite different. The average consumer check was only $145, while the average business check was eighteen times larger at $2636. The average value of a government check had an intermediate value of $1074. Second, the number of days an average check is outstanding before it is paid is also different between groups. For consumer checks, this was estimated to be 3 days, while for business and government checks it was higher, 4.5 and 5 days, respectively.[11,12]

Together, these two factors mean that business checks receive the greatest float benefit because the checks they write have the highest average value and because they are outstanding for a relatively long time. While businesses write 40 percent of all checks, they generate 90 percent of all check float benefits ($35 billion a year a float benefits out of a total of $39 billion). Consumers, who write 55 percent of all checks, only receive 5 percent of check float benefits. For government, the proportion of check usage (5 percent) corresponds to the proportion of float benefits (5 percent).

Private Costs of Business Checks

In terms of unit private costs, each business check written generates $1.09 in net revenue, since the float benefit of $1.88 per check more than offsets the $0.79 unit social cost (table 2–2). For some business checks, this revenue is substantially larger. Both the Federal Reserve System and large correspondent banks offer programs that provide expedited processing and collection services for large-dollar checks. In late 1987, the Federal Reserve was collecting 373,100 items worth $2.5 billion on a dialy basis in its High Dollar Group Sort (HDGS) program. The average value of a check in this program was $6803. Without HDGS, these remotely disbursed items could be outstanding 2 days longer than the average for other business checks; with HDGS, this is reduced by 1 day (to 5.5 days). Business checks expeditiously handled by correspondent banks are often written for much higher amounts. The net revenue raised by writing a business check for $6803 is $5.08, or almost five times the average for business checks. This includes an extra $0.05 per item cost to the payor for maintaining a controlled disbursement account. For the items in the HDGS program, this translates into a net revenue gain to check writers of $1.90 million each business day, or $479 million per year. This revenue gain from writing

Table 2-2. Estimated Social and Private Check Costs for Consumer, Business, and Government Users

Check User Group	Number of Checks Written[a] (billions) (1)	Unit Social Cost[b] (2)	Unit Float Cost (Total Float Cost)[c] (3)	Unit Private Cost (2) + (3) = (4)
Consumer payments	25.8	$0.79	-$0.07 (-$1.8 billion)	$0.72
Business payments	18.8	$0.79	-$1.88 (-$35.3 billion)	-$1.09
Government payments	2.4	$0.79	-$0.85 (-$2.0 billion)	-$0.06
Total checks written:	47 billion	Total value of check float:		$39.1 billion

[a] The total number of all types of checks written was 32.8 billion in 1979 (Federal Reserve Bank of Atlanta 1979, 1). Check growth from 1979 to 1987 was assumed to be 4.8% annually. Hence $32.8(1.048)^8 = 47.7$ billion items, and was rounded downward to agree with the 47 billion figure reported by Federal Reserve staff to the Bank for International Settlements in their revised book on *Payment Systems in Eleven Developed Countries* (1985). The estimated number of checks written by the user group shown were derived by applying the percentage composition estimates in table 2–A3, column 1, to the 47 billion figure.

[b] Real resource costs of check disbursement and collection differ by user group, but such differences are difficult to estimate and appear to be relatively small. For example, remote and controlled disbursement of business checks, which arguably use the most real resources, are estimated to use $0.3217 per item in additional resources. However, these items constitute such a small percentage of total business checks as to add only a negligible amount to the average social costs for business checks. These additional real resource costs include (1) the extra processing and accounting costs borne by the paying corporation and the payor depository institution ($0.0460 per item); (2) the extra costs borne by payees and collecting institutions in expediting collection ($0.1559 per item); and (3) the increased risk exposure to the payee imposed by the extra float ($0.1350 per item). Partly offsetting these extra costs is (4) the value of improved cash management control for the disbursing corporation ($0.0152 per item), for a net increase in social costs of $0.3217 per item. The additional payor costs in (1) consist of a controlled disbursement maintenance fee ($125.00 per month) plus an incoming wire charge ($5.00 per business day). These are spread over 21 business days and 5000 checks per month, for a cost per item of ($125.00 + ($5 × 21))/5000 = $0.0460. The extra collection costs in (2) are

assumed to equal 10% on average (although they are 100% on the margin) of the value of the float benefits obtained by improving collection time by 1 day on these items. Assuming an average check size equal to that for HDGS checks, $6803, an average Treasury bill rate of 5.775%, and 252 business days per year gives $(0.10 \times \$6803 \times (0.05775/252)) = \$0.1559$ extra collection costs per check. The increased risk exposure of the payee in (3) results from having to wait longer than on other business checks to determine whether the check will be dishonored, even when expedited collection is used for these remotely disbursed items. Assuming this delay is 1 extra business day on average and that the value of this uncertainty is 50 basis points on an annual basis gives an average cost per item of $\$6803 \times (0.0050/252) = \$0.1350$. Note that we exclude from these costs the additional risk that the smaller institutions through which these checks often flow may be forced to close because of problems on large-dollar disbursement checks that exceed their capital. Finally, the improved cash management control (4) occurs because delayed or controlled disbursement often allows the corporation to find out disbursement totals earlier in the day when overnight investment markets are thicker and search costs for placing funds are lower. Assuming that 15% of the funds would otherwise be invested later in the day at a loss of 37.5 basis points on an annual basis gives a per-item benefit of $0.15 \times \$6803 \times (0.00375/252) = \$0.0152$ from improved cash management control and earlier in the day investment of funds.

    ^{c} Total float costs (F) were derived from: $F = \Sigma F_i = \Sigma (N_i/365 \text{ days}) (A_i) (T_i) r$ for i = consumers (C), business (B), and government (G) users, where N_i = the estimated number of checks written (column 1); A_i = the estimated average value of checks written (discussed below); T_i = the estimated number of calendar days a check is outstanding (table 2–A3, column 7); and $r = 0.05775$ = the 1987 average 90-day Treasury bill rate. Unit float costs were obtained by dividing total float costs (column 3) by the number of checks written (column 1). The average value of checks written by user group (A_i) are $A_C = \$145$, $A_B = \$2636$, and $A_G = \$1074$. A_C is from a comprehensive survey of family use of transaction accounts in 1986. The average size of a check written on a family's main checking account was \$133. Eighty-five percent of all families owned such an account, and 97% of all owners used it, writing an average of 17 checks per month (Avery et al. 1987, table 3, 182). The average size of a check written on a family's other checking accounts (excluding nonbank money market accounts) was \$186. Twenty-two percent of all families owned such an account, but only 75% of all owners used them, writing an average of 11 checks per month (same source, table 4, 183). Since the rate of inflation between 1986 and 1987 was 4%, the weighted average size of a family's check from all checking accounts was $0.89 \ (\$133) + 0.11(\$186)]1.04 = \$145$ in 1987. The weights are, respectively, $0.89 = a/(a + b)$ and $b/(a + b)$, where $a = 0.85(0.97)$ (17 checks) and $b = 0.22(0.75)$ (11 checks), as noted in the text above. A_G reflects only U.S. government checks and is reported in the Board of Governors of the Federal Reserve System 1987a, table 11. The Federal Reserve is the payor bank for all U.S. government checks and, as a result, these data are publicly available. Data on A_B, in contrast, was not observed but instead was computed using the average value of all checks written, \$1188. The \$1188 figure is derived by taking the average value of all checks written in 1979 of \$757 (Federal Reserve Bank of Atlanta 1979, 73) and multiplying it by 1.57, which reflects the amount of inflation that occurred from 1979 to 1987. Thus, A_B was found by solving $0.55(\$145) + 0.40(A_B) + 0.05(\$1074) = \$1188$, which yielded $A_B = \$2636$.

large-dollar business checks would be several times higher if the volumes of these checks handled by correspondent banks were included.

If the check float barrier to electronic payments could be removed, the market failure in the use of business checks could be corrected. As noted in the chapter by Stone, some form of electronic business data interchange (EDI) would likely be the preferred electronic substitute for many types of business checks, although ACH could be used in other applications. While EDI will likely be somewhat more expensive than ACH alone, we assume for illustrative purposes that most business check payments could be shifted to ACH transfers. Thus, a first approximation to the possible savings in social costs for business payments could be obtained by multiplying the difference between check and ACH social costs ($0.50) by the volume of checks that could be shifted. Virtually all payroll and business-to-business payments could probably be shifted to electronic payments, while perhaps half of other business payments could be so shifted (16.45 billion items). This illustrative exercise suggests a real resource savings of $8.2 billion.[13] The elimination of remote or controlled disbursement of large-dollar business checks collected through the High Dollar Group Sort program would add only $30 million to this estimated cost savings, and possibly several times this amount if remote and controlled items collected by correspondent banks were eliminated as well (see table 2–2, note b).

Private Costs of Consumer and Government Checks

Consumer checks, on average, have a positive private cost. At $0.72, the consumer user cost is only $0.7 lower than its social cost.[14] As a result, there is little evidence of market failure for consumer use of checks. Because of the relatively small size of float for consumer check payments, the elimination of market failure for these checks is unlikely to provide much additional relative price incentive for consumers to shift to electronic alternatives. Consumers, on average, already face check costs ($0.72) that are higher than ACH ($0.29), so removing check float and raising further unit check costs (to $0.79) is unlikely to have much impact on this decision. Obviously, consumers continue to use checks for reasons that cannot be easily quantified (and thus are not reflected in the relative prices computed here). In addition, the pricing practices of banks often obscure the user cost of checks and other payment instruments. The bank price for checks is typically a complex combination of minimum balance requirements, per-check fees, and monthly account maintenance charges. However, if consumers could be induced to shift to electronics, a real resource savings of perhaps $8.0 billion could be obtained.[15]

Government checks, like business checks, have a negative unit private cost (and thus could generate revenue), but this is much lower, -0.06. While there is market failure in the use of government checks, this is being reduced voluntarily, especially at the federal level, as discussed later. If all government checks shifted to ACH, the resource savings would be relatively small, $1.2 billion.

In sum, an estimated $17.4 billion could potentially be saved by shifting from checks to electronic payments. However, only about half of this would likely be forthcoming if the check float wedge were removed. Consumers and government users do not appear to be substantially affected by float, since it is small for consumers and voluntarily disregarded by government. Only business check decisions will likely be significantly impacted by removing the check float wedge, saving perhaps $8.2 billion in real resources.

Historical Causes of, and Responses to, the Check Float Wedge

From a legal standpoint, checks are essentially sight drafts whose payment is subject to signature verification, examination of the account to determine if sufficient funds are available, and other inspection rights. Float is created because it takes time to receive, process, and transport a check for presentment. This process has evolved historically with few major changes, other than those aimed at standardizing the size of the check, the placement of the payment information, and the magnetic ink encoding of the payor bank and customer account number. These changes expedited the processing, collection, and presentment functions but have not altered the essential character of a check as a sight draft that must be physically delivered, creating float benefits for the user.

Responses to Check Float in Canada

A different treatment of checks has evolved in Canada, which, like the United States, relies heavily on checks for payments. Canadian banks have negotiated away much of what would otherwise be payer float benefits by agreeing that virtually all checks will be paid on a same-day basis (Cumming 1983). The float that would otherwise be created by this process is removed by the use of retroactive interbank settlement entries. This is equivalent to an as-of adjustment, taking away any benefit from the time lags inherent in the interbank check processing and collection process

(Dingle 1986). In Canada, this time lag is one day, so the debiting and crediting of bank reserves by the central bank for settlement is back-dated by one day, removing any benefits from bank float. Checks are thus paid and settled when deposited by customers, not when they are presented to the relevant payor bank branch for payment, as in the United States. These voluntarily negotiated arrangements were possible because the Canadian banking system operates nationwide and is very concentrated, and the largest banks have similar market shares of the consumer deposit (and hence check) market.

Checks require relatively few handlings to be collected in Canada. This is because of the nationwide banking in Canada and the fact that checks drawn on one office of a bank can be paid on a same-day basis when presented (through a clearinghouse) at another office distant from it. In contrast, transit items in the United States are on average handled by 1.9 intermediaries plus the payor and collecting bank (Berger 1985). Legally, presenters in the United States are required to deliver checks to the bank office identified by the routing-transit number in order to be paid. Both of these conditions tend to increase check processing costs and lengthen average collection times for the United States compared to Canada.

The fact that banking in Canada is very concentrated makes it easier to negotiate the cooperative arrangements that have voluntarily reduced market failure by eliminating bank float on checks, although mail and recipient float remain. The six largest Canadian banks account for more than 75 percent of payments volume and act as clearing agents for the remaining 25 percent, which is generated by the over 100 smaller institutions offering checking accounts. These six banks also account for 90 percent of total banking assets, while in the United States this level of coverage would require more than 3000 institutions. Lastly, the fact that the major Canadian banks have similar market shares means that the principals to the negotiation of the redistribution of bank check float had roughly equal stakes in the outcome, and adverse distributional effects were minimized. Here the loss of float benefits by one bank's payor customers is basically offset by the improved availability these customers receive when they are payees and deposit checks drawn on other institutions. On balance, none of the major banks are disadvantaged relative to each other by the elimination of bank check float for their customers.

In the United States, by contrast, elimination of bank check float would produce significant redistributions of revenue among banks. Large banks often charge business customers to provide them with float benefits through remote or controlled disbursement and charge them again, as payees, to expedite the collection of checks drawn on other banks to reduce their float costs. Similarly, Reserve Banks provide collecting banks with expedited collection services and would also lose revenue if the check float wedge were eliminated. In all of these cases, the social costs expended in either float-generating payment activities or float-reducing collection activities would fall if check float was eliminated, benefiting society as a whole.

Responses to Check Float in the United States

The response to check float by consumer payees, particularly in the case of payroll checks and other individual payments, has been to absorb it. This conclusion follows from the observation that consumers lack market power, and perhaps sufficient financial interest, to negotiate a higher wage if paid by check rather than cash or ACH direct deposit (both of which would typically give faster availability to investible funds than payment by check). In contrast, business payees often have the needed market power and the financial interest (because of the total value of checks they receive) to have incorporated over time most or all check float costs directly into the prices of the goods or services sold to payors. Check float costs to businesses are equivalent to a working capital expense for receivables. Indeed, when very large dollar payments are involved, the choice of payment instrument is sometimes negotiated along with the price. More often, however, business payees raise the prices of their products or services to cover some weighted average of the float and handling costs they incur as a receiver of different payment instruments rather than attempting to recover the different costs for each instrument separately. Thus, the price paid is typically not a function of the payment instrument used, even when these costs vary.

Part of this response by business payees has been custom, and part of it has been legal. In terms of custom, as long as a merchant charging a single price is covering all costs and earning a normal return, there is little additional incentive to price discriminate by payment means. First, the cost differences to merchants are a relatively small portion of the value of the transaction. The greatest cost difference is between cash and credit cards where, as a percent of transaction value, cash is two percentage points cheaper to accept than a credit card (Board of Governors of the Federal Reserve System 1983, 58). Thus, price differences based on cost differences by means of payment are not large, and some extra costs would likely be associated with running a two- or three-tiered retail pricing structure. Second, there would be consumer resistance from all those who typically use the (now) higher-priced instrument, and this may not be balanced out by increased sales from those who already use the (now) lower-priced instrument.

There also exists a legal restriction on some types of price discrimination by payment means. For example, in 1984, it was illegal to assess a surcharge on purchases by credit card, although the economic equivalent, a price discount to those who did not use credit cards was not prohibited. Today, a surcharge is legal but is subject to Truth-in-Lending Act restrictions applying to finance charges and, for that reason, has been little used by merchants. Some merchants reportedly would prefer the surcharge arrangement, since their advertised price could then be the cash price, which would be lower. Credit card companies prefer the discount approach, since credit card users would not be as explicitly penalized (although most would prefer no price discrimination at all by payment means).

Even with these difficulties, some businesses have chosen to specialize or otherwise discriminate by payment means. This occurs when establishments refuse to accept credit card payments or accept them only for payments above some minimum amount. Others have a cash-and-carry policy (no checks) or impose cumbersome credit verification procedures as nonprice barriers. Still others (primarily gas stations) offer a discount for cash or POS compared to a credit card purchase.

Prospects for Reductions in Market Failure

Business Payments

The market failure associated with business payments is by far the largest. Indeed, these payments generate 90 percent of total check float, with the result that the private cost of a business check is −$1.09. Unlike government, business does not have the power to absorb higher user payment costs (when lower social cost alternatives are used in place of checks) and to recoup this higher cost through taxes. Also, the United States banking system, unlike Canada's, is probably too disaggregated to be expected to develop on its own a negotiated solution to redistribute check float costs away from payees and to payors and to remove the market failure for check users.

The one negotiated solution to have been tried for business payments did not succeed. This was the ACH Corporate Trade Payments program. A small number of business participants agreed to (1) calculate the average float benefit for check payments among them; (2) alter their trade credit terms to one another to preserve these float benefits; and (3) use ACH payments in place of checks to reduce payment costs. This arrangement had the appeal of preserving the distribution of check float benefits while saving real resources through the use of ACH. More important for the participants was that this program was expected to be able to save even more resources through the associated automation of their accounts payable and receivable processing, along with the automation of the business payment. For a variety of reasons, including bank and corporate disagreement over what format would best meet their respective needs, this program did not expand much beyond a small pilot group, and volume remained very low. Its succeeding concept, Electronic Data Interchange (EDI), is discussed in the chapter by Stone.

The policy issue to be faced here is whether some sort of public intervention may be useful to reduce check market failure and thereby provide a stronger incentive for business check users to shift to electronic payments. The arguments in support of such intervention would consist of cost-benefit analyses indicating that some type of action is in the public interest, both in terms of quantifiable economic costs and in terms of less quantifiable payment risk considerations. For example, it may be time to reconsider an earlier Federal Reserve policy proposal to establish a high-dollar electronic image transmission service for checks above, say, $50,000 or $100,000. Under this arrangement, a digitized image of both sides of a check, including the signature, date, endorsements, MICR line, and dollar amount, would be transmitted to the payer bank for collection. Many things have changed since 1981, when a similar service (called Electronic Check Collection) was last seriously considered. Transmission technologies have improved substantially since that time, potentially lowering costs. There may also now be an increased recognition of the risks that very large dollar checks can create for the payment system, especially when speedier and more secure forms of electronic payments exists (wire transfers). In addition, speedier collection should reduce the incidence of remote disbursement and speed up large-dollar return items.

Consumer Payments

The benefits of check float are small per individual consumer. Correspondingly, market failure is lowest here. Survey information indicates that the average household writes 28 checks per month (Avery et al. 1987). With an average estimated float benefit from writing checks of only $0.07 per consumer check written (table 2–2), the average benefit is just under $2.00

per household per month. This level of market failure would seem insufficient to justify much policy concern.

Alternatively, these results for the average consumer can mask the extent of check market failure at points other than at the mean of the distribution of households. For example, check users in rural areas can generate significantly greater-than-average real resource costs and float benefits from check use because of the difficulty and expense for banks and the Federal Reserve to collect checks written there. In effect, this is a consumer variant of remote disbursement. This situation is currently being addressed through voluntary cooperation by rural banks and the Federal Reserve in a pilot project concerning a so-called electronic clearing zone in the Upper Peninsula of Michigan. In the pilot program, checks will be presented electronically for payment. Thus, the switch from checks to electronics is partial, not total, and involves check truncation with ACH presentment. Such an arrangement allows consumers to write checks, but the back-office processing, transportation, and collection will be through electronic means, saving real resources in the process. This concept is developed in the next section within the context of interstate banking.

Government Payments

The market failure associated with government payments, at least at the federal level, has been directly addressed through administration decisions. The result has been a strong effort by the U.S. Treasury to reduce check use and shift as many federal government payments as possible to electronic means using ACH and wire transfers. This has covered social security payments, federal payroll and military retirement benefits, and even large-dollar federal contract payments. And, even when checks are used, there has been an emphasis on mailing them early so that mail float is lower than it otherwise would be.

The private cost of checks to the government has been extensively investigated (Dudley 1983b; Avery, Dudley, and Synder 1984) and is similar to our estimates for all government checks for 1987 (table 2-2). In 1983 the social cost of an ACH direct deposit of a federal government payment was estimated to be $0.27, while the same payment by check would cost $0.40. Thus, for each payment shifted from checks to ACH in 1983, $0.13 in real resources could be saved. But for each payment made by ACH, the Treasury would have given up $0.66 in check float benefits. This meant that the private cost faced by the Treasury was negative, −$0.26 (from $0.40 real resource cost less $0.66 in check float benefit).

While government user costs clearly favored the continued use of checks (bringing in $0.26 in revenue for each check written), the social costs did not (as each check cost $0.13 more in real resources). Even so, decisions have focused appropriately on the social costs of checks and ACH and therefore have benefited society as a whole. While in principle the power to tax would allow the government to recoup the rise in user costs by taxing those segments of society who benefit from the shift to electronics, this has not been done. Instead of special taxes, a broader approach has been used, where general revenues have (implicitly) been used to cover the higher user costs.

A Partial Solution to Market Failure Through Interstate Banking

While it is the users of payments whose decisions are distorted by the float wedge, there is reason to believe that payment suppliers will in the future reduce some float through the use of improved back-office technologies. These technologies reduce float time on paper payments by speeding up the interbank collection process. In some cases, this involves making the collection process for paper items at least partly electronic. The advantage of back-office technologies is that they require little or no institutional changes on the part of payment users and no imposition of fees on users to counteract float subsidies, which would be difficult to implement in practice. Instead, from the user's viewpoint, the float wedge is simply reduced on paper payments, so that the decisions to use paper versus electronic payment methods are based on comparisons of private costs that are closer to social costs.

The primary motivation for payment suppliers to implement these technologies would not be to reduce float but to reduce payment collection costs. Most of the economies associated with these technologies cannot be achieved without a substantial level of cooperation among payment suppliers, however, and this level cannot easily be achieved within the context of the current unconcentrated structure of the U.S. banking industry. Interstate banking will increase concentration and reduce the costs of cooperation, making these technologies and the associated cost savings and float reduction possible. Thus, the elimination of one source of market failure (high cooperation or negotiation costs among participants) can help to reduce another market failure (float).

The three back-office technologies discussed here are (1) replacement of transit payments with on-us items, (2) improved physical collection of paper items, and (3) electronic collection through data transmission.[16] In practice, (2) and (3) are mutually exclusive, so the total effect will either be (1) plus (2) or (1) plus (3), not all three together. We provide estimates of the reduction in check float associated with each of these possible effects.

Replacement of Transit Payments with On-Us Items

The most efficiently cleared payments are on-us items, those where the payor's and payee's accounts are at the same financial institution. On-us items are internal to a bank and are cleared electronically by transferring funds between accounts. In contrast, transit items, those where the relevant accounts are at different institutions, require interbank transfers (often involving Reserve Banks or correspondent banks) as well as interaccount transfers. In the case of a transit check, interbank and Federal Reserve float is created because the item must be sorted to one of several thousand different end points, handled on average by 1.9 intermediaries, and physically presented to the payer's bank before funds are transferred. On-us checks, by contrast, virtually eliminate bank and Federal Reserve float, although mail and recipient float may remain (see appendix table 2–A3).

As bank concentration increases with interstate banking, some checks and other payments that would otherwise be transit items will become on-us items, reducing bank and Federal Reserve float. When two banks merge, the affected items are those for which one of the merged banks formerly had the payor's account and the other had the payee's account. The average float reduction for the checks that become on-us items is likely to be larger than the average float on the universe of transit checks, since mergers pursuant to interstate banking deregulation will largely be between banks in different cities, where float time is relatively high and where average dollar amounts per check are also larger.

Berger and Humphrey (1988) estimated that almost 4 billion items may shift from transit item to on-us status, with an average float reduction of 1.4 days. Combining these figures with the average value of a check written and the interest rate gives the estimated float reduction from the shift to on-us status (table 2–3, column 1). The total reduction in the value of float across consumer, business, and government checks is only $1.37 billion, or 3.5 percent of the total value of check float.

Improved Physical Collection of Paper Items

Interstate banking will produce an industry with fewer, larger, and more geographically integrated end points, reducing the time required for private-sector banks and the Federal Reserve to collect the remaining transit items. The changing structure of the banking industry under interstate banking will likely have substantial impact on check collection patterns (Berger and Humphrey 1988). First, in the more highly concentrated banking industry resulting from interstate mergers, there will be fewer end points to be served, reducing the number of sorts and deliveries required on transit checks. Second, the larger banks created by interstate banking will take advantage of scale and scope economies in check processing and transportation, reducing the need for intermediary handlings of checks. Third, the greater geographical dispersion of the merged banks, with branches located in different cities, will expedite incoming check transportation, increase opportunities for direct exchanges of checks among clearers, and expand the use of local clearinghouses for presentment of nonlocal items.

The econometric model of the check-clearing market developed in the Berger-Humphrey (1988) study simulated the effects of the entire nation having the banking structure of either California or New York State, as these are large states where statewide branching is allowed. The model predicted that the Federal Reserve's market share would fall by 43–60 percent as a result of bank mergers under interstate banking.[17]

Note that while part of the motivation for reducing the number of intermediary steps in check collection is to reduce interbank and Federal Reserve float, further motivation is also provided by the real resource savings in collection costs. A processing step by a correspondent bank that is eliminated from the endorsement chain saves over \$0.09 on average, in the collection costs for each check, while eliminating a Federal Reserve Bank processing saves over \$0.03 (Berger 1985, table F, footnote j). In effect, therefore, the external costs from check float creation will be reduced in part because of the external benefits from real resource savings in check collection.

The float savings from improved physical collection of paper items will be concentrated in reduced collection time for interzone items, those checks for which the payor's bank and payee's bank are located in two different Federal Reserve check-clearing zones (of which there are 48 nationwide).[18] Anywhere from 0.25 days to 1.5 days may be saved and distributed over 9.3 billion transit items, resulting in estimated float savings of \$1.0 billion, or 2.6 percent of the total value of check float (table 2–3, column 2).

Electronic Collection Through Data Transmission

An alternative to improved physical check collection is electronic collection. Here transit checks are not physically presented to the payer bank

Table 2–3. Sources of Check Float Reduction Associated with Interstate Banking

Check User Group	Source of Total Reduction ($ billions)			Total Effect	
	(1) Shift from Transit to On-Us[a]	(2) Faster Physical Collection[b]	(3) Electronic Collection Through Data Transmission[c]	(4) Shift from Transit to On-Us plus Faster Physical Collection (1) + (2)	(5) Shift from Transit to On-Us plus Electronic Collection (1) + (3)
Consumer Payments	$0.048	$0.059	$0.086		
Business Payments	$1.32	$0.901	$2.56		
Government Payments	0	$0.040	$0.058		
Total float reduction: (percent)	$1.37 (3.50%)	$1.00 (2.56%)	$2.70 (6.91%)	$2.37 (6.06%)	$4.07 (10.41%)

[a] The proportion of on-us checks for Federal Reserve District 12, which contains California and other statewide branching states, was 7.3 percentage points higher than it was for the nation as a whole (Federal Reserve Bank of Atlanta 1979, vol. 2, table 2–11). This district is likely illustrative of how the nation as a whole may look under full interstate banking. Since branching restrictions will likely be slightly less binding under full interstate banking than is currently the case in District 12, this figure was rounded upward: it was thus assumed that on-us volume under full interstate banking will be 8 percentage points higher than the current nationwide level. It was also assumed that the proportion of business checks will be 60% of the total items switched from transit to on-us status (2.256 billion items), reflecting the interstate character of the mergers, and that the remaining 40% to be switched (1.504 billion items) are consumer checks. Government checks were assumed to have no change in on-us status. An average float reduction of 1.404 days was used for these items (consistent with average float on nonlocal transit items in the Federal Reserve Bank of Atlanta 1979, vol. 1, 161). Combining these figures gives an annual reduction in the float subsidy to consumer check use of $0.048 billion, or 2.67% of the value of total consumer check float. For business check writers, the reduction in float earnings is estimated to be $1.32 billion, or 3.74% of the total value of business check float. Combined, these give a total reduction in float benefits of $1.37 billion, or 3.50% of the total. The reduction in consumer check float is $0.048 billion = 1.504 billion checks × $145 per check

× 1.404/365 years of float per check × 0.05775 interest per year. The reduction in business check float is $1.32 billion = 2.256 billion checks × $2636 per check × 1.404/365 years of float per check × 0.05775 interest per year.

^b For each interzone check shifted from Federal Reserve to private-sector processing, float time is assumed to be reduced by 1 day if one Federal Reserve office was processing the check and 1.5 days if Federal Reserve offices in two different zones were processing the item. (In private-sector processing, we include fine-sorted items on which the Federal Reserve provides some transportation and presentment services.) In addition, there is expected to be a 0.25 day float savings on interzone checks that switch to private-sector processing and a 0.25 day float savings on in-zone Federal Reserve items that switch to private-sector processing and a 0.25 day float savings on interzone checks handled entirely by the private sector. The latter items are currently in the private sector but will be handled by fewer correspondent banks and be presented increasingly through local clearinghouses. The econometric simulation model used predicts a reduction in interzone checks processed by one Federal Reserve office from 11.8% of all checks to 6.4%, a reduction in interzone checks processed by two Federal Reserve offices from 3.1% to 1.8%, and a reduction in in-zone Federal Reserve items from 14.4% to 8.5%, using California state assumptions (Berger and Humphrey 1988). In addition, 7.1% of all checks are interzone checks that are currently in the private sector and will remain there. This last group of items has a one-half higher than average proportion of business checks, so that 60% of them are business checks, 36.7% are consumer, and 3.3% are government. From all this, the estimate of float reduction for consumer checks is $0.059 billion = 47 billion checks × [(55% × (11.8% − 6.4%) × $145 per check × 1/365 float years) + (55% × (3.1% − 1.8%) × $145 per check × 1.5/365 years) + (55% × (14.4% − 8.5%) × $145 per check × 0.25/365 years) + (36.7% × 7.1% × $145 per check × 0.25/365 years)] × 0.05775 interest per year. For business (government) checks, this float reduction is $0.901 ($0.040) billion and derived similarly except that 40% (5%) replaces 55% in the formula, 60% (3.3%) replaces 36.7%, and $2636 ($1074) replaces $145. The predicted reduction in the annual float subsidy to checks from faster collection of transit items is $0.059 billion for consumer checks (3.28% of consumer check float benefits), $0.901 billion for business checks (2.55% of business check float), and $0.040 billion for government checks (2.00% of government check float). These total to $1.00 billion, or 2.56% of float benefits.

^c All checks other than on-us and local clearinghouse items were assumed to be candidates for electronic collection. Currently about 54% of all checks are in this category. Assuming that 6 percentage points out of the 8 percentage point increase in on-us checks comes out of this category leaves 48% of all checks. It was judged that 75% of these items could be collected electronically, with the remaining non-on-us, non-clearinghouse items being directly exchanged in reasonably efficient fashion between respondents and correspondents or between nearby banks not in local clearinghouses. Thus, 36% of all checks, or 16.92 billion items, potentially could be collected electronically. Assuming that electronic collection would allow same-day collection of 20% of the items, and next-day collection of 80% of the items, reduces the current 1.404 interbank collection days to 0.80 days, for an average float savings of 0.604 days. As before, it is assumed that the electronically collected checks have a business check proportion one-half higher than the universe of checks. The consumer float reduction estimate is from $0.086 billion = 36.7% × 16.92 billion checks × $145 per check × 0.604/365 years of float × 0.05775 interest per year. The business float reduction estimate is from $2.56 billion = 60% × 16.92 billion checks × $2636 per check × 0.604/365 years of float × 0.05775 interest per year, and the government float reduction is $0.058 billion = 3.3% × 16.92 billion checks × $1074 per check × 0.604/365 years of float × 0.05775 interest per year. These figures represent reductions of 4.78%, 7.25%, and 2.90%, respectively, of the float benefits to consumer, business, and government check users.

before payment, but instead certain information from the check is sent electronically to the payor bank. The collecting bank (or an intermediary acting on its behalf) would send an electronic message to the payor bank, or to its intercepting correspondent, containing the MICR line and dollar value encoded data, which are read electronically off the check. The data could be sent by means of an ACH message or other electronic form not as yet implemented. Settlement of aggregated interbank check totals could take place through conventional means, such as adjustments to interbank correspondent balances or Federal Reserve reserve or clearing accounts, or through Fedwire funds transfers. The physical checks could either be truncated at the transmitting bank or be sent to the payor bank in a slower and less costly manner than occurs today.[19]

Analysis in Berger (1985) shows that both the collecting and payor banks could save real resources through electronic collection of items that currently require the use of an intermediary. The collecting bank would save by eliminating its cost of sending the physical item to an intermediary in an expeditious fashion plus the costs of intermediary services, which would generally be greater than the additional costs of transmitting the data electronically. Net savings would likely be made even for small collecting banks that may have to continue to send the physical items to their intermediaries to be collected electronically from that point onward. Payor banks could save resources by avoiding the costs of receiving and sorting the physical items for daily posting, since the required information would be received electronically.

The problem with electronic check collection is that it requires a high degree of cooperation between collecting and payor banks, because for payor banks, the float losses generally outweigh the real resource gains (see Berger 1985). Also, under current law, checks are sight drafts subject to physical inspection and signature verification. Although payor banks do not inspect signatures except on large-dollar or questionable items, they can legally demand physical presentment for the purpose of capturing float benefits.

Under the current structure of the banking system, with thousands of banks and only one nationwide intermediary (the Federal Reserve), widespread adoption of electronic collection seems difficult because of the high costs of cooperation. Under interstate banking, however, the greater concentration of the banking industry and the greater number of nationwide intermediaries may make this feasible. Perhaps an arrangement similar to that in Canada may evolve. Canadian banks exchange items nightly at eight Regional Settlement Points (RSPs, similar to local clearinghouses), giving each payor bank the checks drawn on *all* its branches. The MICR line and dollar amount encoded data are stripped off the interzone items and transmitted electronically to bank offices in the other seven RSPs the same night. The physical items are then transported by coast-to-coast air courier later that evening.

Electronic collection in the United States could affect 36 percent of all checks, or almost 17 billion items. The average float savings from electronic collection is estimated to be 0.6 days. As shown in table 2–3, column 3, this gives an overall reduction in the value of float of $2.70 billion, only 6.9 percent of total check float benefits.

The total reduction in the check float subsidy from these three back-office technologies is small when compared to total check float. This is mainly because these technologies can only reduce bank and Federal Reserve float, which together constitute less than half of all check float. Since the improved physical collection of transit items and electronic collection of checks are mutually exclusive, the total reduction in the value of check float from interstate banking is estimated to be $4.07 billion (10.4 percent of the total) if electronic collection can be implemented and $2.37 billion (6.1 percent) if it cannot be implemented. It is doubtful whether a 6–10 percent reduction in float benefits will substantially reduce the market failure associated with checks.

Conclusions

This chapter discusses the market failure in the U.S. payments system created by float. The float associated with certain payment instruments creates a substantial wedge between the private costs of using the instrument faced by the user and the social or real resource costs expended in producing and processing the instrument. The misallocation of resources resulting from these faulty market signals constitute an important public policy problem.

The payment instruments with substantial float benefits to users are checks and credit cards, while cash imposes float costs on users. As a result, the former are overused and the latter are underused, from a social viewpoint. The float wedge is greatest for checks, where the $0.83 per check float benefit for the average user outweighs the $0.79 social cost, yielding a *negative* private cost per check of −$0.04.

Electronic payment instruments such as ACH and POS are viable alternatives for many or most check payments. Electronic payments have lower social cost, but because they generate virtually no float, their private costs are higher than checks. As a result, electronics are underused, from a social viewpoint. Checks currently constitute 85 percent of noncash payments, while all electronic payments total only 2 percent. A difficulty in encouraging users to switch to electronics is that no amount of cost reduction for electronic instruments, as through scale economies or productivity improvements, can match the negative private costs of checks.

The float benefits of writing checks are not evenly distributed across users. These benefits vary by both the dollar value of the check and the expected collection time. Business checks, which tend to have both high dollar values and relatively long collection times, generate $1.88 in average float benefits per check, giving a −$1.09 private cost. This represents a substantial market failure, which contributes to a potential real resource loss on the order of $8 billion annually, the amount that may be saved if most business checks were replaced by electronic payments. Consumer checks have only a small float benefit, so that private costs are positive ($0.72) and almost as high as the social costs ($0.79), indicating only a minor market failure. Government checks have higher float, giving a negative private cost of −$0.06. However, the federal government is actively internalizing the social costs and substituting electronic payments for government checks voluntarily, which corrects the market failure.

The market failure caused by float persists for several legal and institutional reasons. The time it takes for a check to be processed and presented to the payor bank for payment in investible funds creates float. In principle, check float could be negotiated away between the payor and payee, or the bank float portion negotiated away between payor and payee banks. However, unless there are other benefits involved (as there may be with EDI), such negotiations would be more expensive than the resource savings from switching a payment from check to electronic form. Using the average business check float time of 4.5 days and an interest rate of 5.775 percent, a business payor's float benefit is only 8 basis points of the amount of the transaction. Even on the large-dollar checks that are collected through the High Dollar Group Sort program, the float benefits are only about $5 per item, which is apparently too small an amount to negotiate over on a transaction exceeding $6000. Thus, negotiation is generally not an institutionally acceptable method for reducing float between individual payees and payors. While the benefits from negotiating away float may be larger for banks, such negotiation has proved difficult because of the current unconcentrated nature of the U.S. banking industry.

From a legal perspective, payors themselves have legal rights to float. Unless otherwise specified by contract, payment is deemed to have been made when the payment instrument has been tendered, not when investible funds are actually transferred. These rights could in principle be offset by negotiation over the forms of payment allowed, or by making the contract price a function of the payment instrument. However, float rights are generally not offset, because of (1) relatively high negotiation costs that outweigh potential real resource gains, (2) institutional inertia and consumer resistance to merchant price discrimination by payment instrument, or (3) a lack of market power on the part of payees.

Finally, there is the possibility of a partial solution to payments market failure through interstate banking. Interstate banking would speed collection of checks between the collecting and payor banks by switching some transit checks to on-us status. Interstate banking would also speed collection of many of the remaining transit items through either improved physical collection or electronic collection through data transmission. However, the likely effect of these innovations is surprisingly small, on the order of only 6–10 percent of total check float.

Of greater potential impact would be a program that concentrated on business checks alone. These items account for 40 percent of all checks written but generate 90 percent of all check float. In particular, a service whereby a digitized image of a check is electronically transmitted to payor banks for payment could eliminate a significant portion of business check float and reduce market failure. Such an arrangement could best be applied first to very large dollar items (say, those in excess of $50,000 or $100,000), because the market failure is largest there. A similar concept was developed in 1981 (Electronic Check Collection) and may usefully be revisited today. Speedier collection means less incentive to continue remote disbursement. Speedier collection also means a speedier return, if these items have to be returned for insufficient funds.

On the whole, it appears that public policy alternatives are limited in the extent to which they can, by themselves, eliminate the market failure created by float. Efforts by the Federal Reserve in accelerating the collection of checks through programs such as High Dollar Group Sort and encouraging electronic collection of high-dollar items may significantly reduce bank and Federal Reserve float, but these components comprise less than half of all check float. Mail and recipient float alone are sufficient to make the average business check have negative private costs. Thus, even if all bank and Federal Reserve float were eliminated, an important market failure would still exist for business checks. The only apparent solution to this remaining cause of market failure is for a substantial number of businesses *voluntarily* to agree to stop writing checks to each other and instead use some form of electronic business data interchange (EDI) to exchange funds and make payments.

Notes

1. For a good survey of the market failure concept, see Layard and Walters (1978, 22–26 and chapter 6), or Bator (1958).

2. At that time, envelopes were not in common use and the nature of what was being delivered could more easily be determined before opening the letter. Letters were merely one or more sheets of paper folded in half and sealed shut.

3. Production costs for credit cards, money orders, and travelers checks are as large or larger than the estimated processing costs. For all other instruments, production costs are small compared to processing costs. See appendix table 2–A2 for more detail.

4. These costs were quite difficult to obtain. The exact procedures used to derive them, including data sources and assumptions made, are shown in appendix tables 2–A1 and 2–A2. This documentation should permit other researchers to determine the impact of other assumptions or approaches they may deem more relevant. Similar methods were used earlier in Humphrey (1984) and Berger and Humphrey (1986) but have been reworked and updated to 1987.

5. In other countries, where crime is significantly lower than in the United States, cash is even more heavily used (e.g., Japan and Switzerland; Bank for International Settlements, forthcoming).

6. The ATM transfer costs reported here refer only to the costs of making a payment, not to the costs of withdrawing cash, making account transfers, or making deposits.

7. Business practice and case law considers a payment as being tendered when cash or a negotiable instrument (e.g., a check) is given at the point-of-sale or when it has been mailed. Once mailed, the instrument cannot be retrieved and the postmark will typically indicate the date and time (a.m. or p.m.) of postal receipt. This is the point where we start our float clock for checks, so mail float can exist for some types of payments. More recently, businesses receiving mailed checks have attempted to take away mail float by using lockbox collection procedures and altering their contracts with payors so that, along with a due date, a later date is specified beyond which time the receipt of a mailed check will lead to a penalty fee. The due date and the date of the penalty charge are sometimes the same but usually differ, to allow for mailing and other frictions. Although the impact of these developments on mail float is difficult to quantify, our estimates of the mail float component of total check float are shown in appendix table 2–A3.

8. While the incentive to underuse cash applies to all users, those in the "underground economy" have likely found that the benefits of avoiding taxes on cash payments for services rendered and the increased ability to cover illegal activities exceeds the float cost of holding idle cash balances.

9. In this regard, we believe our errors are in omission rather than commission. There are, in principle, many "costs" that cannot with any reasonable degree of accuracy and consensus be quantified; some of them were noted in the text (e.g., convenience, speed, reliability).

10. This value for total check float ($39.1 billion) is close to an earlier estimate by Dudley (1983a). His $36.08 billion estimate for 1983 becomes $45.6 billion in 1987 if the likely annual growth in the number of checks written is accounted for ($45.6 = $36.08(1.048)^5$). Left out, of course, is the corresponding rise in the average value of a check and the fact that interest rates are lower today than in 1983.

11. The methodology used to compute these values is described in the notes to table 2–2 and 2–A3. Business checks are outstanding longer than consumer checks primarily because (1) business-to-business checks typically have mail float (1.5 days), and (2) business-to-

consumer checks typically have long recipient float (1.75 days). Similarly, most government checks are for social security payments, payrolls, or retirement payments, which are also typically mailed and not immediately cashed by the recipient. Indeed, the 5-day figure for all government check payments is close to the 5.7 day figure found for a comprehensive study of U.S. government checks (Avery, Dudley, and Snyder 1984, 1, footnote 3). In contrast, close to half of all consumer checks are written at the point-of-sale or for cash acquisition. Here mail float is zero while recipient float is low.

12. The definition of float used here differs from that used by the Federal Reserve and the banking industry. Our float concept is the time period for which the payor has investible funds after payment has been tendered. This is a float benefit that accrues to the payor and can influence the decision to use one payment method versus another. The concept of float commonly used in the banking industry refers to the difference between a bank's or the Federal Reserve's availability schedule and the actual time it takes to collect an item. Even if actual collection times perfectly matched availability schedules, payors would still receive float benefits for the time it took to collect the item.

13. This estimate, of course, needs to be considerably refined. First, the savings estimate should be adjusted downward to reflect the one-time adjustment costs of shifting from paper to electronics and the likely extra costs of providing EDI. Second, it needs to be increased by adding in the additional potential savings in internal business accounts payable/receivable costs from EDI.

14. The $0.07 value of float figure may be understated. If the credit card loan rate of around 18 percent better reflects a consumer's opportunity cost of funds than does the average 90-day Treasury bill rate of 5.775 percent used here, the float benefit to consumers rises to $0.21 per check. This would reduce the private cost of a check to consumers from $0.72 to $0.58.

15. It was assumed that all consumer bill payments (25 percent of all checks) and half of consumer retail purchases (9 percent) could be shifted from checks to electronic payments if consumers found such a shift to be in their interest. Thus, the estimate in real resource savings is from $8.0 billion = $(0.25 + 0.09) \times 47$ billion checks $\times$ $0.50, where the last figure is the difference between check and ACH social cost.

16. Two other back-office improvements that are not discussed in the text are expedited return item handling (which will discourage the writing of high-float checks with insufficient funds) and credit card paperwork truncation at the point-of-sale (which will generally reduce processing time by at least one day).

17. Any reductions in the absolute volume processed by the Federal Reserve would likely be small, however, because of a gradual phase-in of interstate banking and offsetting growth in the number of checks written over the intervening time period. Thus actual volume losses at Reserve Banks might average only 1-3 percent per year.

18. Data availability problems prohibit focusing directly on interstate items, although in most cases, interstate items are also interzone.

19. Electronic collection through data transmission differs from high-dollar electronic image transmission. In the former, only the bank routing-transit number, customer account, and check number (which will make up the MICR line), along with the dollar amount of the check, is transmitted. This is all the information that is normally used to debit an account, since the signature, date of the check, and the endorsements are not normally inspected (but may be important if high-dollar checks are being paid).

References

American Express. 1983. *Annual Report.*

Avery, Robert, Gregory Elliehausen, Arthur Kennickell, and Paul Spindt. 1987. "Changes in the Use of Transaction Accounts and Cash from 1984 to 1986." *Federal Reserve Bulletin* 73 (March): 179–196.

Avery, Robert, William Dudley, and Eugene Snyder. 1984. *Social Security Check Float.* Washington, D.C.: Board of Governors of the Federal Reserve System.

Bank Administration Institute. 1985. *Banking Issues and Innovations.* Chicago.

Bank for International Settlements. 1985. *Payment Systems in Eleven Developed Countries,* rev. ed. Chicago: Bank Administration Institute.

Bator, Francis M. 1958. "The Anatomy of Market Failure." *Quarterly Journal of Economics* (August): 351–379.

Berger, Allen N. 1985. "Electronic Payments Technology, Deregulation, and Interstate Banking." Working Paper, Board of Governors of the Federal Reserve System, Washington, D.C.

Berger, Allen N., and David B. Humphrey, 1986. "The Role of Interstate Banking in the Diffusion of Electronic Payments Technology." In *Technological Innovation, Regulation, and the Monetary Economy,* ed. Colin Lawrence and Robert Shay. Cambridge, Mass.: Ballinger.

———. 1988. "Interstate Banking and the Payments System." *Journal of Financial Services Research* 1 (January): 133–145.

Board of Governors of the Federal Reserve System. *Federal Reserve Bulletin,* various issues. Washington, D.C.

———. 1983. *Credit Cards in the U.S. Economy,* Washington, D.C.

———. 1986. *Functional Cost Analysis.* Washington, D.C.

———. 1987a. *Annual Report.* Wasington, D.C.

———. 1987b. *Planning and Control System Expense Report* (PACS). Washington, D.C.

Carreker, J. D., and Associates, Inc. 1985. *Return Item Study: Final Report.* Prepared for the Bank Administration Institute.

Cirrus System, Inc. 1985. *Madison Report.* Proprietary consultant's report on retail payments in the U.S.

Cumming, Bruce D. 1983. "Understanding and Managing Canadian Availability: A Neglected Cash Management Opportunity." *Journal of Cash Management* 3 (February–March): 26–31.

Curtin, Richard T. 1983. *Payment Method Costs: Assessments by Retailers.* Ann Arbor: Survey Research Center, University of Michigan.

Dingle, James F. 1986. "Technical Note: Introduction of Retroactive Settlement for the Daily Clearing of Cheques and Other Payment Items." *Bank of Canada Review* (August): 3–7.

Displacing the Check. 1983. Special Issue of *Economic Review* 68 (August). Federal Reserve Bank of Atlanta.

Dudley, William C. 1983a. "The Tug-of-War over 'Float.'" *Morgan Guaranty*

Survey (December): 11–14.

————. 1983b. A *Comparison of Direct Deposit and Check Payment Costs*, 2d ed. Washington, D.C.: Board of Governors of the Federal Reserve System.

Faulhaber, Gerald R., Almarin Phillips, and Anthony M. Santomero. 1989. "Payment Risk, Network Risk, and the Role of the Fed." In *The U.S. Payment System: Efficiency, Risk, and the Role of the Federal Reserve*, ed. David B. Humphrey. Boston: Kluwer Academic Publishers.

Federal Reserve Bank of Atlanta. 1979. *A Quantitative Description of the Check Collection System*, vols. 1 and 2.

Humphrey, David B. 1984. *The U.S. Payments System: Costs, Pricing, Competition, and Risk*. Monograph 1984–1/2, Salomon Brothers Center for the Study of Financial Institutions, Graduate School of Business Administration, New York University, New York, N.Y.

Jackson, D. Mark. 1987. "Are ATM Strategies Changing?" *Magazine of Bank Administration* 63 (April): 16–18.

Kutler, Jeffery. 1988. "Payment System Gains Ground But Progress Is Slow." *American Banker* (March): 21.

Layard, P.R.G., and A.A. Walters. 1978. *Microeconomic Theory*. New York: McGraw-Hill.

National Commission on Electronic Fund Transfers. 1977. *EFT in the United States*. Washington, D.C.

Penzer, Michael L. 1978. "The Nature and Size of Money Order and Traveler's Check Markets in California and the Nation." Mimeograph, Economic and Financial Information Division, California State Banking Department.

Pierce, James L. 1977. "The Users of Money Orders." Mimeograph, Department of Economics, University of California, Berkeley, Calif.

POS News. 1988. (January). Chicago: Barlo Communications Division of Faulkner and Gray, Inc.

Robinson, Michael A. 1987. "Travelers Check Industry Rebounds." *American Banker* (September 3).

Scheele, Carl H. 1970. *A Short History of the Mail Service*. Washington, D.C.: Smithsonian Institution Press.

Stone, Bernell K. 1989. "The Electronic Payment Industry: Change Barriers and Success Requirements from a Market Segments Perspective." In *The U.S. Payment System: Efficiency, Risk, and the Role of the Federal Reserve*, ed. David B. Humphrey. Boston: Kluwer Academic Publishers.

Survey Research Center. 1978. *Household Mail Stream Study*. Prepared for the Mail Classification Research Division, Rates and Classification Department, U.S. Postal Service. Ann Arbor: Survey Research Center, University of Michigan.

————. 1980. *Nonhousehold Mail Stream Study*. Prepared for the Mail Classification Research Division, Rates and Classification Department, U.S. Postal Service. Ann Arbor: Survey Research Center, University of Michigan.

The Nilson Report. 1987. Los Angeles: HSN Consultants, Inc.

Trans Data Corporation. 1988. *1988 Bank Pricing Program*. Salisbury, Md.

U.S. Postal Service. 1986. *We Deliver: The Story of the U.S. Postal Service*. Publication No. 1. Washington, D.C.

———. 1987. *Costs and Revenue Analysis Report*. Washington, D.C.

Wall Street Journal. 1985. "Canceled Checks Are Destroyed at Some Banks, Producing Savings." (February 21): 1.

Zimmer, Linda Fenner. 1987. "ATMs: An Industry Status Report." *Magazine of Bank Administration* 63 (May): 30–37.

Appendix

Table 2–A1. Volume, Value, and Growth of Different Payment Instruments, 1987

Type of Payment Instrument	Volume (millions)	Total Value ($ trillions)	Average Dollar Value	Annual Growth (1986–1987)	Percentage Volume Composition
	(1)	(2)	(3)	(4)	(5)
Nonelectronic					
Cash[a]	278,600	$ 1.4	$ 5	8%	83.42%
Checks[b]	47,000	55.8	1,188	5	14.07
Credit cards[c]	5,111	0.317	62	7	1.53
Travelers checks[d]	1,354	0.047	35	9	0.40
Money orders[e]	811	0.07	86	4	0.24
					99.66%
Electronic					
ACH[f]	936	$ 3.6	$ 3,882	26%	0.28%
Wire transfers[g]	84	281.0	3,300,000	7	0.03
POS[h]	55	0.000822	15	59	0.02
ATM bill payment[i]	29	0.002	70	3	0.01
					0.34%

[a] *Cash.* Cash transactions are not directly reported. An educated guess by a national commission put cash transactions at two-thirds of all types of transactions (National Commission on Electronic Fund Transfers 1977, 333). A comprehensive survey of retail establishments (covering food-supermarkets, automotive, general merchandise, gas stations, restaurants, hotel-motel, airline, car rental, home improvement-hardware, apparel, furniture-furnishings-appliances, drugstore, nonstore retailers, liquor, and jewelry stores) reported 94 billion cash transactions worth $468 billion, for an average value per cash transaction of $4.98 or $5.00 (Cirrus 1985, 11–12). Cash transactions (expenditures) comprised 87% (43%) of all retail transactions, while checks and credit cards were each used 6% of the time (26% and 18%, respectively, for check and credit card expenditures). But retail sales are primarily consumer purchases rather than purchases by business or government. Business or government purchases, no matter where from, would in any event almost always be by check, ACH, or wire transfer rather than

cash. Therefore, the estimate of the total value of cash transactions used in the table relies upon an estimate of cash transactions by consumers. This, in turn, is based on a household survey of currency and transaction account usage (Avery et al. 1987, special computer run), which indicated that the average family (which includes more than one adult) spends $829 per month in coin and currency transactions compare1 to $2228 a month on check transactions (excluding checks used to obtain cash). Thus, for every $2.69 spent via check, $1 is spent using cash ($829/$2228 = $1/$2.69). Dividing the $3.748 trillion value for check expenditures by consumers by $2.69 gives $1.393 trillion as an estimate of the total value of consumer cash transactions. The $3.748 trillion value for consumer check expenditures is from the 55% of all checks written by consumers (table 2–A3) times the number of all checks written (47 billion—see below) times the average value of a consumer check ($145, table 2–A3), or $3.748 trillion = 0.55(47 billion)($145). Dividing the $1.393 trillion estimate of the total value of consumer cash (and therefore all cash) transactions by the $5 average value per transaction gives 278,600 million as a very approximate estimate of the total number of cash transactions. This volume figure represents 83% of the total of all types of transactions shown in the table. The annual growth of cash transactions shown reflects the actual growth in coin and currency in circulation, assumed to equal the growth in transaction value.

    b *Check*. The number of (private) checks written in 1979 was 32.8 billion (Federal Reserve Bank of Atlanta 1979, 1) and the growth rate between 1979 and 1987 was estimated to be 4.8% annually. These data suggest that 47 billion checks would have been written in 1987. The average value per check transaction in the Atlanta study was $757 in 1979 (p. 73) and was increased to $1188 for 1987 using the 57% inflation (cost-of-living index) experienced between 1980 and 1987. The value per check transaction is skewed upwards due to a small number of exceptionally large-dollar checks that are written.

    c *Credit Cards*. Data on credit cards covers purchase transaction volumes for retail (30%), bank (44%), and oil company (26%) cards for 1986 (*The Nilson Report*, March, May, and June issues, 1987). Dividing total value ($317 billion) by the total number of transactions (5.111 billion) gave an average value per transaction of $62 in 1986 (Bank for International Settlements, 1985, table C, and Avery, et al. 1987). Transaction volume growth was approximately 7%.

    d *Travelers Checks*. The average number of days a travelers check was outstanding at American Express in 1986 was 70 days, from [(365 days) (average daily value of outstanding travelers checks of $3.3 billion)/(total sales of travelers checks in 1986 of $17.1 billion)] = 7, as reported in American Express, *Annual Report*, 1983. Assuming this figure applies as well to all nonbank travelers checks issued, the total value of nonbank travelers checks is estimated to be $36.5 billion (from (365 days/70 days) times $7.0 billion in average daily value of U.S. dollar-denominated outstanding nonbank travelers checks reported in the money supply statistics in the *Federal Reserve Bulletin*, December 1987, table 1.21, p. A13). Bank travelers checks are included in demand deposits and not separately listed, but the combined market share of BankAmerica and Citicorp travelers checks is around 23% (Robinson 1987). Thus, the total travelers check market is estimated to be $47.4 billion in 1987 ($36.5 billion/(1 – 0.23)). Since actual data are proprietary, we assume that $50 and $20 travelers checks were issued in equal proportions (and neglect the $100 and $10 face value checks), giving an average face value per travelers check of $35. Transactions volume was thus estimated as 1354 million (from $47.4 billion/$35 = 1354 million). This is very approximate, since some transactions require more than one travelers check while for others one is too much and cash is received back as change. Annual growth was computed from data on the value of outstanding travelers checks reported in the *Federal Reserve Bulletin* referenced above.

    e *Money Orders*. Accurate data on money orders exist only for those issued by the U.S. Postal Service. Penzer (1978, 26) estimatec that postal money orders constituted between 15% and 21% of the value of all money orders issued by bank holding companies, private firms, and the U.S. postal service in 1976. We take the midpoint of 18% as the Postal Service's market share. Having no other information, we assume that this market share can be applied to the value ($12.511 billion) and volume (146 million) of postal money orders processed in 1987 (Board of Governors of the Federal Reserve System, *Annual Report* 1987a, table 11). Under this assumption, the value of all money orders in 1987 is estimated to be $70 billion, with 811 million being issued. The implied average dollar value per postal money order is $86. Growth of postal money orders processed by the Federal Reserve was 4% between 1986 and 1987.

[f] *ACH.* ACH transaction volumes and growth are from the National Automated Clearing House Association, reported in Kutler (1988). The data include Federal Reserve and private-sector processing volume (the latter of which is almost entirely from the New York Clearing House). Total ACH volume was 936 million in 1987. The value per commercial ACH transaction averaged $6390. This number is strongly influenced by the ACH transfers that occur on the night cycle, which is primarily used for concentrating corporate cash balances from receiving banks to disbursing banks. The average government ACH transaction value was $628 (largely payroll), while the average value for all ACH transactions was $3882. Multiplying $3882 by 936 million transactions gives $3.6 trillion as an estimate for total ACH value transacted.

[g] *Wire Transfer.* Wire transfer volumes are for Fedwire and CHIPS. Volume data for Fedwire and CHIPS are adjusted downward to correct for transfers counted twice when handled by two Federal Reserve offices. Fedwire had 53 million transfers worth $142 trillion, or $568 billion per day over 250 business days (Board of Governors of the Federal Reserve System 1987b, table 11). CHIPS had 31 million transfers worth $139 trillion, or $556 billion per day over 250 business days. The average value per transaction was $2.7 million for Fedwire and $4.5 million for CHIPS. Putting these figures together gives the values shown in the table.

[h] *POS.* There are 82 million POS or debit card transactions per year. However, some of these represent cash withdrawals or "cash-backs" from a purchase transaction. Of the total monthly value of $193.7 million of POS transactions, purchases accounted for 35.4%, or $68.5 million per month. Thus, for 12 months, the value of POS purchases was $822 million. Since the average POS purchase transaction was $15, the implied volume of yearly POS transactions was 54.8 million (all these data are from *The Nilson Report*, October 1987, 3). Average yearly growth in POS purchase transaction volume, is obtained by using the 6-month growth in POS terminals (26%) between June 1987 and January 1988 (*POS News* 1988, 1), yielding a 59% annual growth rate ($1.59 = 1.26^2$).

[i] *ATM Bill Payment.* The ATM transfers in the table refer only to bill payment transactions (excluding cash withdrawal, balance inquiry, and account transfer transactions). Zimmer (1987) estimates that there were 69,161 ATM machines being used, with an average of 5,000 of all types of transactions per month per machine, giving a total estimated volume of 4.150 billion in 1986. ATM bill payments were between 0.4% (Jackson 1987, 16) and 1% (*Displacing the Check* 1983, chart 6) of this total. The average figure (0.7%) yields an estimated ATM bill payment volume of 29 million. We concentrate on the bill payment aspect of ATM usage because we are interested in the payment method used for the final transaction. Since cash transactions have been included in the cash category, ATM cash withdrawals are excluded here. The average value of an ATM bill payment was assumed to be the same as the average value of all ATM transactions, which was $70 in 1984 ($90 billion in ATM withdrawals plus $182 billion in ATM deposits divided by 3.91 billion ATM financial transactions for 1984). The total ATM bill payment transaction value of $2 billion is from the 29 million bill payment transactions times an average value per transaction of $70. Annual ATM transaction growth of 3% was from reported growth in ATM net installed capacity (from 61,177 to 69,161 machines between 1986 and 1987; Zimmer 1987, 31) and the reduction in the estimated number of transactions per machine per month (from 5,500 to 5,000, same period and source).

Table 2–A2. User Prices and Social Costs of Different Payment Instruments, 1987 (in $ millions or unit costs)

Type of Payment Instrument	Production Cost (Unit Cost)	Processing Cost (Unit Cost)	Total Social or Real Resource Cost (Unit Cost)	Float Transfer Payment (+ for Cost, – for Benefit) (Unit Cost)	Total User Charges (Unit Price)[p]
	(1)	(2)	(1) + (2) = (3)	(4)	(3) + (4) = (5)
Nonelectronic					
Cash	$ 419[a]	$10,858[b]	$11,277	$13,283[c]	$24,560[d]
	(0.00)	(0.04)	(0.04)	(0.05)	(0.09)
Checks	1705[e]	35,641[f]	37,346	–39,100[g]	–1754
	(0.04)	(0.76)	(0.79)	(–0.83)	(–0.04)
Credit cards[h]	2257	2249	4506	–2257	2249
	(0.44)	(0.44)	(0.88)	(–0.44)	(0.44)
Travelers checks[i]	995	609	1604	0	1604
	(0.73)	(0.45)	(1.18)	(0.00)	(1.18)
Money orders[j]	933	518	1451	0	1451
	(1.15)	(0.64)	(1.79)	(0.00)	(1.79)
Electronic					
ACH	$0	$273[k]	$273	–$1[l]	$272
	(0.00)	(0.29)	(0.29)	(–0.00)	(0.29)
Wire transfers	0	616[m]	616	–2[j]	614
	(0.00)	(7.33)	(7.33)	(–0.02)	(7.31)
POS[n]	0	26	26	0	26
	(0.00)	(0.47)	(0.47)	(0.00)	(0.47)
ATM bill payment[o]	6	13	19	1	20
	(0.21)	(0.45)	(0.66)	(0.03)	(0.69)

[a] *Cash.* Production costs were estimated by multiplying the number of currency notes outstanding (11,776 million) times an average production cost of $26 per 1000 notes produced at the Bureau of Engraving and Printing (giving $306 million). The weighted average cost of

coin issue is $0.0107 per coin at the U.S. Mint for approximately 154 billion coins outstanding (giving $1648 million). This production cost for all currency and coin outstanding is transformed into a yearly cost as follows. Since the average $1 bill (37% of currency notes outstanding) is replaced every 1.5 years, with other denominations replaced at more infrequent intervals, all currency was assumed to be replaced every 2 years. Coin has a very long lifetime but requires replacement over time as individual coins are lost. For our purposes, coin was assumed to be replaced every 15 years. To these replacement costs are added the cost of producing new currency and coin due to yearly growth in demand, a function of inflation and population growth. The yearly growth of cash has been 8% over 1985–1987. In sum, the yearly production cost of cash is $419 million ($306 million/2 + $1648 million/15 + ($306 million + $1648 million) × 0.08 = $419 million a year).

b *Cash.* Payee costs of accepting cash for retail sales include point-of-sale and accounting costs, the costs of theft and loss of cash, safekeeping and security costs, along with deposit costs and fees paid to financial institutions (Curtin 1983). These costs, expressed as a percentage of the average cash retail transaction amount, were 2% (and 2.5% for check). Studies have suggested that the share of retail sales paid for by cash is around 30%. Applying this 30% share and the 2% cost percentage to all retail sales in 1987 of $1505 billion yields a total payee cost of cash of $9030 million (0.02 × 0.30 × $1505 billion). This payee cost estimate covers payee bank cash costs as well. Payor costs of using cash cannot be reliably estimated but would include the cost of lost cash and theft along with the cost of obtaining cash from a bank. The bank costs of giving cash over the counter when checks are cashed are estimated to be $1674 million. This estimate is derived primarily from the 1986 *Functional Cost Analysis* (FCA) data for the 76 banks with over $200 million in deposits. The smaller banks were discarded to offset the bias toward smaller banks in the FCA sample, although the difference would be negligible. The per-transaction cost of giving cash is estimated to be $0.314. The number of checks cashed per personal account was estimated by taking the total on-us plus transit checks cashed by the average bank per year and dividing by the average number of personal accounts per bank (for those banks reporting a separate breakout by type of account), giving 48.55 cashings per account per year. The aggregate number of personal accounts was estimated to be 109.8 million (from Avery et al. 1987, special unpublished computer run). Total check cashing costs were therefore estimated to be $0.314 × 48.55 × 109.8 million = $1674 million. Federal Reserve costs in transporting and processing currency and coin, including the cost of retiring old and counterfeit currency, was $154 million (Board of Governors of the Federal Reserve System 1987b). Thus, the payee ($9030 million), payor and bank ($1674 million), and Federal Reserve ($154 million) processing cost of cash is $10,858 million.

c *Cash.* The opportunity cost of holding idle coin and currency was derived from evaluating the $230 billion in coin and currency in circulation in 1987, which is less than the $271 billion outstanding, at the average 90-day Treasury bill rate in 1987 (5.775%), giving $13,283 million. This figure excludes coin and currency held by the U.S. Treasury and Reserve Banks but includes idle cash balances at depository institutions. That vault cash at banks can be used to satisfy reserve requirements reflects the fact that effective reserve requirements were lowered in 1959, not the possibility that the seigniorage benefits to the government were reduced and that vault cash costs are now part of reserve requirements.

d *Cash.* This figure excludes the government production cost of $364 million and the portion of processing costs borne by the Federal Reserve, $154 million, both of which are provided free. The remaining private-sector costs are assumed to be passed onto cash customers through higher prices.

e *Check.* Check production costs were estimated by taking the actual production costs per standard consumer-type check (2.5¢ per item) and business-type check (5.0¢ per item) for a large East Coast check printing firm and multiplying these average production costs by the volume of the types of checks written. The number of consumer, business, and government checks estimated to be written are, respectively, 25.8, 18.8, and 2.4 billion (table 2–2). Government checks are more like business checks and are included there. Thus the total check production cost is estimated to be ($0.025 × 25.8 billion consumer checks) + ($0.05 × (18.8 billion business checks + 2.4 billion government checks)) = $1705 million.

[f] *Check.* Check-processing costs were composed of accounting and disbursing costs of business and government payors, postage ($0.22) and envelope costs ($0.02) for all payors (business, government, and consumer), and bank costs. The opportunity cost of consumer payors in taking time to write and mail checks was not included because few consumer payors actually have the opportunity of getting paid for the time saved if they did not write checks. Accounting and disbursing costs for business and government payors is estimated to be $0.24 per check or payment transaction, based on the $0.239 per payment transaction cost for the U.S. Treasury's direct deposit program (Dudley 1983b). This excludes all postage, commercial bank, and Federal Reserve check-processing and collection expenses. Thus, $0.24 times the sum of business and government checks written (21.2 billion items, table 2–2) gives $5088 million in business and government payor costs. According to U.S. Postal Service sources, there were 153.9 billion pieces of mail handled in fiscal 1987. Earlier analyses by the University of Michigan's Survey Research Center (1978 and 1980) indicated that 82.5% of all mail sent originated in the nonhousehold sector, while 17.5% originated from households. Of nonhousehold originated mail, 35% was bill payment related and typically included checks sent to pay for bills received. In contrast, 75% of all household originated mail was bill payment related. Overall, some 42% ($0.75 × 0.175 + 0.35 × 0.825 = 0.42$) of all mail (153.9 billion items) is estimated to be payment-related, either sending a bill to be paid, paying a bill through the mail using a check, or both. At $0.24 each, the 64.638 million in payment-related items generates $15,513 million in consumer, small business, and corporate payor stamp and envelope costs. Since almost all of these mailed items are likely to be first-class mail, and the number of first-class items was 78.9 million in 1987, bill payment related mail comprises 82% of all first-class mail in this estimate. Bank processing-transportation costs per check were estimated to be $0.32, which includes (1) costs of crediting a deposit account of $0.057, (2) costs of processing and transporting transit items (either by the payee bank or its intermediaries) of $0.049, (3) costs of an on-us debit of $0.177, (4) costs of handling return items of $0.012, and (5) the cost of returning canceled checks to account holders of $0.029. These estimates were based primarily on data from the 1986 *Functional Cost Analysis* (FCA) data for the 76 banks with over $200 million in deposits. The smaller banks were discarded to offset the bias toward smaller banks in the FCA sample, although the estimates would not be substantially different if these smaller banks were included. The estimate in (1) was determined by dividing the cost of handling a deposit ($0.3627) by the number of checks per average deposit (6.386). The estimate in (2) was determined by multiplying the cost of a transit check deposited ($0.0975) by the proportion of total handlings accounted for by transit items (0.507). (Note that this proportion is less than the proportion of transit checks overall, since all transit checks are also handled as on-us items by other banks). The estimate in (3) is simply the FCA's estimate of the cost of an on-us debit. The estimate in (4) was determined using data from a return item study by J.D. Carreker and Associates (1985). It was estimated that 350 million out of about 40 billion items in 1985 were returned, for a ratio of 0.00875. The estimated costs to reject the item are $0.71, and the estimated costs to send the item each step backward through the endorsement chain is $0.43. We assume that the $0.43 also applies to returning the item to the payee. The average return item cost of $0.012 was therefore determined to be $(0.00875) × ($0.71 + $0.43 + ($0.43 × (0.507)))$, where 0.507 is the transit-handling proportion discussed above. The estimate in (5) was determined by taking the check safekeeping savings of $7.00 per account

per year (i.e., the savings from not returning canceled checks to payors) reported by Valley National Bank (*Wall Street Journal* 1985) and dividing by the number of checks written per account per year (237.28). Thus, bank processing costs are $0.32 × 47 billion checks = $15,040 million. Together, the business and government payor accounting and disbursing costs ($5,088 million), the mailing costs for all payors ($15,513 million), and the bank costs just derived total $35,641 million in check-processing costs. Bank costs will include Federal Reserve check-processing and transportation costs.

[g] *Check.* The total value of check float in 1987 is estimated to be $39.1 billion (table 2–2, note c). Dividing by 47 billion checks written gives a per-item float benefit of $0.83. The cost of holding funds earning little on or interest in a checking account is assumed to be a soft-dollar payment for services and is therefore implicitly included under production and processing costs rather than float costs.

[h] *Credit Cards.* According to a Bank Administration Institute study (unpublished) referenced in the *American Banker* (April 9, 1985, 16), bank credit card transactions are outstanding an average of 45 days. Thus, total credit card float costs are estimated in the *American Banker* (April 9, 1985, 16) to be $2257 million (from $317 billion in yearly charge volume in table 2–A1 divided by 365 days times 45 days a transaction is outstanding times the 90-day Treasury bill rate of 0.05775). Credit card production costs—which include the costs of issuing the cards, maintaining the account, and paying the merchants—on average equaled the cost of float (*American Banker* referenced above) and is presumed to do so today ($2257 million). Retail or merchant processing costs were $0.44 per credit card transaction, giving a total processing cost of $2249 million (from 5111 million card transactions in table 2–A1 times $0.44 from Board of Governors of the Federal Reserve System 1983, 43). Thus, the total social (user) costs of credit card transactions are estimated to be $4506 ($2249) million, with a unit cost estimate of $0.88 ($0.44) per transaction.

[i] *Travelers Checks.* Production, processing, and operating costs for travelers checks is proprietary. Thus, it was assumed that revenues associated with issuing travelers checks equaled the costs involved. Generally, an issuing fee of 1% of the face value of the travelers check is assessed, yielding a revenue flow of $470 million (from 0.01 times $47 billion in table 2–A1). Further revenue to the issuer is obtained from float, since the average travelers check is estimated to be outstanding for 70 days (see table 2–A1, note d). (Penzer (1978, 32) estimated that a travelers check was outstanding for an average of 57 days in 1976). Float revenues to the issuer are $525 million (from 0.05775—the 90-day Treasury bill rate in 1987—times $7.0 billion/(1 – 0.23), which was the average daily value of outstanding travelers checks noted in table 2–A1, note d, adjusted upwards to account for bank travelers checks). Thus, the costs of issuing and paying travelers checks, which would also cover the expense of funding lost checks, is $525 million plus $470 million for a total of $995 million. The retail cost of handling and processing travelers checks is assumed to be equal to that for cash of $0.45 per transaction (Board of Governors of the Federal Reserve System 1983, 43), which yields a cost of $0.45 times 1345 million transactions (table 2–A1) = $609 million. While there is float associated with travelers checks (($525 million in float divided by 1345 million transactions) = $0.39 in float cost per travelers check), we have assumed that all float revenues in fact cover operating costs, so float in the same sense as check float, or the opportunity cost of holding idle funds, in the same sense as applied to the issuance of cash by the government, does not exist. Put differently, travelers check float is not the same thing as a redistribution of income between payor and payee but rather an alternative method of covering operating expenses for the issuer of the travelers check. Since this is a reasonably competitive industry, we have assumed that there is no monopoly power on the part of the issuer to obtain above normal profits (such a situation does not apply to the issuance of currency by the government). In sum, the user and social unit costs of a travelers check are the same at $1.18 per transaction (($995 million plus $609 million) divided by 1345 million transactions).

^{j} *Money Orders.* Federal Reserve cost in processing 146 million postal money orders in 1987 was $2.8 million (direct and allocated costs plus overhead (39% of total activity costs), from Board of Governors of the Federal Reserve System 1987b), or $0.019 per money order. This unit cost figure was applied to the 811 million money orders estimated to have been used in 1987 (from table 2–A1), giving $15 million. Merchant or receiver processing costs were assumed to equal that reported for checks at a sample of retail stores of $0.50 per item for a total merchant processing cost of (811 million money orders) × ($0.50) = $406 million (Board of Governors of the Federal Reserve System 1983, 43). It was assumed that one-half of all money orders are mailed by the user, giving an extra user cost of $97 million (from postage ($0.22) plus envelope costs ($0.02) times 0.5 (811 million items) = $97 million). This assumption is supported in a survey of money order users in California by Pierce (1977), who found that the payment of utility and other monthly bills plus sending money to relatives or friends accounts for almost two-thirds of the responses as to why money orders were used (his appendix table A–3, 8). Total money order processing costs are thus estimated to be $518 million. Money order production costs, including all costs of distributing them to users plus the costs of redemption, are taken from postal money order fiscal year data for 1984 (and thus will not exactly agree with the volume and value figures for postal money orders processed by the Federal Reserve in calendar year 1987). The directly allocated production costs for postal money orders were $0.79 per item ($112 million in directly allocated cost divided by 142 million items in fiscal year 1987, from U.S. Postal Service 1987). Revenues, however, were $1.15 per item ($148 million from fees plus $16 million from float, giving $164 million total, divided by 142 million items). Money orders are estimated to be outstanding between 5 and 11 days (Penzer 1978, 8). Taking the midpoint (8 days) generates an estimated float benefit of $16 million for postal money orders ($16 million = $12.511 billion annual value of postal money orders times 8/365 of a year outstanding times 0.05775 interest rate). Revenues from money orders ($164 million) in excess of directly allocated costs ($112 million) are allocated to Postal Service overhead for all services offered. These overhead costs are viewed as joint costs and are reallocated back to the individual services according to certain criteria, one of which is the value of the service to the user (Ramsey pricing). Thus, it is impossible to determine if postal money order revenues cover all costs or if excess profits (or losses) are being incurred and cross-subsidization exists. Penzer (1978, 6) has noted that use of postal money orders peaked in 1952 and subsequently lost market share to bank-issued money orders and private firms. This implies that postal money orders face a competitive market and, if anything, may be cross-subsidized rather than be used to cross-subsidize other postal services. As a result, we assume here that all postal money order revenues are used to cover all costs, even though it is likely that costs may exceed total revenues by some unknown amount. This implies that the fully allocated cost of a postal money order is at least $1.15 per item, and this is used to approximate the unknown production cost of all money orders. Thus, total production costs of all money orders is estimated to be $1.15 × (811 million items) = $933 million, for a total social cost of $1451 million. Total user costs are the same because total money order float costs of $89 million (from $0.11 times 811 million items) are presumed to be fully used to cover real resource costs and represent an alternative charging method rather than a transfer payment.

^{k} *ACH.* Payor ACH costs are estimated to be $0.18 per ACH item, based on the government's direct deposit ACH costs (Dudley 1983b). Applying this origination cost to the total volume of ACH items originated (936 million items, table 2–A1) gives $168 million as an estimate of government and business payor costs. Payee and bank ACH costs were derived by multiplying the 1987 weighted average per item commercial bank price for ACH ($0.089, from Trans Data Corporation 1988, 42) by 1987 ACH item volume (936 million), giving $83 million. This includes per-item fees, tape-handling costs, and other ACH charges. The commercial bank prices used included all Federal Reserve costs ($71 million, from Board of Governors of the Federal Reserve System 1987b, including a 16% PSAF). Lastly, some bills paid through an ACH are first mailed to payors as a notification prior to debiting a customer's account. These costs ($0.22 for postage plus $0.02 for an envelope) are assumed to apply to 20% of ACH commercial volume, which is around one-half of total ACH volume of 936 million. Thus, mail costs of $22 million ($22 million = $0.24 × 0.10 × 936 million) are added to ACH costs of $251 million, giving total ACH processing costs of $273 million.

l *ACH.* ACH debits do create some float, like checks, but there is no float associated with ACH credits (which are like European giro payments). ACH debit float, evaluated at the 90-day Treasury bill rate cited above, gives less than $1 million in float value in 1987. Wire transfer also can create some float, and fluctuates between debit and credit float (none for CHIPS). Over 1987, wire transfer debit float valued at less than $2 million was created. Debit float is a user benefit; credit float is a user cost.

m *Wire Transfers.* Wire transfer volume in table 2–A1 (84 million) was multiplied by a weighted average commercial bank charge for wire transfers ($7.33, from Trans Data Corporation 1988, 72) to give the total cost of wire transfers ($616 million). The Federal Reserve wire transfer cost components, from Board of Governors of the Federal Reserve System 1987b and the PSAF, was $66 million and was assumed to be fully passed on to final users in these bank fees.

n *POS.* Some POS networks utilize a direct debit to an account (like an ATM withdrawal or bill payment with a unit cost of $0.66). Other networks are configured to work more slowly through an ACH, which has a unit cost of $0.27. Lacking strong evidence on the real cost of POS, we assumed that it is likely to lie between that for an ATM direct debit and an ACH transfer. The simple average of these two unit costs was $0.47, which was used to approximate the cost of a POS transaction. There is no float associated with POS transactions (except for those functioned through an ACH, but the value of this float is small), so the user costs and the social costs ($0.47 × 55 million POS transactions = $26 million) are the same.

o *ATM Bill Payment.* The cost per ATM transaction was reported to be between $0.50 and $0.60 (Bank Administration Institute 1985, 4). A per-transaction cost of $0.55 was used plus $0.089 for ATM bill payments processed through an ACH, giving $0.639 as a unit social cost. Total ATM bill payment social costs were estimated from $0.639 times 29 million transactions, shown in table 2–A1, giving $19 million. There can be a float cost associated with ATM usage for bill payment, since, if the ACH is used to credit the payment receiver's account at another institution, a customer-initiated bill payment (an ACH credit transfer) will be processed the next day on the ACH day cycle with at least a one-day funds availability schedule for the payee. Thus, an ATM bill payment processed through the ACH will cost the payor two days in float, or around $1 million (from 2/365 times $2 billion in bill payments (from table 2–A1) times the 90-day Treasury bill rate of 0.05775). That is, the customer's bank will debit the customer's account on the day the ATM transaction is initiated, but the bank will itself be debited perhaps two days later if the bill payment is processed through an ACH, giving the customer's bank two days of float.

p *Unit Costs.* User and social unit costs were all derived by dividing the total user and social costs in this table by the volume figures in table 2–A1. The result is a per-transaction cost estimate.

Table 2–A3. Estimated Composition of Check Payments and Number of Days They Are Outstanding

| | Percent Composition[a] | Component Weights | Number of Days Checks Are Outstanding for: | | | | |
| | | | Mail Float | Recipient Float | Bank Float[b] | FR Float[b] | Total[c] |
	(1)	(2)	(3)	(4)	(5)	(6)	(-)
Consumer Payments	55%	1.00					3.00
Cash acquisition	7%	0.13	0	0	0.25	0	0.25
Retail purchases	18%	0.33	0	1.00	0.75	0	1.75
Bill payments	25%	0.45	2.50	0.25	0.75	1.00	4.50
Other	5%	0.09	2.50	0.25	0.75	1.00	4.50
Business Payments	40%	1.00					4.50
Payroll	10%	0.25	0	1.75	0.75	1.00	3.50
Other payments to individuals	10%	0.25	2.50	1.75	0.75	1.00	6.00
Business to business	20%	0.50	1.50	1.00	0.75	1.00	4.25
Government	5%	1.00	1.50	1.75	0.75	1.00	5.00
Weighted number of days checks are outstanding, by float components: (percent composition):			1.38 (37%)	0.89 (24%)	0.71 (19%)	0.75 (20%)	3.73 (100%)

[a] Estimated percent check payment composition is from *Displacing the Check* (1983), table 6, 37. This composition breakdown is, in turn, based on three earlier surveys summarized in *Displacing the check* (1983), table 3, 30.

[b] It is emphasized that the estimates here give the number of days a check is outstanding from the *payor's* viewpoint. Every day a check remains outstanding means more float benefit for the payor to use a check. The fact that availability schedules provided by banks and the Federal Reserve on the *collection side* of the transaction may or may not create collection float is immaterial for our purposes. Collection float may be zero, if availability schedules are set to perfectly match the time funds are made available to depositors at banks (or collecting banks at the Federal Reserve) with the time these funds are made available to banks (or the Federal Reserve). But zero collection float by no means implies that the float benefit to the payor is zero as well.

[c] The total number of calendar days an *average* check is outstanding represents our best guess, based on discussions with certain industry and Federal Reserve experts. The total for consumer and business payments is derived as a weighted average of the components, using the weights in column 2 (which were obtained from column 1). The total shown for government payments is assumed to cover *all* government checks (local, state, and federal) but is slightly lower than the figure derived earlier in a very comprehensive study of all federal government checks (5.7 days reported in Avery, Dudley, and Snyder 1984, 1, footnote 3). In an earlier study, Dudley (1983a) used 8 calendar days (p. 38), but this figure was based on preliminary data from the more comprehensive study just noted and was subsequently adjusted downwards.

COMMENTARY

by Donald R. Hollis

David Humphrey and Allen Berger are to be congratulated for quantifying the present float situation. I am overwhelmed and impressed by the data they have gathered and extrapolated. I have had neither the time nor the resources to validate it, although, based on my experience, the calculated float values seem, on the whole, reasonable. Given the extensiveness of the data analysis, I almost failed to see the forest for the trees. Upon reflection, however, I have concluded that the author's underlying premise—that the market has failed—is seriously misleading.

I am especially concerned about the suggestion that given the fragmentation in the payment system, more government intervention may offer the most hope. I feel strongly that government intervention should be used only as a last resort for achieving efficiency, and when it cannot be avoided, it should only be used on an interim basis. What is especially ironic about the authors' argument for additional intervention is that we do not normally face market failure when there is intense competition. And certainly today, the U.S. banking system suffers from excess capacity and intense competition.

The market should be presumed to be efficient unless there is compelling proof of the contrary. In corporate-to-corporate payments, with the largest float dollars, float is a zero-sum game. However, as most businesses receive more dollars than they pay out, net float is a slight loss. In a market where there is a competitive equilibrium for cash management services (and we have certainly reached that point), few companies can reasonably expect to beat the float game systematically. So they work at achieving a balance, minimizing lost float on receivables while achieving some positive offsets on the payments side.

Furthermore, most cash management services, which may include float-producing or float-reducing activities, do not represent incremental costs but involve replacement costs. For example, the deposit preparation and accounts receivable functions of a lockbox processor have to be done by someone, and these tasks may be done more efficiently in the lockbox setting because of scale and specialization.

If one presumes that the market is efficient until proved otherwise, then there must be other factors that determine the method of payment. And I submit that regulation is a major contributor. Unfortunately, we haven't had a free market in U.S. check clearing (or in many other aspects of the payment system) in my lifetime. In fact, ever since the government (in the form of the Fed) began to compete with private banks in the provision of payment services, we haven't had a free market. I'm not questioning the fact that there were problems leading to the original congressional mandate and subsequently the Fed's initial intervention. My concern is with the form that intervention has taken. And while I advocate private-sector solutions, I acknowledge the many contributions the Fed has made in check collection. But as Don Tucker asserts in his chapter, there is a fundamental conflict inherent in the Fed's dual roles.

Clearly, the Fed's availability schedules over the years have played a major role in creating the opportunity for the float, which ultimately was built into various corporate and bank processing systems. So I submit that the float the authors want to eliminate is a by-product of government regulation. If anything has failed, it is the form of that regulation, not the free market. As corporations expanded nationally, these problems multiplied and the resulting float dollars became huge. In essence, the companies went national, but the banks were constrained to local operations— in some cases to statewide operations, in others to citywide operations, and in some states even to a single location. In fact, this is another failure of regulation and legislation that inhibited the evolution of the free market.

The authors' Canadian examples are further evidence of the power of free markets to develop superior solutions. It is my understanding that no other country in the world has the float problem the United States has. And no other banking system is saddled with both the huge burden of restraints on national banking and significant competition in payment services from its central bank. Thus, my solution is radically different from that of Humphrey and Berger. I would focus the central bank's role in check clearing exclusively on safety and soundness and free the commercial banks to compete on a national scale.

I do agree with the observations that checks are overused; that national banking will significantly help reduce float, even under today's regulations and Fed involvement; and that it is very difficult to get 3000, let alone 14,000, banks to voluntarily do anything. However, I feel certain nonpecuniary factors of concern to selectors of payment options may have been understated, such as the role of safety and convenience versus direct costs. Clearly, for millions of consumers, convenience overrides direct costs when selecting the credit card options over a variety of lower-cost loan options.

Similarly, the driver for electronic data intercharge (EDI) is greater competitiveness through improved quality and responsiveness, plus manufacturing and distribution efficiency. Any settlement gains (and any changes in float) are only a by-product of the EDI option. One of the major obstacles that must be overcome before electronic payments are adopted universally is the issue of payment terms. I believe that corporate America will deal with the renegotiation of terms as businesses quantify the benefits from electronic processing, such as electronic updating of accounts receivable systems, electronic exception handling, and appropriate level of data security. There is no case for government intervention, as it is only a matter of time until corporations voluntarily adopt EDI. In fact, leading corporations have already started using EDI. Just in the past week, the Ford Motor Company stated that eventually EDI will be mandatory for all of its suppliers.

The discussion of the automated clearinghouse (ACH) and corporate trade payments also caused me to reflect on what has really happened. And here I would argue that remoteness from the market was the culprit, not the inherent float advantages of checks. Commercial banks and Fed operations officers designed the ACH for interbank efficiency and treated customer information fields as "indicative data" without quality controls. The main problem with corporate trade payments is not the allocation of check float or payment terms but the fact that the format is inflexible and cannot meet corporations' needs when making vendor payments. Although the new Corporate Trade Exchange (CTX) format does, to a certain extent, resolve the format and transmission efficiency issues, it does not fully solve the other ACH weakness. It is no wonder that GM insisted on having its own standards rather than putting up with a fairly inflexible bank-driven alternative.

ACH/EDI systems will almost always involve incremental costs (rather than substitute costs) because most companies will still need check systems to pay to, and receive from, nonrepetitive or unsophisticated trading partners. Second, the setup costs to establish new linkages for ACH or EDI payments are high and may only be recovered via volume over time. Third, the ACH has not been efficiently designed for applying payments in accounts receivable. When the cost of applying payments is taken into account, there may be little cost advantage to the ACH, especially in cases of multiple invoices, adjustments, disputes, and so on. Finally, in many cases, production costs for ACH are not really less than checks. Companies using direct deposit of payroll still print stubs, use envelopes, and so forth. As Bernell Stone stated in his chapter, only five of ten trade payment requirements are being aggressively addressed. Therefore, I contend the inefficient design of the ACH has been a contributing factor to the prolonged preference for checks, not the inherent float advantage of checks. As we all know, the Fed subsidized the first dozen or so years of the ACH with government payments. At the time, many banks applauded. What is now clear is that the original ACH should not have been kept alive by government force-feeding. Rather, the market should have been allowed to force its replacement. If we had not had so much government assistance, we might not be so far behind much of the rest of the world in ACH-type services.

The market has decided that it needs something more responsive than the current ACH. As the participants have gotten a truer picture of total costs, the market has worked, through its call for new services. The question is, how can we respond by making the payments process more efficient while lowering net societal costs and evolving from the current ACH to more market-driven solutions?

Another market-driven success story is the insurance industry's draw-down collection service, which predates the ACH. It worked because it is based on sharing the benefit with insurance buyers. Both parties traded off some of their historic float gains for improved convenience and efficiency.

The depository transfer check (DTC) draw-down, first in check and then in ACH form, is another success story, which private-sector corporations and banks created to help their clients solve the float problems that stemmed from past regulation. In the early 1970s one of the nation's major automobile manufacturers began using DTCs to collect for cars delivered against floor plan loans. The savings that accrued from not having to issue invoices, clear checks, and deal with the uncertainty of when the funds would arrive more than offset the loss of float. In fact, in order to get the dealers to participate in this program, the automobile manufacturer locked in for the dealers the actual average settlement time that they were experiencing. This was done even though the average settlement time was two days longer than the stated terms. Nonetheless, the certainty of the arrival of funds on a predictable date allowed the automobile manufacturer to maximize the return on its investment portfolio. This advantage, coupled with the efficiency in reducing paperwork and reconciliation activity, led the automobile manufacturer to adopt DTC draw-downs as a superior approach to the collection of receivables by check. Other automakers soon followed. Once again, the float involved did not impede the adoption of more efficient overall methods.

Netting schemes have also arisen in the private sector. At Petroclear, for example, sets of participants voluntarily gave up large-dollar float for the common benefit of the payors, even though those benefits did not accrue evenly to each.

Another interesting example is the credit card sales draft, which in the early 1970s had extensive out-of-area draft-clearing times. Bank card issuers asked the Fed to include these drafts in check clearings. The Fed, fortunately, declined to do so for two reasons: it was not sure this action was appropriate, given the Fed's charter; and the Fed was busy opening Regional Check Processing Centers (RCPCs).

In turn, the card-issuing banks installed truncation at the initial merchant-processing bank and leapfrogged the check system in efficiency—to everyone's benefit. At the same time, they reduced the risk of fraud and lowered credit exposure. Thank our lucky stars for the free enterprise system! Note, the banks adopted true truncation, not the dual approach (and double work) of costly full-image transmission as advocated in the authors' electronic check-clearing proposal. The credit card drafts do not follow the transmission, and only posting information is transmitted. If a copy is needed, a facsimile is transmitted. This low-cost approach has worked well for over ten years. However, while it is useful for credit card transactions, I am not advocating its adoption for large-dollar checks. Rather, I am advocating letting the market work out the best payment mechanism for large-dollar items.

If the Fed will auction off its check-processing sites and revert to a pure safety and soundness role, I contend, the float problem will be solved by the market. Today, commercial banks have little or no incentive to invest in improved check clearing, as their largest competitor is also their regulator and thus can materially change the profit dynamics of the business on short notice. I assert that an unfettered free market will invest and work to maximize efficiency and minimize risk while reducing float.

Also, deregulated private enterprise provides much more promise for improving EDI and other payment mechanisms than government intervention. My model assumes certain standards are perserved or finalized, for example, MICR, Cash Items in the Process of Collection (CIPC) reduced via netting (as in California), expedited return item deadlines, and presentment fee elimination.

I do agree that large-dollar checks are especially risky and that the Fed's safety and soundness role should focus on reducing this risk at its source. Perhaps a surcharge based on the face value, which funds a loss reserve, would discourage the use of checks for large amounts. We have an excellent large-dollar payment system (FedWire/CHIPS)—let's use it and not impose all of its risk control features on our high-volume (low-value) ACH/check payment mechanisms.

While I am opposed to the addition of ongoing regulation, I would be willing to consider interim regulations that materially reduce risk, overcome the inertia inherent in today's perference for checks, and are phased out over time as change occurs. The real key is to eliminate today's regulations so as to free market forces.

I am also concerned about the added costs, risks, and inconvenience that electronic check collection would involve. I remain unconvinced that the benefits offset the incremental costs. Further, I believe that collecting banks have incentives to expedite collection if the barrier of presentment fees is eliminated and if the Fed turns the tasks over to the private sector.

In summary, I believe Humphrey and Berger have done the industry a real service in documenting some of the float by-products of past regulation. While thanking them for their contribution, we should avoid new regulations to eliminate float (or to address other efficiency issues in the payment system). In fact, if the authors would quantify the costs now incurred to manage the risks caused by so many parties commingling large-dollar items with low-value check/ACH items, we would have a better case for assigning each payment mechanism its most appropriate role. We should use regulation to achieve safety and soundness objectives.

3 THE CANADIAN PAYMENT SYSTEM: AN EVOLVING STRUCTURE

Mohsen Anvari

Canada is reputed to enjoy one of the most efficient payment systems in the Western industrialized world. It is generally thought, particularly in the United States, that the determining factor leading to this efficiency is the existence of a small number of large banks with branches across the country. The large size of these banks fosters a high degree of automation; their coast-to-coast branching lends itself to the development of nationwide networks; and their small number is conducive to a streamlined process of exchange and settlement. One can also observe that although a specific historical process has led to this structural peculiarity of the Canadian banking system, through technology adoption nations with fragmented banking structures can, in principle and to varying degrees, emulate the infrastructure of the Canadian payment system. What may not be as well known, however, are the ongoing institutional changes that are taking

The author's research is currently supported by a grant from the Social Sciences and Humanities Research Council of Canada. The author gratefully acknowledges the assistance of the Canadian Payments Association in the preparation of this chapter; all remaining errors are his own.

93

place in Canada to accommodate the evolving character of the payment system. The experience of Canadians with their system therefore, may be of benefit to others as they develop, adopt, and grapple with the resulting challenges and opportunities of payment system innovations.

This chapter is an attempt to describe the current payment system in Canada, to shed light on the legislative and institutional infrastructure of the system, and to trace the current trends and developments. In the course of this discussion, the attention of the reader is particularly drawn to the challenges of adopting new payment technologies on a large scale. Given an infrastructure handsomely amenable to the rapid incorporation of innovation in payment methodology, the slow pace, albeit in a relative sense, of technology adoption in Canada, despite the alleged real benefits, can only highlight the complexities of the processes that lead to alterations in the payment habits of households, firms, and governments. A discussion of the status of particular payment alternatives in Canada can provide a fuller appreciation of these complexities.

This chapter is organized as follows. In the first section, a brief discussion of the deposit-taking institutions is presented, with heavy emphasis on chartered banks. The main points of the debate leading to the formation of the Canadian Payments Association, its mandate, structure, organization, and operations are briefly described. The clearing and settlement process in Canada is detailed. Then, the next section presents current payment statistics in Canada in an attempt to set the stage for a discussion of the forces operating to alter payment method preferences. This is followed by a discussion of the current initiatives in the payment system. A number of developments are individually discussed, with an emphasis on describing those factors inhibiting their development as well as the economic forces favoring their adoption. A brief set of concluding observations are contained in the final section.

Background

Historically, the Canadian financial system has been characterized, in the main, by the "four pillars," i.e., chartered banks, life insurance companies, trust and mortgage loan companies, and investment dealers. The distinction between various types of institutions are becoming increasingly blurred in the face of deregulation of the financial services industry. The latest concrete example of this was the entry of banks into investment dealership, which has resulted in a substantial takeover of brokerage firms by banks. Of the four pillars, the chartered banks, so-called because of the requirement to obtain a charter, historically granted by the Parliament of Canada, have been the mainstay of the payment system, particularly with reference to transferring bank deposits. Further, until the advent of the Bank of Canada in 1935, they were also allowed to issue paper currency. The operations of the banks are covered under the Bank Act, which was first proclaimed in 1871 and, with minor delays, has been revised on a decennial basis by Parliament. The Bank Act originally intended the banks to be commercial banks and permitted them to open branches "...at any place or places in the Dominion." Revisions of the Act in 1954 and 1967 expanded the permissible scope of their operations, notably by permitting them to engage in mortgage lending and consumer lending. The latter revision also removed all interest rate restrictions and limited the ownership of these banks so that no one group or individual can hold more than 10 percent of the outstanding stocks of these firms. The latest revision, proclaimed on December 1, 1980, introduced two major changes relevant to the present discussion and, in addition, created the Canadian Payments Association (CPA).

The first pertinent change in the Act of 1980 relates to data processing. For all intents and purposes, the banks were prohibited from offering data-processing services to their customers save and except payroll services. This provision resulted from a desire to protect the independent Canadian service bureaus from competition from the banks and came on the heel of a court ruling in favor of a bank that had offered general ledger accounting services to a client (Crawford and Falconbridge 1986, sec. 3801). As discussed later, this provision of the Act has important implications for the development of certain payment alternatives.

The second change of importance to this discussion was that wholly owned subsidiaries of foreign banks were permitted to operate in Canada upon issuance of letters patent by the Minister of Finance. These banks, known as Schedule B banks, are currently restricted as to their asset size and branching activity. It should be noted that through grandfathering, resulting from the amalgamation of Schedule B banks and small Schedule A banks, there are certain Schedule B banks with more branches than are normally permitted. Also, as of September 1987, a Quebec-based bank, being the only bank operating under a federal law known as the Quebec Savings Bank Act, has operated as a Schedule B bank.

By and large, the Canadian banking system is still dominated by the six large Schedule A banks. Selected data on concentration in Canadian banking (table 3-1) indicates that 90 percent of all bank assets and deposits are accounted for by these large institutions.

Table 3–1.   Concentration in Canadian Banking, 1987

Banks[a]	Assets ($ millions)[b]	Percentage of Total	Deposits ($ millions)[b]	Percentage of Total
Royal	$103,328	21.42	$ 85,042	21.33
CIBC	89,872	18.63	73,100	18.33
Montreal	84,873	17.59	72,158	18.10
Scotia	70,150	14.54	59,149	14.83
TD	57,423	11.90	47,786	11.98
National	30,208	6.26	24,737	6.20
Others (2)[c]	292	–	232	–
Total Schedule A	436,146	90.41	362,204	90.84
Total Schedule B[d] (59)	46,241	9.58	36,512	9.16

Source: Canada Gazette 1988.
Note: Numbers are rounded.
[a] Continental Bank of Canada and B.C. Bancorp are excluded.
[b] All dollars in millions as of October 31 1987, as revised.
[c] "Others" represents Bank of Alberta and Western & Pacific Bank.
[d] Schedule B banks include Laurentian Bank of Canada.

The Canadian Payments Association (CPA)

As regards the payment system, the most significant recent development in Canada has been the formation of the CPA, a private membership corporation, as a result of the 1980 amendment of the Bank Act. All banks, as well as Bank of Canada, must be members of the CPA. Other deposit-taking institutions may become members. Membership is classified, mainly, into Direct Clearers (DCs), each of which have to account for at least 0.5 percent of the national clearing volume, and Indirect Clearers, which clear their items through arrangement with a DC. The CPA Board of Directors is structured based on types of member institutions and is presided over by a representative of the Bank of Canada. Subject to government approval, the Board can make by-laws and, in conformity with these, any rules respecting clearings and settlement matters.

The CPA is charged with two mandates: (1) "to establish and operate a national clearings and settlements system," and (2) "to plan the evolution of the national payments system." The CPA Board has organized two committees corresponding to its two mandates: the senior planning committee, which is concerned with the longer-term mandate, and the national clearings committee, which is charged with monitoring the operations of the system. Prior to the creation of the CPA, clearings and settlements in Canada were entrusted to the Canadian Bankers' Association, which was empowered (under an Act dating to 1900) to establish rules and regulations pertaining to these activities subject to the approval of the Treasury Board. On February 1, 1983, the CPA assumed the responsibility for clearings and settlements, inheriting essentially the system then in existence. The details of these activities are described in the next section.

The second mandate of the CPA, although not too specific, is indeed a novelty. Coupled with the organizational structure of the CPA, it will prove instrumental in the process of implementing large-scale changes in the Canadian payment system. The impetus for the creation of the CPA, and the reasoning behind its particular form and its mandates, are reflected in a government White Paper issued in 1976. The discussion in the White Paper highlighted the following facts: (1) as compared to currency, the importance of deposits transferable by checks and other means has increased; (2) nonbank deposit-taking insitutions are becoming more active participants in the payment system (see table 3–2); (3) while banks have made arrangements to clear items belonging to nonbank deposit-taking institutions, these entities have no voice in the operation of the system; (4) nonbank deposit-taking institutions have no access to lending facilities at the central bank nor are they obliged to maintain (non-interest-bearing)

Table 3–2. Annual Clearing Volumes by Class of CPA Member, March Year End (Millions of Items)

Class	Receipt and Deliveries For Own and Non-member Accounts		Percentage of Total	
	1986	1987	1986	1987
Banks	2,549.23	2,709.21	75.93	76.02
Centrals	390.99	412.59	11.65	11.58
Trust and mortgage loan companies	164.77	191.83	4.91	5.38
Other financial institutions	65.57	70.47	1.95	1.98
Bank of Canada	186.80	179.72	5.56	5.04

Source: Leishman (1987).

reserves with the Bank of Canada; and (5) there will be a move to augment the current paper-based system with an electronic system and it is desirable for all deposit-taking institutions to be involved in the process of implementing the impending changes.

In response to these issues, in the interest of promoting competition, efficiency, and equity, and to ensure the continuing operation of a secure payment system, Parliament decided to create a broad-based entity open to all deposit-taking institutions for national clearing and settlement. It was also recognized that the development of alternative payment systems is an evolutionary process best accomplished through the participation of all categories of deposit-taking institutions and that the structure of the CPA enables it to plan this evolution. As a consequence, the CPA has become the central forum for implementing changes respecting the payment system. This is not to say that all new ideas and payment venues originate from the CPA. Rather, once economic forces in the market have indicated the viability of new payment methodologies, as in the case of electronic funds transfer and point-of-sale (EFT/POS) for example, the CPA provides the apparatus for dialogue among the clearing institutions and between these institutions and other economic entities with an interest in these developments. This function of the CPA will ascribe to it a pivotal role in the process of incorporating technological innovation in the payment system in Canada.

Clearing and Settlement System

The backbone of the clearing system in Canada is the computer and communication facilities of the Direct Clearer members of the CPA. Direct Clearers maintain data centers in eight locations across the country. Data centers are used by the branches of deposit-taking institutions for extended back-room operations and, in some cases, are electronically linked with its branches. Payment data processing takes place overnight at these centers on a batch basis and may involve processing of items that have been partially processed during the day at the branch level. Each institution operates electronic links between its own centers for processing intra-institution items. Items exchanged between data centers of different institutions are the so-called national clearing items. The nature of the items thus exchanged, and the rules and regulations covering these exchanges, fall within the purview of the CPA, which in addition facilitates the process of settlement among different institutions that takes place via the adjustment of balances of DC member institutions at the Bank of Canada.

Subject to the requirements of the CPA rules, payment items qualifying for clearing and settlement should fall within one of three categories: (1) "paper-based payment orders including bills of exchange, promissory notes, drafts, settlement vouchers, money orders...," (2) "payment orders recorded on magnetic tape and capable of being reproduced in alphanumeric characters on paper, microfilm...," and (3) "payment orders trabsmitted in any other electronic message medium capable of being reproduced by both sending and receiving institution on paper,...." The CPA rules specifically identify "debit or credit items contained on magnetic tape or bulk paper or transmitted in any other electronic message medium," and "shared automated banking machine (ABM) cash withdrawals" as items acceptable for clearing. Of these two, the former falls under (2) and the latter under (3) above.

To understand the clearing and settlement process, consider the procedure for treating a check on a typical business day, i.e., one not preceding a weekend or a holiday. A check drawn on a deposit-taking institution, X, is deposited at a branch of another deposit-taking institution, Y, before 3 p.m. Depending on the operations of Y, the check may be immediately entered into Y's computers or may be forwarded to the appropriate data center for batch processing that evening. In either case, the depositing customer is given "provisional" credit for the deposited amount immediately, i.e., "same-day availability." The credit is "provisional" in the sense that it may be reversed if it is not honored by the drawee institution. Note that this arrangement notwithstanding, some deposit-taking institutions have policies for placing a "hold" on consumer deposits for varying lengths of time. The check is forwarded with all others to the data center of Y, if it is a Direct Clearer, and to the assigned Direct Clearer's data center otherwise (for simplicity, suppose Y is a Direct Clearer). By approximately 6 p.m. the item is put in a computer-readable form if not so already. Y's data center sorts all items into on-us and exchange items. The on-us items include items drawn on Indirect Clearers for whom Y acts as a Direct Clearer. These items do not enter the national clearing system and are processed as intra-institution items. Large-value checks, i.e., $50,000 and over, are processed separately, are given special handling, and are subject to tighter control. Exchange-items, which include tape items as well as paper items, are physically forwarded to data centers of appropriate Direct Clearers along with totals for each bag. Via a computer terminal the total is entered as a "claim" against the relevant receiving institution into the CPA's Automated Clearing and Settlement System (ACSS). The ACSS, operating from a host computer in Toronto, was introduced in November 1984 as a means of tracking interinstitution exchanges and to confirm the resulting balances for later use at the Bank of Canada. By monitoring the ACSS statistics throughout the night, the DCs are in a position to track their gains and losses as exchanges take place. This process ensures meaningful interest rate quotation in the overnight funds market during the early hours of each business day. X's data center receives the bag on a "said to contain" basis and proceeds to verify the contents and, as a result, may make entries into the ACSS. It will immediately debit the account of the customer whose check is being traced here and may arrange for the return of the check to the branch. The exchange of items continues until midnight with minor regional variations. The ACSS closes for further entry at 9:30 a.m. the following day.

Between 9:30 a.m. and 4 p.m. several adjustments may be made to the net positions available from ACSS, at which time the Bank of Canada's accounting procedures establish the clearing balances of each Direct Clearer (See Dingle 1988 for more details). As can be seen, the exchange of value takes place one day after the depositing customer received provisional credit and the check issuing customer lost good funds. Until recently, this resulted in credit float and debit float in the settlement process, a major source of distortion as well as a source of controversy, particularly in bank compensation schemes. As of July 16, 1986, the postings to the accounts of the Direct Clearers are backdated one business day on the books of the Bank of Canada and thus, de facto, there is no clearing float in the system (see Lindwall 1986). It should be clear from this brief description that the clearing system is in effect operated by the clearing agents themselves, with the CPA acting as a coordinating body only. It should also be noted that the CPA assumes no responsibility regarding liquidity of its members.

As discussed above, a depositing customer receives immediate provisional credit for deposited items. This immediacy is in the sense of on-line crediting of the item to the account or in the sense that all credit and debit items are batch processed at the same point in time. On very rare occasions, it may also involve immediate withdrawal of funds by the drawer. When an item is refused by the drawee institution, e.g., due to insufficient funds or signature problems, the item flows back through the system in the opposite direction. This feature of the system raises the question of finality of payment. The main point here is not that once a payee is in possession of funds the payer may seek to repossess the funds by recourse, for example, to the legal system. Rather, the issue is that, given the CPA clearing rules, can a provisional credit granted to the payee be reversed, through the actions of the drawee bank or the payer, resulting in the flow of a payment item in an opposite direction through the clearing system? The CPA rules specify that the drawee bank branch can refuse an item and return it if it acts in a speedy manner, i.e., during the next clearing cycle after receipt of the item at the branch. Two past cases may illustrate the type of problems that may arise.

The first case involved the payee depositing a check, drawn on the Toronto-Dominion Bank (TD), at the Bank of Nova Scotia (BNS), which in turn called the TD and confirmed the existence of sufficient funds in the account to cover the check. BNS then permitted the payee to withdraw the funds in question. Having gone through the clearing system, the item ended at the TD branch after two days. It was approved and stamped PAID later that day or the next morning. The drawer however, instructed TD in the afternoon of that day to place a stop-payment on the item. TD complied and returned the item to BNS, which refused to accept the item, invoking CPA rules. TD agreed, but the customer subsequently sued the drawee bank for failure to carry out its instructions. The action was dismissed. The second case involved a trust company that did not honor, as "insufficient funds", and returned to a Schedule B bank a number of checks after a period varying between four to eight days. In the interim, the payee had withdrawn the funds in question and had become insolvent, so that the bank in question could not indemnify itself for the full amount of the items involved. In the follow up dispute, the court ruled in favor of the presenting bank on grounds of time delays. For a full discussion of these and other cases dealing with returned items, the reader is referred to Lederman (1988). It should be noted, however, that the problem of returned items is normally not a serious issue in Canada. Returned items totalled approximately 1.3 million, with a value of $981 million for the year ending December 31, 1987, which corresponds to only 0.07 percent of the total volume and 0.008 percent of the total value of exchanged items.

Changing Payment Venues

Ever since the advent of computers and their initial utilization to automate the back-room operations of deposit-taking institutions, the promise, and according to some interpretations, the specter, of the "cashless-checkless" society has been touted by North American observers. The tempo has been intensified as computers and telecommunication technology have become more advanced and more accessible. In particular, as the relative costs of traditional payment instruments, e.g., currency and paper-based transfer orders, have soared, the prospect of widespread substitution of these items with electronic payment alternatives has become bright. Yet, in actual fact, the transformation has proved to be a slow process, suggesting that simple indicators of relative advantages of different payment instruments do not capture the overall economics of substitution.

Payment System Statistics

An examination of the clearing system statistics can be a useful prelude to a discussion of the changes that are under way in the system. Tables 3–3 and 3–4 provide data on items that have cleared through the CPA for 1983 and 1987 by categories of items. Although not evident from these data, a month-by-month analysis of more detailed data indicates that the implied trends are indeed persistent over time. The first two categories of items are self-explanatory. The third consists of paper items that are not MICR-encoded that flow through the system, mainly counter checks. Over the past few years, the CPA has tried, it appears successfully, to reduce the volume of these costly items. The fourth category of items, magnetic tapes, refers to the exchange of items among Direct Clearers of both credit items, e.g., payroll deposits, and debit items, e.g., insurance permium and mortgage payments. These are prepared originally by the deposit-taking institution in a variety of ways, upon the instructions of their customers, possibly using value-dates, are processed at the data centers, and are exchanged among the members. Shared automatic banking machine (ABM) transactions (called ATMs in the United States), the only truly electronic items,

Table 3–3.   Clearing Statistics, Volume, Year Ending December 31
(Millions of Items)

Class of Items	1983	1987
Paper under $50,000	1174	1715
	(97.36%)	(92.84%)
Paper over $50,000	3	6
	(0.26%)	(0.34%)
Uncoded paper	12	10
	(1.02%)	(0.56%)
Magnetic tape	15	80
	(1.21%)	(4.34%)
Shared ABM	–	34
		(1.85%)

Source: Canadian Payments Association.

originate from the members' ABMs and are directly transmitted to the CPA's ACSS for inclusion in the settlement process.

It should be kept in mind that the data pertain to interinstitution items only. It is estimated that 23 percent of all transfer items are intra-institution items that do not enter the national clearing system (Leishman 1987). An interesting question to examine is whether in-house items have the same mix as those entering the national clearing system. In the absence of any data on the composition of in-house items, it may be safe to assume, particularly as regards small paper items, that the mix of items in that stream resembles that of the national clearing items, although it should be kept in mind that cash managers, for operational as well as cost considerations, may direct certain activities, e.g., cash concentration, to individual banks. Similarly, because of the present scope of shared ABM networks and the prevailing service charge structures, cash withdrawals and deposits at these machines are expected to be concentrated at individual institutions.

As can been seen from tables 3–3 and 3–4, most of the volume is accounted for by paper items of less than $50,000. Of these, about half is estimated to be accounted for by bill payments (Speake 1985). In addition, the federal government checks represent 10 percent of all checks (Murray 1986), the vast majority of which are included in this stream. Despite this very large volume, note that the value of these items is about 7 percent of the total value of the exchanged items. By contrast, paper items over $50,000 represent a miniscule percentage of the exchanged volume but account for the lion's share of the value. Two points have to be kept in mind when examining these items. First, all major payments related to

Table 3–4. Clearing Statistics, Value, Year Ending December 31 (Billions of Dollars)

Class of Items	1983	1987
Paper under $50,000	$536	$912
	(10.45%)	(7.09%)
Paper over $50,000	$4562	$11,894
	(88.95%)	(92.42%)
Uncoded paper	$16	$10
	(0.33%)	(0.07%)
Magnetic tape	$13	$51
	(0.25%)	(0.40%)
Shared ABM	–	$2
		(0.02%)

Source: Canadian Payments Association.

securities transactions are typically made via certified checks and thus appear in this stream. Second, all interinstitution electronic transfers, e.g., those originating at the terminals of cash management systems of the banks and SWIFT transactions, lead to creation of a paper item, which is exchanged between the financial institutions involved. This situation arises principally because the chartered banks have been traditionally reluctant to allow a direct link between their computer systems. The only exception in this regard has been the INTERAC network, which links the ABMs of the member institutions (see, for example, McMorran (1988) for a systems diagram). Therefore, although to a corporate user, for example, a transfer order involving a large sum may appear to be entirely electronic, and indeed most of the processing takes place electronically, eventually a paper item is exchanged between the member institutions and enters the national clearing as a part of this stream. Magnetic tape items, representing a clear low-cost alternative to small-value paper items, have shown the largest growth in terms of volume over the past four years. Tape clearing of credit items and debit items date, respectively, to September 1977 and August 1983. It should be noted that since a magnetic tape is neither a bill of exchange nor a promissory note, the federal Bills of Exchange Act does not apply and consequently, the exchange of these items has taken place under private arrangement between the clearers, in particular, the inter-bank indemnity agreement for preauthorized debits arranged by the Canadian Bankers' Association as early as 1960s. Finally, shared ABM network exchanges have grown in importance since their institution in April 1986.

A few words about the relative costs of various payment alternatives are in order. The author is not aware of any publicly available studies dealing with this issue. As regards checks, Adamek (1987) estimates the processing costs to be between $0.75 and $1.00. A more detailed examination at two major banks (Anderson et al. 1987) yields a range of $0.60 to $1.00 and furthermore, estimates the "electronic" aspect of check processing, i.e., costs incurred after the item is in a computer-readable form, to be between $0.04 and $0.11. The cost of paper processing also depends on the tasks that are performed by the clearing institution. That is, if the overall activity were to be broken down, a cost could be ascribed to each subtask. If some of these subtasks were to be performed by the consumer or eliminated altogether, the costs would naturally change. An example of this is check truncation and bulk delivery of processed checks, which will be discussed later. The problem of cost estimation for these bank services is, as in other countries, confounded by the difficult issue of allocating a significant amount of fixed costs over a large number of products.

Consumers

The two main sources of innovation in the payment system are (1) the attempt by corporations to reduce their payment costs by devising new payment alternatives, and (2) the effort by financial institutions to woo consumer loyalty, increase market share, and enhance profitability by providing new services in an era of rapid deregulation. Consumers influence developments in the payment system by affecting the viability of different payment alternatives as they shift their payment method preferences.

Over the past few years, consumers have become increasingly aware of the earning power of their bank balances, partly as a result of the high level of interest rates in the early 1980s and, partly as a result of the competition among the deposit-taking institutions for consumer deposits through offering of checkable savings accounts and daily interest demand deposit accounts. The ratio of notice and personal term deposits to M2 (defined as currency plus all checkable notice and personal term deposits) increased steadily from approximately 70 percent in 1976 to over 80 percent in 1987, indicating a shift away from demand deposits. More specifically, the ratio of personal checking deposits to checkable savings deposits decreased steadily from a high of over 53 percent in 1982 to a low of 11 percent in 1987, confirming this trend. Thus, consumers are availing themselves of the interest-earning potential of bank balances, a factor that will positively contribute to the use of checks on their part.

Nevertheless, the fees associated with using checks have steadily increased, partly, at least, reflecting the real cost escalations experienced by deposit-taking institutions. The levels of these fees aside, consumers have become increasingly cognizant of their importance, as the fierce competition among different types of financial institutions in the retail market has led to frequent revisions of service charges and has heightened consumer awareness. A recent event highlighting this trend is a class action suit against the banks regarding bank charges now in progress. The House of Commons Finance Committee is also holding hearings on the subject. Responding to these charges the Canadian Bankers' Association recently released a study that indicates that the level of bank charges have not been out of line with those in the United States, and at least two chartered banks have announced new programs aimed at allaying consumers' concerns about bank charges.

A major development in consumer payment alternatives has been the development of ABMs. Proprietary ABMs can be accessed using credit cards or client cards issued by the deposit-taking institution. They can be

Table 3-5. Automatic Banking Machines

	1978	1983	1986	1987	1988
Number	250	1960	4033	4884	5269
Inhabitants per machine	94,580	12,755	6273	5212	4861[a]
Percentage due to banks	–	–	75.33%	71.38%	73.5%

Notes: Numbers for 1978 and 1983 are year end (*Source:* Bank for International Settlement 1985); others are as of July 31, except 1988, which is as of January 31 (*Source: Forum— Canadian Payments Association*, various issues).

Population figures beginning of year for 1986 and 1987 (*Source: Bank of Canada Review*); others (*Source:* Bank for International Settlement 1985).

[a] Estimated.

used to withdraw cash (approximately 70 percent of all transactions), make deposits, pay bills, transfer from one account to another, and to obtain reports on account balances. As noted previously, they are also components of a shared domestic network and, in addition, are part of some international networks such as CIRRUS and PLUS. It should be noted that, by virtue of CPA rules, shared ABM transactions are final.

A point commonly raised in connection with the move to introduce electronic payment methods relates to consumer acceptance of the technology. The record to date mainly relates to the adoption rates of ABM transactions. Table 3–5 shows the rate of introduction of these devices in Canada. It is estimated that there are in excess of 10 million cardholders who can access these machines in the country. Toronto-Dominion estimates (McMorran 1988) that between 4 and 5 million transactions clear through its ABMs each month. Assuming that the volume of TD transactions is in proportion to the size of its deposits, an estimate for transactions going through ABMs of Schedule A banks is between 30 and 38 million items per month, or a sizable 20–25 percent of all national clearing items. It is clear that consumer acceptance of ABMs has been very rapid. The process has presumably been aided by the introduction of computing and communication technologies in the society at large, which has familiarized consumers with the technology itself. This is a good omen for introducing similar technologies.

Two other areas of shifting payment patterns should be noted. More and more firms are encouraging consumers to subscribe to direct debit options. The increasing volume of these items indicates that consumers are softening their resistance to the use of this payment option for fixed payments. Conversely, more and more firms are shifting to direct deposit of recurring payments to consumers, e.g., pension, salaries, dividends.

Initial negative reactions, particularly from unions, to the use of this payment method for payroll, seems to be waning, as evidenced by the steady rise in the volume of items clearing the national system.

Finally, as in the United States, Canadian consumer advocates have become involved in the debates that are taking place regarding the adoption of new payment technologies. The major concerns expressed by these organizations concern the following issues: privacy, security, error correction, liability, disclosure, documentation, freedom of choice, and consumer redress. In addition, consumer advocates argue for a stronger role in the development of electronic alternatives, a position that is not, in principle, opposed by the CPA, which encourages liaison with interested parties that are not members of the association. A number of detailed studies on the impact of electronic payment innovations on consumers in Canada have been conducted (see Valcin 1988).

Corporations

One can classify corporate cash management activity into four categories: cash mobilization, cash forecasting, short-term investment and borrowing, and company-bank relations. The first category impacts on the payment system as corporations attempt to reduce costs associated with receipt and disbursement procedures. The last category also affects the development of the system, since it encompasses such issues as costs and prices of banking services and compensation arrangements.

The author has elsewhere contrasted the practice of corporate cash management in Canada with that in the United States (Anvari 1988). Nevertheless, several areas of particular importance to the payment system merit examination here. The first is the problem faced by the trade biller collecting from other corporations. The two dimensions of this problem are the use of lockboxes and electronic payment alternatives. Lockboxes are used in Canada, in the main, to combat the inefficiencies of the postal service. The product is a mature bank product offered by the Schedule A banks. The major problem in its operation is the nonstandard form of documents accompanying payments that are received by the banks on behalf of their customers. Whereas the check itself can be converted to an electronically readable item immediately, the nonstandard form of the payment document leads to paper processing and necessitates the transfer of paper to the customer (Pelletier 1985). The ultimate solution to this problem is, of course, widespread application of electronic data interchange (EDI) concepts linking the trading partners and their financial institution. An intermediate solution was put in place by the CPA through its Standard 017 relating to uniform invoice formats for utilities. The standard permits the lockbox processor, be it the bank or the receiving firm itself, to process the invoice in the same manner as the check and thus reduces the overall paper-processing costs. It also facilitates the processing of the so-called "acceptance of payment of accounts." This refers to payment of bills at a financial institution that collects payment on behalf of a collecting corporation. With standardized formats, the process of summarization of payments received and reporting of payments to the corporate client is facilitated.

The next aspect of this problem concerns intercorporate electronic payments. It would appear at first glance that in the absence of any clearing float in Canada, substantial incentives exist for converting payments from checks to electronic funds transfers. To be sure, mechanisms for effecting these payments via computer terminals located at the treasurers' offices are readily available through the automated cash management services offered by the banks. The use of electronic payment mechanisms by non-financial corporations, however, is very limited in Canada, as in the United States. The reasons for this are similar in the two countries. Note that following the 1980 Monetary Control Act in the United States, there has been almost a total elimination of Federal Reserve float and the so-called clearing-house slippage. Thus, one incentive for the design of sophisticated check-issuing systems aimed at exploiting these inefficiencies has disappeared. The payment systems in the two countries are in fact converging insofar as clearing lag advantage is concerned, i.e., there is none. The only, albeit very important, qualification to this situation is the use of availability schedules as a marketing tool by United States commercial banks, which, coupled with the inefficiencies of smaller banks, may open the door to opportunities for non-zero-sum games and possibly lead to E. F. Hutton-style abuses (see Financial Executives Research Foundation 1986 for surveys of "questionable cash management practices" relating to this and other issues dealing with payment system inefficiencies). The incentive for corporations to convert to electronic payment, therefore, has to emanate from other components of value transfer delay, i.e., processing lag and mail lag, and, possibly more importantly, from internal transactions costs involved with different payment alternatives.

There is a burgeoning literature dealing with the economics of electronic payment in the United States, which has a direct application in this country and sheds light on the issues, including the determination of benefit-sharing rules that are pertinent to a wholesale switch to electronic corporate payments (see Hill and Ferguson 1985). Three points however merit mentioning. First, mail lags are substantial in Canada and since, at least legally, Canada Post is the agent of the receiver, there is an incentive to continue using the mail. Second, for electronic payments to be of value to the receiver of funds, it should have timely information regarding its bank balances. Thus, for example, agreeing to give a discount to a buyer in exchange for electronic receipt of payments will immediately entail the explicit cost of subscribing to a balance-reporting system as well as the more substantial cost of revising the internal accounting and control procedures involved in using such systems. Finally, a classic case of economies of scale faces both the electronic payor and electronic receiver. Whereas it may be beneficial to convert all corporate customers, or at least a significant class of customers, to a new payment regime, it may be uneconomical to do so for a small number of customers. The problem of inducing a large number of customers to adopt a different payment method then may entail (1) devising an optimal differential pricing structure by the seller, and (2) offering the option of different prices based on the method of payment to different classes of customers. The analytical work necessary for the first task is in a stage of infancy, and the legal underpinnings of the second are not very clear either in Canada or the United States (see Johnson and Maier 1985).

Another cash management issue of relevance to the payment flows is the notion of check truncation. This, of course, is not new in the United States. A subsidiary benefit of this process, which is more easily attainable in Canada, however, is to capitalize on the centralized nature of the clearing process to introduce additional savings in the truncation process by eliminating data entry duplications. An example relating to a multidivisional transportation company can illustrate the process (details can be found in Anvari et al. 1989). This company is decentralized with respect to its disbursement activities with a large number of subsidiaries issuing checks on their own bank accounts. The company arranged for special MICR encoding of all checks, regardless of the actual printings that bear subsidiary specific markings, so that all checks are in effect written against a single bank account in Montreal. The financial institution processing the incoming items produces a tape containing data on the checks that have been presented the previous day and returns the tape along with all paper items (in bulk and unsorted) to the company each morning. As a result, direct check-processing costs are reduced as the bank avoids sorting, transportation to branches, and branch paper processing. These savings are passed on to the company. In addition, by avoiding the cost of entering cleared item data into its computers, the company realizes substantial savings in check reconciliation. Finally, as the subsidiaries are linked electronically, the company requires all check-writing units to report their activities and has available a current record of its outstanding checks. By processing the record of outstanding checks against the record of checks presented the previous day, the firm is able to greatly improve its cash forecasting capability and thus substantially reduce its bank balances.

Finally, a word should be said about cash concentration and its analogue, disbursement funding. The process of transferring funds from local depository accounts and transferring funds to local disbursement accounts is extremely efficient in this country. By structuring these accounts within a single Schedule A bank, a firm can avoid the costly creation and handling of paper that will be entailed if several financial institutions were involved, as may be the case in the United States (see Anvari 1983).

Information Technology Adoption: Opportunities and Obstacles

Nowadays, the notion of innovation in the payment system invariably conjures up images of technology adoption, particularly those of a computing and telecommunication genre. The overwhelming importance of these technologies notwithstanding, it should be kept in mind that payment system innovation can take many different forms. The introduction of credit cards, for example, regardless of the manner in which the processing of the transactions takes place, is a major innovation. When investigating the path of change in the system, therefore, one needs to stay cognizant of this fact and not lose sight of the forces that lead to these "nontechnological" aspects of change. In the discussion that follows, attention is focused on the process of payment system innovation in general but emphasis will be placed on the technological aspects of change.

It is estimated that over the past ten years the cost of information technology has decreased by 30 percent per year whereas the cost of labor has increased 5 percent annually. It would therefore be reasonable to conjecture that the replacement of labor-intensive payment processes with those heavily relying on information technology will lead to positive welfare effects. One can pursue this argument further and observe, using the tenets of classic microeconomic theory, that from the point of view of individual firms whose actions affect the structure of the system, investments leading to increased automation of the system will lead to enhanced profitability. Although these hypotheses are essentially correct, they are too simple to capture the complexities of the process of change.

To gain a better understanding of the issue, three points should be noted at the onset. First, although reducing the overall costs of the payment system is a desirable social goal followed by governments through their various agencies, and although through adoption of a variety of public policies the course of these developments can be influenced, ultimately, in Canada at least, it is the free play of market forces that defines the path of change. Second, innovations in the payment system result as a by-product of firms' actions in pursuit of their other objectives. In Canada, for example, no firm will simply undertake investments to contribute to the social objective of reducing the overall costs of making payments. Rather, as they adjust their procedures and products, firms alter existing payment venues and create new alternatives. Third, there is increasing evidence that when deciding on adopting major changes, particularly technological changes of the type that will influence the payment system, firms are not guided by simple measures of project effectiveness, such as return on investment. This is especially true during times when the industry organization is undergoing rapid change because of such factors as de-regulation and increased global competition. The search for the forces affecting the payment system should therefore focus on the dynamics of technology adoption by those firms whose actions can influence the system structure. This is not to ignore the importance of legal, institutional, cultural, or other relevant influences. Rather it is a way of drawing the attention of observers of the payment system to some of the economic considerations that may be missed when one relies exclusively on a narrow interpretation of microeconomic concepts.

A cursory examination of the literature on the process of technology adoption by firms reveals that the external use of information technology by firms, i.e., the type that may affect the payment system, is closely linked to the desire of firms to gain sustainable competitive advantage. Much of the work related to the operationalization of the concept of sustainable competitive advantage is founded on the seminal work of Porter (1980). In analyzing a firm's competitive situation, Porter identifies five factors of importance: threat of new entry, rivalry among existing competitors in the industry, pressure from substitute products and services, bargaining power of suppliers, and bargaining power of buyers. He identifies three broad strategies that can be followed by firms to protect their competitive posi-tion in the market: becoming a low-cost producer, differntiating products and services, and sharpening focus or niche (see Wiseman 1985, 47–49). More specifically, McFarlan (1983) uses Porter's framework to examine the strategic use of information technology (IT) by posing five questions regarding such systems: (1) Can IT be used to increase barriers to entry? (2) Can IT lead to a favorable change in the basis of competition in the industry? (3) Can IT be used to generate new products and services? (4)

Can IT be used to increase the switching costs of buyers if they were to shift to a competitor? and (5) Can IT be used to increase bargaining power with suppliers? An observer of the payment system cannot but appreciate the importance of these issues to financial institutions, among others, as they examine the potentials of IT systems in the age of deregulation.

Elaborating on these themes further, Wiseman (1985) identifies five types of strategic thrusts that can be followed by firms to use IT in order to improve their competitive position. Differentiation aimed at increasing the costs of new entrants and the switching costs of customers can be enhanced by IT through improving delivery, terms, support, payment convenience, and so on, as well as introducing augmented products. Costs can be reduced by utilizing economies of scale, economies of scope, and economies of information. Innovation as a strategic thrust relates to the use of IT either to develop new products or to effect changes along the value-added chain of the firm's processes. Growth strategies can take place along the product line, i.e., lengthening, deepening, and widening the product line, or functionally through forward and backward integration. Finally, strategic alliances aimed at, among others, enhancing differentiation, reducing costs, and developing new products, forms the last category of strategic thrusts. Wiseman (1985) describes these in great detail and provides numerous cases to illustrate the underlying concepts. Some of his examples concern the changes that have affected the payment system, e.g., the development of ABMs, cash management accounts in the United States, shared remittance processing programs involving banks and retailers, and so on. Although not within the scope of this chapter, many developments in the Canadian payment system can be traced to the utilization of the above-mentioned strategies by financial as well as nonfinancial institutions.

A rather interesting strand of research in the use of IT for improving competitive advantage is discussed by Williamson (1985). The central theme of his work is the importance of transactions costs in the process of economic exchange. These are distinct from the costs of producing a product or providing a service and relate to such factors as searching for a product or service, obtaining quotations, arranging for financing, waiting for delivery, and the like (see Clemons and Kimbrough 1986). From the present vantage point, curiously missing from the list of oft-mentioned transactions costs are the costs associated with the payment aspect of trade transactions. To the extent that the theory has any validity, the use of IT by firms to establish competitive advantage by reducing the costs of transactions to their buyers and suppliers will lead to innovations in the payment system.

Although the process of information technology adoption by firms is rather ill-understood at the present time (see Farhoomand and Drury 1988), a serious investigation of the formative forces affecting the payment system should address the issue. Further, moving from the general to the specific, such studies need to apply the global concepts of the IT adoption process to those firms whose actions directly affect the payment system, notably the financial institutions. Research of this type is particularly timely as firms increasingly use IT as a competitive weapon in a rapidly changing financial services industry.

Trends and Developments

In this section, some of the current developments in the Canadian payment system will be cataloged. The initiatives currently underway cover a wide spectrum and vary greatly in nature and with differing degrees of inter-dependence. These interdependencies are not explored here. Rather, the objective is to provide the reader with a broad understanding of the direction of change in the system.

EFT/POS

As understood in this country, EFT/POS is a payment system whereby an electronic process is activated at the point-of-sale, causing the transfer of funds from the account of a consumer to the account of the retailer. The time of transfer of the funds can be either immediate or overnight, in which case the activity at the retailer's counter is tantamount to reserving the funds in question in a manner akin to certified checks. An EFT/POS system is an alternative to the use of currency, checks, and credit cards at the retail level. Although checks issued at the point-of-sale currently represent a small percentage of the total number of transactions, nevertheless they represent approximately one-eighth of the total number of checks written in Canada. A wholesale adoption of EFT/POS in this country will have a profound impact on check volumes and currency as well as the role of credit cards.

At the moment, the volume of EFT/POS transactions is almost nil, with only a few pilot projects completed or underway. The first pilot was initiated by credit unions in the Swift Current Saskatchewan in June 1985, with a further experiment in July 1986. A more extensive pilot project was conducted in the winter of 1987 in Montreal and involved Provigo, a major grocery chain, and the National Bank. It should be noted that all grocery purchases in these stores are payable by check or currency, with no credit card purchases permitted. Using debit cards, customers were given the option of using the EFT/POS system and, in addition, were allowed cash withdrawals over and above the amount of their purchases. The results of this experiment indicate that for the system to be viable the card base has to grow; that the economics of the system are not obvious; that widespread adoption of the system requires continuous promotion; and that users have exhibited a high level of approval (Friesen 1988). Based on the results, the company believes that the adoption of EFT/POS system in their industry is inevitable, and although they cannot predict the eventual form of the system, they are convinced that these systems will have to result from close cooperation between consumers, retailers, and financial institutions.

Although in its infancy, EFT/POS is a hotly debated topic, and the concerned parties are actively exploring avenues for arriving at a system structure acceptable to all. To shed light on some of the outstanding issues, it is perhaps appropriate to examine each group's concerns in more detail. Consumers' concerns revolve around the following issues: privacy as regards their purchasing habits, authentication methods, risk of unauthorized transactions, mechanisms for dispute settlement, desirability of having a choice of payment method, and ability to influence the finality of payments. Consumers will be also likely to consider the economics of using debit cards by taking into account such factors as transaction costs, "free credit" involved when credit cards are employed, and the convenience of not carrying cash. The choice parameters open to consumers will, of course, change as EFT/POS systems are introduced in the product lines of financial institutions with concomitant repricing of competing products. It should be noted that as ABMs spread at, or close to, many retail locations, they will also represent an alternative to using debit cards. The uncertainty surrounding consumer adoption of EFT/POS has been a major reason for its slow development, given the over 2 billion-dollar capital outlay estimated for the development of nationwide systems.

Retailers are the other major group in this process. Theoretically, they stand to benefit from these systems by (1) reducing their cash-handling costs, (2) reducing waiting time at checkout counters, and (3) eliminating the cost of fraudulent checks. The extent to which they can benefit from EFT/POS systems, however, critically depends on the arrangements that will evolve between retailers and financial institutions, both regarding capital expenditures and operating charges, as well as the resulting relationship between retailers and their customers. A major demand of the retailers has been that their proprietary cards be used to generate transactions that can flow through the national clearing system. This has been vigorously opposed by the financial institutions and the CPA on the grounds of preserving the integrity of the payment system. The CPA, realizing the crucial importance to retailers of having access to purchase records, has suggested the use of two cards for each transaction; one issued by the retailer for information-gathering purposes, and one issued by a CPA member for completing the financial aspect of the transaction. This alternative appears not to be acceptable to retailers. Furthermore, retailers want to be involved in the process of system development. The CPA has welcomed their involvement, and at the present time, representatives of the Retail Council participate in meetings of the CPA's senior planning committee. These concerns aside, it should be recognized that there is a high degree of concentration in this industry in Canada, which is expected to positively affect the rate of adoption of EFT/POS systems.

The financial institutions' posture vis à vis EFT/POS has been influenced, mainly, by the possible impact of these systems on their current products, especially ABMs and credit cards, loss of revenue from cash handling (the charge for $1000 currency deposit is approximately $1.50), a possible loss of revenue from a reduction in check volumes, and capital expenditures required to support the system. More globally, the long-term impact of EFT/POS on their competitive position in the market has influenced the speed with which they will promote the system. Research indicates that the rate of adoption of EFT/POS systems is slower in countries with more efficient payment systems. Countervailing this, however, is the finding that EFT is used as a major competitive tool as the financial service industries undergo deregulation (see Barnes et al. 1987). The slow pace of EFT/POS adoption notwithstanding, it appears that financial institutions are equally convinced of the eventual widespread adoption of EFT/POS and will continue to resolve the outstanding issues with retailers.

The role of the CPA in the development of the system is critical. EFT/POS squarely falls within the second mandate of the CPA. The organization was very mindful of the need to rapidly develop guidelines and procedures regarding this payment methodology in order to forestall the chaos that could result from the advent of heterogeneous systems in the market. Early statements issued by the Board of the CPA were aimed at limiting access to the deposit accounts of CPA members as well as the requirement for vertification of each and all POS transactions (see Lederman 1988). In September 1986, the Board initiated the process of preparing a policy statement and developing standards. A discussion draft was prepared and was adopted by the senior planning committee in the fall of 1987. The CPA continued its consultations with all interested parties, e.g., the Consumer Association of Canada, the Retail Council, and Treasury Management Association of Canada, through June 1988, at which time the final process of developing guidelines and standards for use of the system in Canada began.

Direct Funds Transfer (DFT)

The term DFT is used here to refer to the interinstitutional system involving exchange, on magnetic tape, of credit and debit items. Despite the fact that preauthorized arrangements, particularly for debit transfers, have been in existence for over 25 years, and that the economic advantages of tape-based transactions versus paper transactions are well understood, these items currently represent a small proportion of the total volume of the clearing system.

Beginning in September 1985, the CPA has encouraged the use of these systems and has set a goal of converting 33 percent of the total volume to DFT by 1990. Efforts to replace checks as a means of bill payments have focused on the promotion of "acceptance of payments of accounts," referred to previously, and streamlining the procedure for effecting preauthorized payments. As regards the latter, the CPA undertook a full-scale review of the rules governing this payment mechanism. After consultation with various interested parties, the CPA updated its rule regarding preauthorized payments, which among others, restricts its use to fixed amounts, and will limit the amount per item to $5000. A separate set of rules are to be developed for larger-value items. On the credit side, as in the United States, a major contributing factor to the success of achieving the CPA goals is the adoption of the system for use in connection with transfer payments from the federal government. These checks, deposited at the branches of CPA members, are presented to the Bank of Canada (a Direct Clearer) and amount to approximately 5.6 percent of the national clearing volume (see Table 3–2). The process of converting government credit transfers to DFT has been under way since 1986. Pilot projects have included Canadian Forces pensions and the National Capital Region payroll. In addition, interest on Canada Savings Bonds are paid by the bank of Canada through DFT. Further applications are under study, with some important considerations being the objections of unions and the need to communicate with an electoral constituency spread across the country on a regular basis (Murray 1986).

Electronic Data Interchange

Electronic Data Interchange (EDI) is a methodology for the electronic exchange of intercorporate trade data. The process also involves the electronic exchange of payment through the deposit-taking institutions. This will necessitate a flow of payment data along with payment instructions among different deposit-taking institutions. A detailed discussion of EDI can be found in Horan (1986), and a concise summary of the current status of this methodology in the United States is contained in Hill, Ferguson, and Stone (1987).

In Canada, EDI has gained reasonable acceptance in the automotive, transportation, grocery, and mass merchandising industries. It is estimated that by the end of 1987 some 700 corporations had adopted this methodology to varying degrees. The process of growth of EDI in Canada is facilitated by the EDI Council of Canada, a Toronto-based interindustry cooperative council created to promote the use of common standards and to maintain these standards, to assist its membership in implementing EDI systems, and to provide educational opportunities for Canadian corporations. Canadian banks have recently shown a great interest in EDI developments and some have joined the Council. Although, as mentioned previously, the permissible limits of banks' involvement in processing payment-related data is not clear under the current Bank Act, the growth of EDI is contingent upon their participation. Anvari and Roy (1987) outline the case for relaxing the current data-processing limitations based on the potential welfare effects of EDI systems. Proposals under review at the present time concede the desirability of expanding the data-processing powers of the banks through bank subsidiaries. Chartered banks prefer to be directly involved, and thus do not seem to fully endorse the current proposals (Cleghorn 1987).

As far as the payment system is concerned, EDI is expected to lead to an electronic infrastructure for intercorporate payments. This will necessitate the development of procedures and guidelines for electronic exchange of payment-related data among the members of the CPA. It will also provide an additional impetus for deposit-taking institutions to streamline the process of exchange of electronic payments. This latter imperative will influence the current procedures for exchange of electronically generated data among the members, which at the present always leads to a paper exchange because of the lack of a link among computer systems of member institutions. The CPA will undoubtedly be involved in the process of developing the required standards and guidelines and will apply the general principles that have evolved concerning shared networks, e.g., authorization/authentication, timing and finality of payment, reversibility, account integrity and control, default, and fraud.

Other Developments

Three additional developments in the payment system merit mention. First, an expansion of the functions of the shared ABM networks is technologically feasible and, possibly, economically justifiable. At the moment, clients of a given financial institution can only use the ABMs of other institutions for cash withdrawals. No deposit-taking can, for example, take place at these machines. An expansion of shared network capabilities is a natural phase in their development. It should be borne in mind that currently ABMs are exclusively used by consumers. A more distant possibility regarding these machines is the extension of their functions to accommodate business transactions, such as small retailer deposits. Second, a more convenient way for the electronic exchange of large-dollar items needs to be put in place. The CPA has been considering this issue for some time. Recently a decision was adopted by the chartered banks to use the SWIFT-based Interbank International Payments System (IIPS) to accommodate the transfer of domestic items of $50,000 or more between pairs of Canadian banks. Although, as mentioned previously, paper settlements in the form of debit vouchers created by a recipient bank are still exchanged, it is expected that a procedure for netting and settlement at the central bank will soon develop under the auspices of the CPA (see Wright 1987). Finally, the scope of operation of the Canadian Depository for Securities is expanding rapidly. Well over $80 billion dollars worth of securities were on deposit at the end of 1987. The flow of funds associated with transactions relative to these securities is estimated to be $636 million on an average day and dividends distributed amount to over $2 billion annually. At the present time, all funds transfers in and out of the depository, save for flows to and from depositories in the United States, are through checks and bank drafts that must clear through the CPA. The process of converting these payments to electronic items, although not imminent, is a distinct prospect in the future.

Conclusions

A rather broad outline of the current payment system structure in Canada and the directions of impending changes were presented. The major force behind the evolution of the system is the quest for reducing the overall costs of transferring value among the country's economic entities. The process is aided by a "technology push," which is the same in Canada as in the United States. Further, a critical factor involved is the cultural profile of consumers, firms, and governments, which again, is very similar to that in the United States. These aside, there are a number of relevant factors that are uniquely Canadian.

The current Canadian payment system is very efficient, and thus new payment alternatives, having lower marginal benefits than in some other countries, are bound to be scrutinized more closely before they are adopted. Second, there is a high degree of industrial concentration in this country. This was pointed out earlier with reference to the banking industry and the retail industry but is equally true in many other sectors. To the extent that concentration may be correlated with rates of adoption of new payment methodologies, one can expect the process to differ from that in the United States, for example. Third, not only is the financial services industry structured in a particular fashion but the process of deregulation under way is unique. As markets are redefined and providers of financial services attempt to gain market share and increase profitability, economic forces will be unleashed that will ascribe a particularly Canadian tone to the process of payment system innovations. This will, in the main, define the path of evolution of the payment system in Canada. The impact of foreign competition, particularly in view of the proposed Free Trade Agreement with the United States, will certainly influence this process. Fourth, given the CPA and its mandates, the mechanics of implementing innovation in the payment system has been, to a large degree, already defined. Innovation will, by and large, emanate from the free interplay of economic forces in the market. Their widespread adoption, however, will be contingent upon the resolution of possible conflicting interests through this participatory organization, which not only encompasses the deposit-taking institutions but as time goes by will have stronger ties with other interested parties. It is important to note that in view of both formal and informal ties between the CPA and the Bank of Canada, the broader issues of public interest that may arise with reference to innovations in payment system methodology are bound to be taken into account.

References

Adamek, P. 1987. "A Credit Transfer System for Canada." *Forum—The Canadian Payments Association* 3 (1): 3–4.

Anderson, G., M. Bhattacharya, R. Coallier, and R. Daigle. 1987. "Electronic Funds Transfer: A Canadian Perspective." Working Paper, Treasury Management Centre, Concordia University, Montreal, Canada.

Anvari, M. 1983. "Cash Concentration Systems in Canada: An Example of National Banking." *Journal of Cash Management* (June–July): 48–56.

————. 1988. "Corporate Cash Management in Canada: A Comparison with the U.S." *Advances in Working Capital Management* 1 (1): 79–95.

Anvari, M., P. Hanley, C. Methot, and C. Fox. 1989. "Cash Disbursement at CN." *Journal of Cash Management*, forthcoming.

Anvari, M., and R. Roy. 1987. "Electronic Data Interchange and Revision of the Bank Act." Paper presented at the Third Symposium on Cash, Treasury, and Working Capital Management, Las Vegas, Nevada (October).

Bank for International Settlements. 1985. *Payment Systems in Eleven Developed Countries*. Chicago: Bank Administration Institute.

Barnes, P., P. Beyrouti, G. Kyte, and M. Tinmouth. 1987. "EFT/POS: Issues and a Canadian Case Study." Working Paper, Treasury Management Centre, Concordia Univesity, Montreal, Canada.

Canada Gazette. 1988. Part 1, Vol. 122, No. 4, January 23.

Cleghorn, J. 1987. Luncheon Address, Cash Management Association of Canada Conference, Toronto (October).

Clemons, E. K., and S. O. Kimbrough, eds. 1986. *Information Systems, Telecommunications, and Their Effects on Industrial Organization*. Proceedings of the Seventh International Conference on Information Systems. San Diego, Calif.

Crawford, B., and Falconbridge. 1986. *Banking and Bills of Exchange: A Treatise on the Law of Banks, Banking, Bills of Exchange, and the Payment System in Canada*, 8th ed. Toronto: Canada Law Books.

Dingle, J. F. 1988. "The Detailed Schedule of the Daily Clearing and Settlement System." Paper presented at the seminar Money and Electronic Banking: The Law of Payments and Clearing, Toronto (February).

Farhoomand, F., and D. H. Drury. 1988. "A Model for Information Technology Adoption." Working Paper, Concordia University, Montreal, Canada.

Financial Executives Research Foundation. 1986. *Cash Management and the Payments System*. Morristown, N.J.

Friesen, D. R. 1988. "EFT in Canada: A Retailer's Perspective." *TMAC Journal* 4 (1): 8–12.

Hill, N. C., and D. M. Ferguson. 1985. "Negotiating Payment Terms in an Electronic Environment." Paper presented at the National Corporate Cash Management Association meeting, New Orleans (November).

Hill, N. C., D. M. Ferguson, and B. K. Stone. 1987. "Electronic Data Interchange: An Introduction and Status Report." Paper presented at the Third Symposium on Cash, Treasury, and Working Capital Management, Las Vegas, Nevada (October).

Horan, T. F. 1986. *Electronic Data Interchange*. Report No. 741. Business Intelligence Program, SRI International.

Johnson, T., and S. F. Maier. 1985. "Making the Corporate Decision: Paper

Checks to Electronic Funds Transfer." *Journal of Cash Management* 5 (6): 30–41.

Lederman, L. T. 1988. "The Canadian National Payments System and the Canadian Payments Association." Paper presented at the seminar Money and Electronic Banking: The Law of Payments and Clearing, Toronto (February).

Leishman, W. 1987. "The Canadian Cheque Clearing System." *Forum—The Canadian Payments Association* 3 (3).

Lindwall, E. 1986. "A Significant Step." *Forum—The Canadian Payments Association* 2 (3).

McFarlan, F. W. 1983. "IS and Competitive Strategy." Note 0-184-055, Harvard Business School, Cambridge, Mass.

McMorran, S. R. 1988. "Technological Components of Electronic Funds Transfer Systems and Automated Cash Management." Paper presented at the seminar Money and Electronic Banking: The Law of Payments and Clearing, Toronto (February).

Murray, J. B. 1986. "Cash Management in the Government of Canada." *CMAC Journal* 2 (4): 35–41.

Pelletier, R. 1985. "The Driving Force for Change in Trade Biller Practices." *Canadian Treasury Management Review* 2 (1): 7–8.

Porter, M. 1980. *Competitive Strategy*. New York: Free Press.

Speake, J. H. 1985. "DFT: The Future Is Now." *Forum—The Canadian Payments Association*.

Valcin, Y. 1988. "Consumer Issues in Electronic Banking: A Policy Action for Canada." Paper presented at the seminar Money and Electronic Banking: The Law of Payments and Clearing, Toronto (February).

Williamson, O. E. 1985. *Markets and Hierarchies*. New York: Free Press.

Wiseman, C. 1985. *Strategy and Computers*. Homewood, Ill.: Richard D. Irwin.

Wright, E. B. 1987. Paper presented at Cash Management Association of Canada Conference, Toronto (October).

COMMENTARY

by James F. Dingle

I am challenged by the opportunity to discuss Professor Anvari's excellent paper. He has described the various streams of payments in Canada and has noted the growing use of electronic payment media over the period 1983–1988. His data were generated by the Automated Clearing and Settlement System, which is administered by the Canadian Payments Association. Consequently, the numbers are not estimates; they are monthly volume and value totals, based on every item that passed through the national system during those five years. The important story in the data can be told in one sentence: the percentage of total volume of payments (excluding currency and credit card transactions) accounted for by electronic media was just 1.2 in 1983 but rose in the subsequent four years to 1.6, 2.4, 3.4, and 6.2 respectively. These are escalating proportions of the total payment volume; the underlying growth rates for the electronic categories are therefore quite impressive. And the trend is continuing. If we move to the last observation, made in February 1988, the electronic proportion is still higher, 8.3 percent. When you plot the proportion on a chart, it looks like a hyperbola with a right-side asymptote. Or, more precisely, it looks like the steep part of the technology assimilation curve.

Professor Anvari has described the various types of electronic payment media now in use in Canada. They have all appeared over the last dozen years because of the principal economic force for change in payment system structure: the rapidly rising cost of labor relative to the cost of communication and computation. This labor-to-capital factor-price ratio also has a steeply rising chart, because of the falling cost of computers. In Canada, the labor-to-capital price ratio went from an index of 100 early in 1983 to 270 at the end of 1987. So, in rough and ready terms, over just five years, people have became almost three times as expensive as machines. (And the wage rate in the financial sector rose only 30 percent.)

It is no exaggeration to say that this rapidly rising factor-price ratio, observed in Canada and in every other developed country in the world, is one of the key economic phenomena of the decade. It ranks with the oil price shock of 1973 in its broad and powerful impact. So we should not be surprised to see the shift to more computer-intensive processes in providing payment services. We should not be surprised when banks actively promote electronic media for payments. The interesting question is, rather, why is the electronic proportion rising only now?

Why has the response to this cheaper technology been, until recently, so slow? Bernell Stone's presentation gives us a number of explanations, which apply in the United States context. The Canadian explanations are variations on his theme. The considerable advantages associated with electronic payment media tend to be coupled with some countervailing disadvantages. Here are a few examples.

First, electronic payment services in Canada are priced cheaply for consumers—indeed, they may have a *zero* price, being offered as a loss-leader by the financial institution. But other payment media, such as credit cards, may be preferred because they provide significant *positive* compensation to the users in the form of free float for several weeks. The Humphrey and Berger analysis makes this clear.

Second, electronic money services provided via ABMs (called ATMs in the United States) are very convenient to use in Canada because of the 24-hours-per-day, 7-days-per-week, coast-to-coast availability of the universally shared terminals of all major financial institutions. But Canadians are still on a learning curve with respect to ABMs; the machine population is still spreading geographically; and there are, of course, the occasional but irritating times when a hungry and cash-short consumer finds the network is "down" at six o'clock on Saturday afternoon.

Third, electronic money protects the confidentiality of personal data, and the privacy of the consumer, very well indeed—those early fears of surveillance by means of the payment system have largely faded away. But electronic money is not nearly as private as bank notes, which are largely untraceable and can therefore be used for nontaxable transactions. In several countries, including Belgium and Canada, the electronic payment services provided by shared ABMs are stimulating, rather than displacing, the use of bank notes.

Finally, for Canadian retailers, electronic funds transfer at the point-of-sale (EFT/POS) may well be as fast as cash and a lot more secure. But the extensive computer system changes necessary to provide electronic payment services at the point-of-sale have to be set in place *in addition* to the long-standing administrative routines still needed to handle bank notes, checks, and credit cards, not to mention the systems that are used for inventory control and corporate cash management. So the changes at the point-of-sale are not undertaken without detailed examination of how the costs and benefits are shared.

In a similar manner, governments that are considering the direct deposit of social security payments also have to face this costly burden of a parallel system. Moreover, in Canada, some of the decision makers have rather liked the idea of millions of checks moving out to the voting public each month, in paper envelopes which also contain a message of some sort. As a footnote, I would remark that the most recent press reports about the Canadian government suggest that the cost savings associated with direct deposits are finally overcoming such barriers in the case of social security payments.

In summary, then, in addition to powerful economic factors, there are clearly a number of what I might call cultural factors, and these must be addressed if one wishes to explain the rate of emergence of electronic payment media in recent years.

Cross-Sectional Analysis

How can we analyze these cultural factors? I suppose the most pleasant way would be to do a sort of cross-sectional analysis of payment system structure; namely, travel abroad, live in six or seven countries for a month or two, and actually use their payment systems. Barring that, some of us go to Basel in Switzerland twice a year and listen to our central-banker colleagues at the Bank for International Settlements (BIS) describe the current developments in eleven national payment systems. Over the period since 1983 every one of those eleven central bankers has talked at one time or another about the key economic force for change—the falling cost of communication and computation. But they have also talked about the effect of many cultural factors. There is the political orientation of each country; this determines the relative importance of market mechanisms in the allocation of resources. And there is the legal structure. Often this shapes the institutional framework within which the various types of financial intermediaries have to function. Also significant is the relative importance of the government as an operator within the payment system and as a participant in the planning of the payment system.

These cultural aspects are fascinating to hear about, and one is often tempted to ask the question: Which culture is most conducive to the emergence of electronic payment media?

Now, I know that former Governor George Mitchell has pondered this sort of question at some length. Many of you will remember the comparative tables he prepared for the 1985 Symposium in Washington. (If you want to refresh your memory, glance at the special edition of the *Journal of Bank Research* that appeared a year later.) In those tables, which used 1983 data for the eleven developed countries, Governor Mitchell calculated the proportion of electronic payments to the total volume of payments. In 1983, Germany and Japan were the only countries for which the electronic ratio was over 50 percent. The United States and Canada had ratios of only about 1 percent.

I recently had that table updated, using the 1985 data assembled at the BIS. In the brief span of two years, Switzerland approached the halfway mark (50 percent), and the United Kingdom rose to about one-quarter. In contrast, France, perhaps the most interventionist country of the eleven, was stalled at about 15 percent. Now, that contrast between right and left might lead a free enterpriser to form a hypothesis or two. But I would discourage anyone from drawing the conclusion that the free enterprise economies are more conducive to the use of electronic payment media than the countries with national plans. The cross-country correlation is simply not that high.

It is more sensible to note that cultural factors have played—and will play—a significant role in the evolution of national payment systems; and to realize that if you want to show exactly how, you have to recount the various major developments, country by country. It is history, not econometrics, that is relevant. Cultural factors are by their nature very hard to quantify.

So let's shift our focus and move away from the five years 1983–1988 to five *spans* of five years running from 1970 to 1995. From this broader perspective, the difference between 15 percent electronic for France and 60 percent electronic for Germany in the year 1985 fades into insignificance. What comes clearly into view is the fact that all eleven countries are currently experiencing the telematic revolution. By 1995 it may well have run its course for most of the eleven. So keep in mind the *sameness*, *not* the international differences. You see the same driving force of that capital-labor factor-price ratio everywhere in the eleven countries. And, on the cultural side, whether you talk about the information society, the post-industrial society, or the global village—it is one and the same thing, and we are all its citizens.

Here are some further illustrations of the sameness I am talking about:

- More closely **synchronized business cycles** within the group of industrialized countries since 1970.
- The *deregulation* of financial institutions at almost the same time, even in countries of contrasting political orientation.
- The *globalization and securitization* of corporate finance; followed —after the October 1987 crash—by retrenchment and reintermediation.
- The current debates about the *service charges* paid by consumers for payment services.
- The extraordinary acceleration of the work on national and international standards for corporate-to-corporate *electronic data interchange* (EDI), work that has a significant payment system component.

I could go on with more illustrations. But I would prefer to suggest that this sameness—this somewhat surprising homogeneity—has both economic and cultural explanations. Both the similarity and the simultaneity of such developments provide a strong reminder that the key economic phenomena are now global in scope—and a strong hint that a shared culture is emerging among the developed countries of the world.

Lessons Regarding Payment Systems

There are several lessons to be drawn regarding the future evolution of our payment systems, and they all spring from the same general idea: We should nudge our *national* payment structures toward what we feel is a desirable *global* mechanism.

Lesson 1

We should think carefully about the telecommunication linkages between our national systems. For example, we must work together to ensure that SWIFT can continue to perform its central role, which is the moving of payment-related messages across borders; and perform it at least as securely, reliably and efficiently as it does today.

Lesson 2

We should think about payment-system stability and integrity—in *global* terms. For example, the best structural change this year for the Japanese payment system—without question—will be the eagerly awaited change in the settlement failure procedures of the New York Clearing House. A major settlement risk for Japanese banks processing payments in U.S. dollars is being eliminated by the New York development.

Lesson 3

We should view our payment system as a plannable structure. I'm not sure if the word *plannable* exists, but if the word doesn't, the planning *process* certainly does, and here are some relevant parts of it that we all share.

For central bankers. The process is the biannual meeting of payment system people, which takes place at the Bank for International Settlements in Basel.

For lawyers. The process is the UNCITRAL effort to develop model rules for electronic funds transfer, which takes place twice a year at the United Nations in Vienna and New York.

For consumer advoctes (government). The process runs in the Consumer Policy Committee of the Organization for Economic Cooperation and Development (OECD) in Paris.

For bank administrators. The process is animated by the International Standards Organization and by the United Nations, which is currently formulating the standards for electronic data interchange, in Geneva.

And finally, for yourselves as "scholars, banking practitioners, and policy makers having an interest in payment system matters"—to quote Robert Black and the conference program—the process is the very pleasant one that we are enjoying here in Williamsburg.

LUNCHEON ADDRESS: PERSPECTIVES ON PAYMENT SYSTEM RISK REDUCTION

E. Gerald Corrigan

Rather than focusing directly on the subject of payment risk, I would like to share with you some of my thoughts regarding the evolution of trade clearing and settlement practices associated with securities and other financial transactions. In focusing on this area, I want to emphasize how we may be able to strengthen clearing and settlement arrangements and thereby strengthen the workings of our financial and payment systems generally.

Specifically, while there has been—and rightly so—a great deal of attention focused on operational, liquidity, and credit characteristics of large-dollar payment systems such as Fedwire and the Clearing House Interbank Payment System (CHIPS), there are literally dozens of other important trade clearing and settlement systems for funds, securities, futures, options, and other financial instruments that also warrant attention. This is especially true since, one way or another, these other systems generally achieve their final settlements on or through Fedwire or CHIPS or both. The importance of these clearing and settlement systems was forcefully illustrated in the weeks of October 19 and October 26, 1987, when the plunge in equity prices in the United States and abroad brought a number of these clearing and settlement systems under great stress. Indeed, many observers, myself included, are of the opinion that the greatest threat to the stability of the financial system as a whole in that period was the danger of a major default in one of these clearing and settlement systems.

Clearing and settlement systems that directly interact with major large-dollar payment systems are of interest from a public policy perspective for a number of reasons, but the most important, by far, is because the linkages inherent in such systems necessarily raise important questions about systemic risks. That is, a major mechanical breakdown, liquidity problem, or, even worse, default in one of these systems has the potential to seriously and adversely affect all other direct and indirect participants in the system, even those that are far removed from the initial source of the problem. Unlike many other types of financial problems, a major disruption in one of these systems can occur suddenly and can spread rapidly. These traits of large clearing and settlement systems can be especially worrisome because all too often their legal, technical, and operational characteristics are so complex that the direct and indirect users may not fully understand the nature and scope of the risks and exposures— including intraday exposures—that they are incurring.

Against that background, I would like to share with you my thoughts about the key characteristics that should be associated with clearing and settlement systems. Indeed, to the extent there is agreement as to the essential characteristics of strong clearing systems, those characteristics can then be used as a yardstick against which particular clearing systems for financial instruments can be evaluated. Taken as a whole, the driving force behind this exercise is to suggest a series of criteria that can work to reduce risks—especially systemic risks—in clearing and settlement systems for financial transactions.

We can look at the whole structure of systems as an inverted pyramid. At the top are the dealers and parties entering into the financial transactions in the pits at the exchanges or over-the-counter. On the next lower level would be trade netting arrangements, such as securities, futures, and options clearing corporations. These trade netting systems then settle through other systems, and the funds settlement for these systems, in turn, are made by clearinghouse checks, or through CHIPS, or ultimately, at the bottom of the pyramid, through Fedwire, where each payment is processed and settled almost simultaneously.

The key to containing and reducing risks in this inverted pyramid is the finality of payment for the maze of underlying transactions associated with each layer of the pyramid. I suspect that any self-respecting group of lawyers could probably debate for hours as to what the term *finality* means, but I will rely on a practical, commonsense definition: In its purest form, finality means that at the very instant an institution receives an advice of payment or confirmation of delivery through a system for a particular transaction, the money in question is "good money," even if at the next instant the sending institution goes bust. Under this definition, there are two elements to consider: first, the prompt discharge of counterparty obligations, and second, the financial strength of the instrumentalities through which obligations and payments are discharged. When these elements are recognized, it becomes apparent that finality is crucial in efforts to contain systemic risk, because the more we do to achieve finality as quickly as possible, the more able we are to contain problems at their source.

To my way of thinking, Fedwire possesses a pure form of finality. At the moment a depository institution receives an advice of credit from a Reserve Bank, the institution and its customers are prepared to have the obligations of their counterparties discharged, because the Reserve Bank provides immediate and irrevocable funds and because reserve balances provide a universally acceptable medium for payment. Some other payment, clearing, and settlement systems operate under procedures where payments or transactions could be revoked after they are made but before they are finally settled. The provisionality within these systems reflects a variety of considerations, including the liquidity and credit risks confronted by the systems. Other systems depend upon preserving the unquestioned credit standing of the central clearing corporation. However, in either case, some reasonable and prudent steps can and should be taken by any clearing or settlement system to minimize potential problems and thereby strengthen the clearing and settlement process.

Achieving true finality when securities or securities derivatives are involved can be even more complex in that most such clearing and settlement systems involve some form of netting before delivery, settlement, and payment mechanisms come into play. In these instances, final payments are generally made against receipt of what is, in effect, netted positions of securities. A first question is whether the netting has effectively discharged the counterparties' obligations on each of the underlying transactions and, with respect to funds settlement, replaced them with an intermediary's credit obligation. A second question is whether participants in a clearing or settlement system are prepared to accept the credit of the intermediary or whether the intermediary's settlement obligations are finally discharged only when net settlement money transfers are made over Fedwire.

The amount of time between the point at which a particular financial transaction is made and the point at which the payment for the transaction is truly final can vary enormously, depending both upon the type of instrument in question and upon whether one is considering the original contractual obligations of the counterparties or the settlement obligations of the clearing corporation and its participants.

In citing the examples in the accompanying table, I do not mean to imply that time alone is the only or the most important factor in seeking to contain systemic risks. Obviously, other factors enter the picture. However, it does seem clear to me that an overriding goal in our efforts to strengthen clearing, settlement, and payment systems should be to reduce to the maximum extent possible the amount of time between when a financial transaction is entered into and when both parties to the transaction know with certaintly that the valuables to be delivered and the payment corresponding to the transaction are final and irrevocable. Being realistic, however, there are both trade-offs and limits as to how far we can and

Clearing and Delivery

Type of Transaction	Maximum Time to Final Payment
Purchase or sale of equities on certain foreign exchanges	Counterparty trades, up to several months
Purchase or sale of mortgage-backed securities	Counterparty trades, up to 30 days
"When-issued" trades in government securities	Counterparty trades, up to 15 days
Purchase or sale of domestic equities	Counterpart trades (net against clearing corporation), discharge within 5 days; clearing corporation to participants, 2 days more; total 7 calendar days
Futures and options transactions	Counterparty trades, immediate discharge, clearing corporation to participants, early next day

Large-Dollar Payments	Maximum Time to Final Payment
CHIPS payments	Bank to bank, up to 11 hours; receiving customer, same day or next day (depending on availability)
Fedwire transfers	Bank to bank, almost instantaneous; receiving customer, same day (depending on availability given by receiving bank)

should go in seeking to narrow the time gap between when financial transactions are made and when they are truly final. Fortunately, there are also
devices that can help manage and reduce the risks posed by the time gaps
in the process. But under any set of arrangements, achieving finality as
quickly and as safely as possible is the key to stronger clearing, settlement,
and payment systems. By extension, a crucial property of such systems is
transparency—they should be structured so that all participants clearly
understand and agree on when transactions and payments are final and
when they are not.

   While transparency and finality are crucial features of clearing and
payment systems, designing systems that achieve these features is not an
easy matter. However, it seems to me that there are three generic groups
of traits of clearing and settlement systems that are relevant to the larger
question of containing both direct and systemic risks in the operation of
such systems. These are the operational, structural, and financial features
of such systems.

Operational Features

While there is consensus that major clearing and settlement systems should
have the highest possible degree of operational reliability and integrity,
it may not be fully appreciated just how important these operational features are and how difficult and expensive it may be to achieve them. For
example, it is clear that a major operational breakdown in one of the
systems—particularly if it occurs while business is in progress or if it lasts
more than one business day—can give rise to serious liquidity if not credit
problems among the participants. In addition, the operational and control
features of such systems constitute a vital link in the ability of participants
to keep track of positions and exposures—including on an intraday basis—
and are thus crucially related to the all-important credit decision-making
process within and among clearing and settlement systems. When looked
at in this broader light, there are several key design and operational features that we should look for in any clearing and settlement system that,
by its nature or its size, carries with it systemic risk considerations. Three
such features strike me as worthy of note:

1. All such systems should be designed with adversity in mind. This
   means having in place systems and multilevel backup that can cope
   with a wide range of potential problems, not simply problems of an
   operational nature. It is clearly not possible to design a system that

is fail-safe, but it is essential to ensure that operational traits of such
systems are capable of dealing with a broad range of contingencies. As
an extension of this, a very high level of security and control devices
to guard against fraud and other abuses is obviously important. In
short, a high degree of availability, reliability, flexibility, and integrity
is essential, even if costly.

2. All such systems should have on-line, real-time information access
   systems so as to provide participants and the system operator—and
   when necessary, the authorities—with prompt access to information
   needed to make informed credit and other decisions. This too is costly,
   but so is the alternative.

3. All such systems should have design and operational features that
   go as far as possible in reducing or at least immobilizing the movement
   of paper instruments and paper flows. This is important in its own right
   but is also relevant from the point of view of risk containment, because
   the reduction of paper flows facilitates more rapid trade comparison,
   netting, and ultimate final settlement of transactions. As an extension
   of this, the possession and control of collateral are also of importance.

These essential operational features of clearing and settlement systems
imply that well-designed systems are going to be expensive systems. In a
highly competitive world that reality raises the specter of competition in
laxity—something we must rigorously guard against. Like it or not, there
is no such thing as a five-and-dime version of a clearing and settlement
system, and users of such systems should make it their business to see
that they are not part of, and are not exposed to, clearing and settlement
systems that are not up to the highest standards of operational design.
Low transactions costs are obviously a great aid to market efficiency and
liquidity but not if they are achieved at the expense of high standards of
operational reliability, security, and integrity.

Fortunately, the track record of all major clearing and settlement systems in the United States is very good, even though we have had a few
near-misses. Thus, I stress these features in the interests of strengthening
an already strong track record—a goal that becomes all the more important as markets and institutions in the United States and abroad become
even more closely linked and as the volume and complexity of financial
transactions increase at a rapid pace.

Structural Features

In considering the structural features of clearing and settlement systems,
one should keep in mind that many such systems rely on one form or an-

other of shared risk or shared liability. While arrangements differ from place to place and from time to time, the general practice is that, in the event of a default of one of the members, the clearing corporation is obligated to make good on the default, either through liquidation of the defaulting participant's margin or collateral, or through some kind of shared assessment on all other members. The credit and financial interdependencies resulting from these arrangements—especially when they arise in the context of otherwise tightly linked and volatile markets—are a main reason why structural features of clearing and settlement systems are so important. Against that background, the following structural features of these systems strike me as especially noteworthy:

1. Standards for participation or membership in clearing and settlement entities should be explicit and meaningful. Criteria for membership—especially in entities that have shared risks—should, at a minimum, include strong capital adequacy requirements, proven operational soundness, and high standards of professional and ethical management as well as demonstrated access to ample sources of credit and liquidity short of the central bank. Open access is important but not at the expense of credit standards. Strong members can sponsor and be responsible for those not ready for direct participation. There is also the question of whether, as a general rule, members of clearing corporations and the clearing corporations themselves should be subject to a higher degree of official oversight.

2. Clearing and settlement entities should have in place clear rules specifying the obligations and rights of clearing firms, their customers, the clearing corporation itself, and the corporation's settlement banks. These entities should have some flexibility in addressing problems, but clarity about their respective rights and obligations is especially important in times of stress, including the event of default or bankruptcy of individual participants.

3. Clearing systems should provide the structural capability for the entities, individual members, creditor banks, and supervisors to be able to assess and limit positions and exposures, including on an intraday basis. Ideally, that capability should exist across instruments, across markets, across exchanges, and across clearing corporations, since it is not uncommon for individual firms or their large customers to have sizable positions in a variety of instruments in a variety of different exchanges. In this regard, there is a question as to whether it makes sense, in the long run, for transactions in a wide range of agricultural, industrial, material, and financial instruments to be cleared and settled in the same clearing entity.

4. The most important structural features of clearing and settlement systems, however, are those relating to the manner and certainty with which the settlement takes place. As noted earlier, a strong clearing and settlement system must have sound information systems, and it must be able to effect trade comparisons in a prompt and efficient manner.

Assuming the above features are in place, settlement systems must also have the following:

5. A well-understood and binding mechanism for netting positions of individual participants and, by extension, their customers, including procedures for failure to deliver securities. This is easier said than done, especially since ill-conceived netting systems can become a smoke screen behind which abuses can occur. It is also true that multilateral netting arrangements present difficult legal and credit problems growing out of the contingent liabilities that can arise in the event of a default by a direct or indirect party. Needless to say, if the netting mechanism is flawed, the achievement of final net settlement also is suspect.

6. Settlement rules should provide ample time and opportunity to secure and deliver the cash or securities required of each participant and their customers. Since the act of settlement may often involve drawing on credit facilities at banks, this implies the need to ensure that creditors are able to make informed and explicit credit decisions. It also implies that seemingly unimportant things, such as disparities in operating hours and days of doing business between banks and exchanges, can become important in times of stress.

7. The settlement mechanism should have access to a reliable and trusted method for achieving final net settlement. Here, too, the manner, timing, and precise circumstances in which final settlement is achieved should be clear and explicit. As a practical matter, in many, if not most, circumstances, clearing and settlement systems will need to have the capacity—through settlement banks—to effect payment for their net settlement obligations over Fedwire. And if net settlement is to be effected over Fedwire, the net settlement transfers should be made so that (as is the case with CHIPS, for example) the purpose of the transfers is explicit and clear to all, including to the Fed itself. In other words, transparency should be a central part of the process of final net settlement so that credit decisions, including those made by the Fed, can be explicit.

Regardless of whether net settlement is achieved via the Fed or otherwise, it is important that the Fed or some other settlement agent have strong assurances that the settlement will stick. That is why the concept of settlement finality is so important. That concept says that the clearing entity seeking to achieve final settlement has in place the financial resources and commitments—whether in the form of reserves, collateral, committed bank lines, guarantees, or some other arrangements—to ensure that, in the event of a problem or a default, settlement will still take place. Absent those resources and commitments, the danger in times of stress is that one or more parties will refuse to participate in the settlement, thereby triggering potentially substantial losses for the clearing corporation and, through it, other members. Needless to say, the consequences of such an event could be very serious indeed.

Financial Features

The last, and in many respects the most important, feature of clearing and settlement systems relates to their financial strength and resiliency. Here, I have in mind the nature and size of the financial, credit, and liquidity cushions that are available with certainty to be able to meet contingencies and problems that may arise. In this regard, the earlier discussion has already referred to the importance of strong operational controls and the transparency of the settlement and credit decision-making processes associated with such systems, but there is more to it than that.

The ultimate line of defense insofar as the financial strength of these systems is concerned is, of course, the capital adequacy of the participating members and the extent to which informed, rigorous, and explicit credit judgments are associated with all aspects of the system. But even if we assume that capital standards are adequate and that all participants are diligent in their monitoring of and control over exposures, the case for further elements of strength in financial and liquidity characteristics within clearing and settlement systems is clear. It is for this reason that most such systems rely on some combination of member deposits or guarantees, together with margins to establish a liquid clearing fund, which is intended to serve as a financial buffer to enable the clearing system to absorb shocks ranging from large and sudden price changes to defaults. However, the size and composition of such cushions can vary appreciably from one clearing system to another—a result that in and of itself may not be bad. But because the consequences of a major default in one of these systems can be so severe, I believe we should err on the conservative side in our judgment

as to what constitutes an adequate measure of capital and liquidity support
for clearing and settlement systems. I believe we should look carefully at
the following:

- The capital structure of firms that are members of clearing corporations.
- The size, composition, and nature of the deposits that members are
  required to post with the exchange or clearing corporation as a condition of participation, including the question of the liquidity and certainty with which such funds are available quickly to meet emergencies.
- The level and structure of margins, with particular emphasis on en-
  suring that margins provide a sufficient cushion to protect the integrity
  of the marketplace generally, and that they can play this role without
  having to rely prematurely on the liquidation of positions in order to
  generate the cash needed to start up in the morning or to keep the
  exchange or the clearing corporation whole. Clearly, the appropriate
  level of margins can vary from one market or clearing system to another depending, among other things, on the amount of price volatility
  and the time to final settlement. However, the potential range of
  factors that can produce a significant default in a clearing mechanism is
  wide. There is no analytical tool that can, with precision, evaluate the
  probability of such events. Yet, however low the probability, the consequences of such a default can be so severe that a conservative and
  prudent standard should be extended toward margins. We need to ensure that margins themselves are not subject to a competition in laxity.
- Major clearing systems should have access to an identifiable pool of
  liquidity or collateral, again, short of the central bank. This might
  include the presence of firm, committed lines of credit at commercial
  banks on the part of members and perhaps the clearing corporation
  itself. It might also involve arrangements for the establishment of
  a pool of liquid collateral in satisfactory form that can be brought to
  bear either to secure positions or to facilitate external financing; or, it
  might involve some kind of financial guarantees. However, its precise
  form is not as important as the concept; namely, seeking to add an
  extra element of certainty to the settlement process.
- We should give greater attention to, or at least consider, whether
  there may be a role for some device that can limit or contain the total
  amount of exposure any participant can incur within and across a series
  of interdependent clearing mechanisms. This would not be easy to
  accomplish, but, in my view, it is worth some thought.

There is no one specific formula that can tell us in a fail-safe manner what constitutes adequate financial cushions for every clearing and settlement system. That is neither achievable nor desirable. Rather, the point is that the financial underpinnings of these systems are of great importance, not least from a public policy perspective. Thus, as I said earlier, judgments about what is adequate should be made with a cautious and conservative bias that realistically takes account of the dangers and the consequences of default.

These remarks are already too long, but I have only scratched the surface of the subject. For example, I have not even referred to the complexities that arise in connection with off-shore clearing and settlement systems or those which, in one way or another, involve multiple currencies cutting across national boundaries. Similarly, I have not touched on the question of direct linkages among clearing systems or on what can be done to better integrate existing systems. Those subjects will have to wait for another time. But, in a way, that is appropriate, because I believe that the primary thrust of current efforts should be to ensure that existing systems are all that they can and should be. As I have said, the importance of the safety and integrity of payment systems is now widely accepted; what I am suggesting is that if we really care about the safety of the payment system, we must also are about the safety and integrity of related clearing and settlement systems, which ultimately operate through the payment system.

II PAYMENT SYSTEM RISK

In the luncheon address preceding the papers in this session, Gerald Corrigan notes a number of payment risk concerns. He focuses on how clearing and settlement arrangements in securities markets are dependent on funds and settlement transfers on large-dollar payment networks. Most independent security transactions, whether they be for equities or government securities, are settled with wire transfers. Further, the value of these transfers often reflect only the net position between parties rather than the (much larger) gross value of the securities traded that day. And it is not always clear whether the parties settling securities trades would be liable for the smaller net value or the larger gross value if settlement problems arise. Consequently, the finality, or nonreversibility, of the settlement transfer takes on great importance.

Another important dimension of a settlement transaction is timeliness. Depending on the security or financial instrument being transferred, the time between when the instrument is traded and when settlement occurs can range from a week (for sales of domestic equities) to several months (for equity sales on some foreign exchanges).

Finally, Corrigan outlines some standards by which the riskiness of securities clearing and settlement systems could be judged, including the underlying legal framework regarding discharge and assignment of liabilities, the adequacy of the financial resources of the clearing entity and its participants to deal with a significant settlement failure, and the ability of networks to recover (in a timely manner) from severe operational disruptions.

The two following chapters discuss payment risk issues in more detail. David Mengle takes up the issue of payment finality, which can assume different forms depending on the parties involved and the assignment of legal liability for monetary losses. These issues have a long history in statutes, case law, and regulatory actions for checks, but there is no similar guidance for electronic payments.

Mengle focuses on payment finality as applied to large-dollar wire transfer networks, particularly on how the different concepts of finality might be applied to CHIPS (Clearing House Interbank Payment System), which has daily dollar volumes on the order of $600 billion. At present, transactions on CHIPS have only sender finality, meaning that once a payment is sent, the sender cannot cancel it. Errors are reversed by having the receiver return the funds sent. In contrast, Fedwire (the Federal Reserve's wire transfer network) processes a similar dollar volume but has sender, settlement, and receiver finality. That is, any transfer made on Fedwire is final for all parties at the time it is made.

In the event of a major settlement failure on CHIPS, many or even all payments made during a day could be reversed under current CHIPS rules. The consequences of such massive reversals have been simulated and could be quite disruptive to financial markets. CHIPS is currently studying settlement finality arrangements that both forbid settlement entries from being reversed and that allocate monetary losses, if any, among participating banks. The objective is to internalize risks and costs created by network participants in order to induce them to behave differently.

In effect, the payment finality issue revolves around assignment of risk. The more risk is concentrated on one party to a transaction, the more incentive that party will have to reduce risk. But Mengle points out two cases in which finality rules could be ineffective. First, if banks anticipate that they would be bailed out of a settlement failure by outside aid to the failing bank, they will have little incentive to control their own exposure to other banks. Second, since unexpected settlement failure is a possible but unlikely event, banks may ignore or seriously underestimate the probability of its occurrence. In such a case, concentrating risks on participants may only increase risks, not reduce them. Still, compared with the current system, any clear rule would at least add certainty to a now uncertain legal environment.

Commentary on the Mengle Chapter is provided by Hal Scott, who presents an extended analysis of payment finality. He focuses on receiver finality and how a mandated (regulatory) approach would displace possibly more flexible and efficient contracting among the parties. Current developments in the ongoing process to draft new statutes dealing with electronic payments for the Uniform Commercial Code are also discussed in some detail.

A related aspect of payment risk is covered in the chapter by Gerald Faulhaber, Almarin Phillips, and Anthony Santomero. While Mengle discussed a legal or nonprice remedy for altering risky payment behavior, Faulhaber, Phillips, and Santomero focus on an economic approach to payment risk. First, they suggest a measure that objectively reflects payment risk, such as the level of daylight overdrafts on Fedwire and net debits on CHIPS. Then the measure is priced in order to alter the risky behavior identified and to compensate the party that bears the risk.

In principle, many of the same results should follow from explicit pricing as from altering payment loss exposures by changing finality rules. In the latter case, decision makers form their own implicit "prices" by internalizing the probability of monetary losses. Of course, for certain practical or philosophical reasons, one approach may be preferred over the other. In this instance, the authors argue for pricing over regulatory quantitative approaches (sender net debit caps, bilateral net credit limits) that have been applied to date. They also suggest that pricing might lead to some decentralization of payments and risks to smaller networks rather than concentrating all activity on the two existing large networks.

Commentary on the Faulhaber-Phillips-Santomero chapter is provided by Robert Litan. He supports the concept of pricing payment risk to alter risky behavior on the part of participants. He suggests, however, that a dual approach using pricing and current quantitative restrictions (caps) may be preferred over use of either one alone. While pricing would induce most or all participants to reduce risk generally, a cap in conjunction with pricing would also serve to prevent any one participant from generating an unacceptable amount of risk by itself.

4 LEGAL AND REGULATORY REFORM IN ELECTRONIC PAYMENTS: AN EVALUATION OF PAYMENT FINALITY RULES

David L. Mengle

Each day, approximately $1.3 trillion changes hands by means of wholesale wire transfers.[1] Of this total, about $638 billion is exchanged on Fedwire, the Federal Reserve wire transfer network, while just under $622 billion moves over the privately owned Clearing House Interbank Payment System (CHIPS). On Fedwire, the average transfer is $2.9 million, while transfers on CHIPS average $4.6 million.

With such substantial amounts involved in virtually instantaneous transactions, it is not surprising that concern has arisen over the risk that a large network participant might fail to settle its obligation to the network. Consequently, the Board of Governors of the Federal Reserve System has adopted risk control measures designed for both Fedwire and CHIPS (Board of Governors 1985; 1987). But despite the measures in place, further changes have been suggested. On Fedwire, for example, pricing

The author benefited from a discussion with Robert Jordan and from comments by Hal Scott and Thomas Baxter on an earlier version of this chapter. The views expressed here are solely those of the author and do not necessarily reflect the views of the Federal Reserve Bank of Richmond or the Board of Governors of the Federal Reserve System.

145

daylight overdrafts has been proposed in order to encourage network participants to reduce them.

On private net settlement networks like CHIPS, however, pricing net debits would be more complex. As a result, risk allocation rules, known as finality-of-payment rules, have been proposed for CHIPS. Finality rules specify when payment between particular parties to a transaction is irrevocable. The purpose is to assign risks to the parties in such a way as to give them incentives to reduce the risks they face. In the language of the economist, the rules seek to internalize the costs of a settlement failure in order to lead market participants to control them. Such rules could either be adopted by private networks on their own, imposed as regulations, or enacted into law. Whatever form risk control measures take, they would help fill the vacuum left by the ambiguous legal framework within which wholesale wire transfer operates.

Finality rules are of particular interest now because of the current effort by the National Conference of Commissioners on Uniform State Laws to draft provisions of the Uniform Commercial Code (UCC) to explicitly codify a law of electronic funds transfer. The outcome of this effort will determine the future statutory environment within which rights, obligations, and risk assignments of network participants are established and clarified. In addition, codifying a wire transfer law will encourage private-sector and regulatory efforts to seek further risk control measures. The more detailed the wire transfer provisions of the UCC, the less scope there is for detailed regulation.

This chapter has two objectives. The first is to evaluate various finality rules that could be adopted, either by law or regulation, to allocate risks of a settlement failure. The second is to evaluate the desirability of using the law versus using regulation to adopt a particular finality rule.

As will be seen, it is possible to write finality rules that assign risks to the parties in the best position to control them. But the effectiveness of such rules depends crucially on two assumptions. First, network participants must have accurate information regarding the risks they face. Second, the parties must actually be required to bear their assigned costs if a settlement failure occurs. If either assumption is violated, the rule will not work as intended and will have little effect on risks. Put more simply, the rule will have no teeth.

Given the problems with finality rules, writing a stringent rule into the law does not appear promising. Even if a finality rule is not undermined by informational or policy problems, the complexity of some rules makes them unlikely candidates for inclusion in the law. It appears, then, that detailed finality rules might better be left to the networks and their regulators, leaving to the law such tasks as specifying when obligations are discharged and clarifying rights and relationships between parties to a transfer.

Background

At present, paper check transactions are governed by Articles 3 and 4 of the Uniform Commercial Code, along with Federal Reseve Regulations J and CC. The consequence of such coverage is that even outside the Federal Reserve check-processing system, check payments take place in a well-defined legal framework. If disputes arise between parties to a transaction, there is a substantial body of law to guide resolution of the dispute. Further, Section 4–103 of the UCC allows "variation by agreement," that is, divergence from Code provisions (subject to some limitations) by private contract, Federal Reserve regulations and operating circulars, or clearinghouse rules. For example, some provisions of Regulation J might conflict with the UCC, but Section 4–103 allows such flexibility while retaining the UCC as a backstop legal framework.

In contrast, electronic funds transfer is covered by a "patchwork of laws and regulations" (Penney and Baker 1980, ch. 10). Consumer (retail) funds transfer is governed by the Electronic Funds Transfer Act of 1978 (and Federal Reserve Regulation E), the Truth-in-Lending Act, Comptroller of the Currency Consumer Protection Guidelines, some state electronic funds transfer laws, and others. Wholesale wire transfer has far less coverage. Regulation J governs parts of the typical Fedwire transaction, while CHIPS is covered by network rules and regulations subject to conditions required for access to Federal Reserve Bank net settlement. There is a smattering of case law regarding wholesale wire transfer, but it hardly represents a coherent framework (see Scott 1983a, 1676–1678).

What does not currently exist is a comprehensive, explicitly codified legal framework for wholesale wire transfer. While some have argued that provisions of the UCC written for paper checks have analogous applications to wire transfer (see, for example, Clark 1969), one court said that "maybe the language of Article 4 [of the UCC] could be stretched to include electronic funds transfers, . . . but they were not in the contemplation of the draftsman."[2] Thus, it is unlikely that current law provides much guidance for wholesale wire transfer.

Hal Scott has pointed out several deficiencies of the current reliance on private contract (in the form of network rules) rather than statute (Scott 1983a, 1674–1676). First, network rules do not cover the relationship between banks and their customers. While such relationships could be covered by private contracts, there is no evidence that such contracts are a common practice. Second, network rules specify relationships among bank participants but not between, say, receiving banks and sending customers in the event of a failure. Finally, it is not clear whether courts will enforce private contracts that do not operate within a well-defined statutory framework.

Recognizing the desirability of a codified body of electronic funds transfer law, the Permanent Editorial Board for the UCC initiated efforts in 1974 to revise Articles 3 and 4 to cover wire transfer along with other payment methods. This led to the Uniform New Payments Code, which was based on principles equally applicable to checks and wire transfers. The draft New Payments Code was submitted to the National Conference of Commissioners for Uniform State Laws in 1983 and was also discussed at a conference later that year. The response was not favorable. In 1985, it was decided to drop the New Payments Code. Instead, Articles 3 and 4 would be revised but still cover only checks. More significantly, a new article (4A) would be added to cover wholesale wire transfer (Miller 1986). The effort is now under way, and a final version of the new article should be ready for consideration by the states by the end of 1989.

William Warren and Robert Jordan, the Reporters preparing the draft articles, originally suggested that Article 4A be based on an underlying theory of wire transfer (Warren and Jordan 1986, 19–33). Specifically, they discussed two separate concepts of when payment by wire transfer should be considered final and irreversible by all parties. The first provides for receiver finality, that is, for payment to be final when the receiving bank accepts it. The second provides a system closer to payment by check, that is, payment is final when the receiving bank receives "good funds" from the sender. The Reporters appeared to favor receiver finality, but the suggestion drew criticism from other participants in the revision effort (Lee 1986).

In response to the criticism, the preliminary draft submitted by the Reporters abandoned any attempt to reflect an underlying theory of wire transfers in favor of a more pragmatic tack (Jordan and Warren 1986). Essentially, the preliminary version provided one set of rules if everything functioned normally and another set effective only in the event of the failure of a bank to settle. If a failure occurred, the "skip rule" might take effect. The rule would initiate a "bypass" of the failing bank in order to allow settlement to proceed. But the skip rule did not hold up under further analysis. The Reporters then returned to a receiver finality rule, but with the twist that receiving banks could enter into agreements with their receiving customers to make payments conditional until final settlement occurs. Subsequent versions scaled back the right to contract for provisional payment except in the event of a general failure of a net settlement network loss sharing agreement.[3]

The reason given for abandoning the earlier "unified conceptual approach" based on an "underlying concept of the nature of a wire transfer" was that it "does not produce good results" (Lee 1988; National Conference of Commissioners on Uniform State Laws 1988). Specifically, the Reporters appeared to wish to avoid imposing liability for huge wire transfers when the benefits to the banks transmitting such amounts would actually be rather small. In other words, banks may reconsider handling wholesale wire transfers at all if the expected liability is out of proportion to the revenue from handling the transfers.

Still, it seems premature to reject any attempt to base laws on an underlying concept of the nature of a wire transfer. Such a concept would provide a coherent way of thinking that would be largely absent from a "pragmatic" approach. More important, a coherent framework would help to avoid contradictions in the development of legal rules. With such advantages in mind, the remainder of this chapter will develop a hypo- thetical model of a wire transfer and then use the framework to explore various finality rules.

Analytical Framework

Consider a hypothetical wire transfer network consisting of four parties to each transaction. The network is diagrammed in figure 4–1. The first party is the customer who originates the transfer, the *sender*. The second is the depository institution used by the sender to transmit the payment messge, the *sending bank*. The third is the bank receiving the transaction, the *receiving bank*, which is acting for the benefit of a customer. Finally, the customer who is the beneficiary of the transfer is the *receiver*. The transaction underlying each transfer is between the sender and receiver. It should be noted that the sender and sending bank can be the same entity, as can the receiving bank and the receiver. It is also possible that the sending and receiving banks could be the same entity, but this would reduce a funds transfer to a set of accounting entries within the institution.

As shown in the diagram, the network is formally composed of its member banks. The banks transmit funds for the benefit of third parties, that is, senders and receivers. Their benefit from doing so is the fees received net of operating costs, along with the benefits associated with having custody of their customers' deposits.

In the network, parties to a transaction can extend credit to those

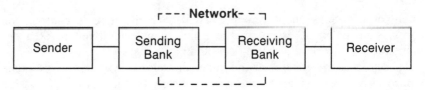

Figure 4–1.   Hypothetical wire transfer Network.

parties with whom they work directly. For example, sending banks can extend credit to senders, receiving banks to sending banks, and receiving banks to receivers. Stated another way, payments in the network are risky, that is, there is some probability that payments will not be covered. This probability leads to credit risk, the risk that loans will not be repaid.

Finally, payment between banks occurs periodically by means of net settlement. Under net settlement, each bank's obligations to and from the other banks are added up so only a net debit or credit amount is exchanged at the end of each settlement period.[4] Net settlement means in effect that receiving banks extend credit to sending banks until settlement occurs.

There are several relationships in the hypothetical wire transfer network in which credit risks arise. The most obvious is in the underlying transaction between the sender and receiver, since it is posible that the receiver will not receive the payment on the transaction. Such credit risk is not unique to payment networks but is part of every transaction involving credit. Still, it is significant to payment network risk allocations because of the crucial question of when the underlying obligation is discharged.

The other risky relationships are due to the presence of risky parties in the chain of transactors that comprises the network. The first such relationship is between the sender and sending bank. If the sender initiates a transfer with the sending bank but does not have sufficient account funds to cover the transfer, the sending bank incurs credit risk if it transmits the payment message before the sender supplies the covering funds. Such risks are normally handled internally by banks as customer account overdraft credit decisions.

The second risky relationship is between the sending bank and the receiving bank. The risk here is that the sending bank will fail to provide funds to the receiving bank at settlement. If the receiving bank has given irrevocable credit to the receiver, then the receiving bank could bear the loss.

Finally, the relationship between the receiving bank and the receiver is risky for both parties. If the receiving bank allowed the receiver to draw on provisionally transferred funds before settlement, the result would depend on whether the receiving bank could successfully revoke the funds to cover its own loss. Even if the receiving bank and the receiver had contracted for provisionality, it is not a foregone conclusion that the bank could recover funds if they had already been withdrawn and spent by the receiver. Thus, the receiver runs the risk of revocation, while the receiving bank runs the risk that it will not be able to retrieve funds from the receiver.

Credit risk, interdependence between banks, and the necessity that settlement take place at a given time give rise to another form of risk, namely, systemic risk. This refers to the expectation that a bank or banks will fail to settle because of another bank's failure to settle.[5] Credit risk is essential to systemic risk because it determines the vulnerability of a bank to losses. Interdependence is important because a bank might depend on receipt of a large credit from one bank in order to meet its obligation to another bank. Finally, the constraint that settlement take place at a given time is important because if one bank fails to settle its net debit, other banks might face liquidity problems. That is, it might be exceedingly costly for them to find sufficient funds to meet their obligations in the time remaining before settlement.

As a real-world counterpart to the hypothetical model, on CHIPS systemic risk would be transmitted by means of a settlement "unwind."[6] If a bank fails to settle, CHIPS Rule 13 provides that payment messages to and from the failed bank be deleted. If all goes well, a new settlement can go through minus the failed bank. But if the other banks are highly exposed to the failed bank as net creditors, they themselves may encounter severe liquidity problems. As a last resort, the rules apparently allow a complete unwind (or "return to storage") of the day's transactions. The consequences of such a drastic revision, in which some banks might walk away from settlement, are unknown.

Measuring credit risk on a wire transfer network poses few conceptual problems. For each bank in a net credit position against another bank, its credit risk is approximated by its expected failure cost, that is, its net credit position with the other bank multiplied by the probability the other bank will fail to settle. To the extent that the costs of the settlement failure are borne by the receiving bank, credit risks represent a private cost to receiving banks, which will take account of such costs in determining their exposure to sending banks.

Systemic risk is conceptually more difficult to measure. While a receiving bank may be expected to take account of risks to itself as a net creditor, it has no incentive to take account of the risk it poses to other banks with which it has a net debit relationship. Thus, the costs of a settlement failure go beyond the exposure of creditor banks to the failing bank. Rather, costs of a failure are equal to receiving banks' exposure plus other banks' exposure to the receiving banks. In other words, if as the result of one bank's failure to settle the receiving bank is also unable to settle, then the receiving bank's creditors will also bear costs. These latter costs, called externalities by economists, will not influence the receiving bank's exposure decisions but are borne nonetheless. It is these externalities that risk control policies are designed to reduce.

Risk control may be accomplished by regulation, statute, or agreement, and may seek to reduce risks by confining them or by creating incentives to reduce them. An example of a regulation that seeks to confine risks is net debit caps. By limiting how much a bank may be in a net debit position with other banks, such a regulation attempts to circumscribe the amount by which the rest of the system is exposed to a bank. The main drawback to such regulation is that, while it may successfully limit risk, it does not reduce the incentives for banks to incur risks. As a result, banks have incentives to seek ways to evade caps through such means as offshore clearings if doing so is less costly than operating within the caps.

Measures that attempt to create incentives to reduce risks differ depending on the network. On Fedwire, pricing daylight overdrafts would create incentives to run lower overdraft levels while leaving banks the option of incurring them (Humphrey et al. 1987). On private net settlement networks, however, it is not clear how explicit pricing would be instituted. While daylight overdrafts, strictly speaking, are possible only on a gross settlement network like Fedwire, net debit positions are the analogous source of risk on a net settlement network. The analogy breaks down at this point because while it is possible to require that Fedwire transfers be fully funded so no overdrafts occur, a net settlement system could not function without at least one party running a net debit position. Thus, levying a fee on net debit positions would penalize behavior that cannot be fully avoided due to the nature of such a network. It is feasible, however, to impose a fee on CHIPS net debits that exceed reserve balances or other clearing balances net of Fedwire daylight overdrafts. The problem is that monitoring and pricing two networks is likely to be costly.

Finality of Payment

As an alternative to explicit pricing of risk on net settlement networks, rules can be devised that allocate risks among parties to a transfer by specifying when a payment is considered irrevocable by each party. These rules, known as finality-of-payment rules, seek to reduce risks by influencing the incentives of the parties on which risks are placed. In economic terms, they are designed to internalize the costs of settlement failure by assigning the costs to specific parties. In effect, because they specify with certainty where the costs of a settlement failure will fall, finality rules may be considered a form of implicit pricing of net settlement risk. If banks judge the price to be too high, they can reduce their risk exposure by means of tighter net credit limits or else bilateral arrangements to net payments outside the networks so actual transfers over the network are reduced (see Mengle, Humphrey, and Summers 1987, 8–9).

It should be noted here that finality rules do not by themselves represent responses to a market failure, that is, a failure of an unregulated market to efficiently allocate resources among transactors. Rather, such rules specify rights and obligations of the parties to a transaction and thereby shape the environment within which the market functions. In other words, finality rules do not attempt to substitute for the market but rather to establish risk allocations within the market and enable transactors to determine what the costs of their decisions are likely to be. While it is true that finality rules could be administratively imposed as regulations, they do not limit transactors' choices. They simply specify who bears the risk of a choice and allow action on the basis of that knowledge. In contrast, net debit caps are designed explicity to limit transactors' options.

Given that finality-of-payment rules could reduce risks, why have they not been voluntarily adopted? One reason may be that such rules would only apply to a highly unlikely situation, namely, settlement failure. Because a failure is unlikely and has not in fact happened, network participants may feel little urgency in preparing for such an emergency. Rather, they may prefer to handle such contingencies when and where they occur (Scott 1983a, 1675–1676).

There is a another factor that could discourage adoption of finality rules. Suppose network participants expect that in the event of a settlement failure they will be relieved of risks. For example, payments could be guaranteed, either explicitly or implicitly, by an insurer, central bank, or other party outside the network. If network participants expect to be so relieved, they will have little reason as individual institutions to limit their own risk exposures or as a group to adopt rules that limit or assign risks.[7] In contrast, stock and commodity exchanges lack both federal insurance and discount window liquidity backup, so they have developed their own risk control procedures along with self-policing and examination policies. Specifically, exchanges have instituted risk-sharing arrangements, margin requirements, and position limits in order to limit risk exposures.

Which Finality Rule?

In traditional economic analysis of regulation, the choice often presented is between an unregulated market outcome and a regulated outcome. A more detailed analysis might present several alternative regulatory scenarios. Here, there is no such neat dichotomy. Instead, there is the regulatory solution, which most likely would take the form of administratively imposed limits on net debit positions of network participants; and there is a set of market solutions under various finality-of-payment rules. Even if no rule were imposed by regulators or law or adopted by collective decision, there would still be an implicit finality rule. In fact, one would expect the implicit rule to eventually find its way into case law and become an explicit rule.

The objective of the analysis of finality rules will be to determine which alternative creates the strongest incentives to minimize the costs due to settlement failure. No alternative will be ideal, and each will create some incentives that will work at cross-purposes with one another. Still, it is possible to express judgments about the relative strengths of the incentives to monitor banks, to shift costs to others, and to otherwise evade the requirements of the finality rule.

Criteria

Various criteria for evaluating laws and regulations have been proposed in the law and economics literature. Guido Calabresi (1970) has outlined two approaches. The first is loss spreading, which seeks to minimize costs to each party by spreading losses as widely as possible. The second is to assign losses to the "cheapest-cost avoider" of whatever causes the losses and thereby minimize the chance of the loss occurring. For example, a driver running into a car in front of him is normally presumed to be at fault because he is generally in the position to avoid the accident at lower cost than is the driver in front. Robert D. Cooter and Edward L. Rubin (1987, 73) call this latter criterion the "loss reduction principle," which assigns liability to whoever can reduce losses at lowest cost. They express the distinction nicely: "Loss spreading presumes that a loss has already occurred and assigns liability to the party that can more effectively spread it, but the loss reduction principle assigns liability for the more complex purpose of affecting human behavior." Thus, finality rules can be evaluated both on how effectively they spread losses and how effectively they could modify behavior.

While loss spreading is fairly straightforward, the cheapest-cost avoider principle requires determining which party fits the description. This involves at least four considerations (Calabresi 1970, 140–152). First, and most obvious, the cheapest-cost avoider must actually be able to take some action that will minimize losses. If the party selected cannot control its exposure, then the liability assignment amounts to no more than a search for "deep pockets." Second, the costs of avoidance must be considered in relation to the value of the activity in which the potential victim is involved. That is, if the cheapest-cost avoider will only exercise care by either ceasing or drastically reducing a valued activity, then it may be preferable either to spread the losses or to find a somewhat more expensive avoider. In Calabresi's words (p. 141), it might be advisable.

...to exclude from consideration as potential loss bearers all those activities that could reduce costs only by causing losses which are clearly much greater, in terms of meeting individuals' desires as expressed in the market, than would result if one achieved the equivalent or greater reduction in accident costs by burdening other activities.

Third, assigning liability to the cheapest-cost avoider must bring about internalization of losses. In other words, the costs must actually be borne by the cheapest-cost avoider in order to induce it to avoid the costs. This means that the party selected should not be able to cheaply avoid the losses by shifting them to another party. Finally, even if it is not clear who the cheapest-cost avoider is, one can assign losses to the party best able to determine the cheapest-cost avoider and to contract with it.

Assigning losses to the cheapest-cost avoider should lead to minimum costs, as shown in the simple supply and demand diagram in figure 4–2.[8] The demand curve (D) represents the benefits of an additional dollar of intraday credit risk exposure to a particular party to a transaction. As is generally the case in economic analysis, the curve is assumed to slope downward because each additional dollar of credit risk exposure is likely to be assigned to a less valuable use than was the previous dollar. The supply curve (S) represents the expected cost of settlement failure and slopes upward because failure costs are assumed to increase with exposure. The potential victim compares the expected costs of settlement failure with the benefits of the credit risk in determining its exposure to a particular party.

Assume a receiving bank's risk exposure in Figure 4–2 is Q_1. At that level, the benefit of the last dollar of risk exposure would be less than the cost. As a result, the bank would have a reason to cut back its exposure. As long as the benefit given up by reducing exposure is less than the avoided failure cost, there is incentive to reduce exposure. Below some level of

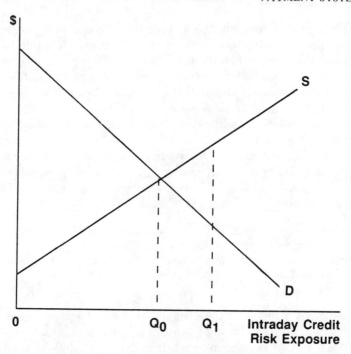

Figure 4–2.   Determination of risk exposure by the cheapest-cost avoider.

exposure (Q_0), however, expected failure costs will fall below what is given up in benefits, and it no longer pays to reduce exposure. At Q_0, then, total costs are minimized.

Assumptions

The analysis of finality rules that follows makes four assumptions within the context of the hypothetical payment network described in the previous Section. First, network participants are assumed to have access at low cost to accurate information regarding the risks of other participants in the network. Second, no regulatory body, central bank, or other outside party will intervene to aid any network participants after settlement failure occurs. Third, when failure occurs only the net obligations to and from the failed bank are relevant. This ignores the possibility that, in bankruptcy, banks might be held to their gross obligations to the failed bank. Finally, settlement failure occurs exogenously. This means there is no action any participant can take to influence the probability of a settlement failure.

The last assumption points out the difference between the economic analysis of finality rules and that of other areas of law. First, while the preceding discussion strongly suggests analogies between tort law and payment law, the assumption here of exogenous settlement failure rules out the possibility of designing a rule that will directly attempt to make failure less likely. In other words, in payment law there is no counterpart to assigning tort liability to the injurer in order to influence behavior. The injurer could, however, be required to post a bond, post collateral, or otherwise guarantee in advance against losses to others. By imposing liability on a firm's creditors or guarantors, there may be incentives for these latter parties to attempt to reduce the probability of failure. The point is that no rule directly influences the failing bank but rather attempts to induce other parties to act to protect themselves.

Second, the externality element in systemic risk implies similarity to environmental law. Again, because the ability to influence the probability of failure is ruled out by assumption, most of the rules to be evaluated are designed to influence the victims' or guarantors' behavior or costs. That is, externalities cannot be internalized by the injurer but only by the victims or guarantors in the form of protective behavior.

The remainder of the section considers various finality rules in the light of the concepts of risk spreading and risk avoidance.

Check Finality[9]

Consider a rule that states that the sender's obligation to the receiver is finally paid when the receiver has access to "good funds." Another way of saying this is that the sender's obligation on the underlying transaction is not discharged until the payment between the banks in the networks is finally settled, for example, by credit to the receiving bank's reserve account at a Federal Reserve Bank.

The rule is called check finality here because it resembles the current rule for when a payment by check becomes final. For example, Section 4–213(1) of the UCC provides that payment by the payor bank is final if the payor bank has (1) paid the check in cash, (2) finally settled without reserving the right to revoke, (3) posted the item to the payor's account, or most commonly (4) failed to revoke the provisional settlement before the deadline for such revocation. Further, Section 4–213(4) gives the payee the right to draw on collected funds after the payee's bank has received final settlement and has had "reasonable" time to verify that settlement was indeed final. This affords the payee's bank a means of protecting itself by debiting the payee's account if the check bounces. Finally, Section 3–802 discharges the payor of the underlying obligation when the check is paid by the payor's bank.

The analogous rule for a wholesale credit transfer is to make the receiving bank liable to the receiver for the amount of the transfer once the receiving bank has received final settlement from the sending bank in accordance with network rules. The underlying obligation between sender and receiver would also be discharged once the receiving bank obtains final settlement.

So who bears the cost if a sending bank fails? The receiving bank is not obligated to release funds to the receiver before final settlement. Unless the receiving bank had already granted irrevocable credit prior to settlement, it will have the right to debit the amount of the transfer to the receiver's account. Thus, the underlying obligation remains unsatisfied, so the receiver has a claim against the sender. But the sender may have already provided funds to the sending bank, which has since failed. In this case, the sender appears to end up bearing the risk of having chosen the "wrong" sending bank.

If it is the sender that bears the risk, one must ask whether the sender meets the criteria for cheapest-cost avoider or most effective risk spreader. In wholesale wire transfer, the sender is most likely a corporation, possibly a bank. Given the size of the transfers, it is plausible that senders are of sufficient sophistication to monitor the soundness of the banks with which they do business. Failure of a sending bank is something against which a prudent sender can protect itself.

The risk assignment breaks down, however, if the sending bank is not a network participant but enters the network through a correspondent that is. It is possible that the correspondent sending bank might fail, and even the most sophisticated sender would not choose and probably would not even know which banks stand between its bank and the sending bank on the network. To find out such information would in fact be costly for the sender. Thus, it is not likely that the sender meets the first criterion for cheapest cost avoider, that is, it is not necessarily in a position to take some action to minimize losses.

The sender also may not meet the criteria for cheapest-cost avoider because it may be able to evade the costs of a settlement failure and pass them on to other parties. Specifically, even if the receiver has a claim against the sender on the underlying transaction, it is possible that the claim will not be recovered without protracted and costly litigation. Further, if the receiving bank had provisionally released funds to the receiver before settlement, the receiving bank may not successfully recover the funds from the receiver. Thus, while the incidence of losses in check finality may nominally be on the sender, actual incidence is ambiguous. And since it is not clear who will bear the cost, it is not clear that the check finality rule will be effective at modifying behavior to reduce losses.

While check finality might not be an effective rule from the standpoint of the cheapest-cost avoider principle, the very ambiguity of the risk allocation might make it effective as a means of risk spreading. Even if the rule did not reduce risk avoidance in any one party, it might reduce risks to individual banks by distributing the risks among the parties to a transaction. But since there is no rule for spreading the risk, the risk might be spread among the parties only on the basis of ability to evade the costs. This means that the risk would be spread in an unpredictable manner and possibly would be concentrated on one party. So it is by no means that the check finality rule would be an effective risk spreading rule.

Settlement Finality I (Ex Ante)

Settlement finality rules make settlement entries between banks irreversible. If a sending bank fails to settle, some bank or group of banks is required to provide funds to allow settlement to go through. Whether the final incidence of the costs remains with the banks depends on the rule chosen.

Ex ante settlement finality would in essence have the failing bank guarantee settlement in advance by posting sufficient collateral to cover its net debit with the network. This is equivalent to a performance bond posted by the bank. As long as no failure occurs, the bank earns a return on the collateral. If the bank fails, then it forfeits the collateral.[10]

By its nature, *ex ante* settlement finality makes no attempt to assign risks to the cheapest-cost avoider. Rather, it simply seeks to ensure that settlement will go through in the event of failure so that credit risks are covered and systemic risk is eliminated. The rule is actually a risk-spreading rule, since the credit risks are transferred outside the network to the deposit insurance funds and unsecured creditors. The more collateral used to cover the net debit, the less available to parties with a claim to the assets of the failed bank.

Credit risks in the system would probably not be affected by the *ex ante* rule because no costs would be borne by banks in the network other than the failing bank. That is, collateralization of sending bank net debits would not affect the incentives of other banks to control their exposure to the failing bank [11] But while the sum of risks in the system might remain the same, the element of interdependence would be broken, so systemic risk is not a consideration. Thus, *ex ante* settlement finality would be effective for eliminating the risk of a chain of settlement failures but would not directly reduce expected losses from a settlement failure. It would merely shift them.

Settlement Finality II (Ex Post)

An *ex post* finality rule allocates the losses from a failure to a bank or banks after a failure occurs. This first version of an *ex post* settlement finality rule would divide up the costs among all the banks in the network (except the failed bank) either equally, by size, according to network usage, or by some other criterion unrelated to exposure. Because all are required to come up with funds to complete settlement, the risk of failure is initially assigned to network banks. Since nothing in such a rule prevents banks that are creditors of the failed bank from attempting to charge back funds provisionally released to receivers, however, some of the risk could ultimately be borne by receivers. Whether senders would bear risks would depend on when the law specifies that the sender's obligation is discharged.

Because the rule attempts to reduce the ability to shift costs by means of a settlement unwind, it creates incentives for banks to monitor sending banks and therefore to reduce credit risks. If the option of an unwind can be eliminated, for example by requiring each bank to post collateral sufficient to cover its largest possible loss under the rule, incentives to monitor will be stronger. Further, the rule should lead to a reduction but not elimination of systemic risk. While the incentives to monitor should make a settlement failure less likely to disrupt the network, there is still some chance that the remaining risk exposure could threaten some secondary failures.

The major disadvantage of the rule is that it does not allocate risk according to exposure and therefore would have limited effects on behavior of receiving banks. Banks would have some incentives to monitor sending banks because they will wish to avoid the costs of failure, but the incentives are weaker than they would be if costs were related to exposure. An externality effect is present here because some banks may take on greater exposure in the knowledge that the costs of failure would be spread among all the banks in the network. Thus, credit and systemic risk are not reduced as much as would be the case under a rule more sensitive to actual exposure.

While the rule does not create strong incentives to monitor risks, it does tend to spread risks among the network participants. More important, as long as the risk-spreading criterion were known in advance, risks would be spread in a predictable and roughly equitable manner. Thus, if one were to conclude that risk spreading is the preferred criterion for a rule, this type of settlement finality rule would be superior to check finality.

Settlement Finality III (Ex Post)

This rule allocates costs of failure among receiving (creditor) banks on the basis of their exposure to the failing bank. For example, costs could be divided among banks on the basis of their net credit positions against the failed bank at the time of failure. Alternatively, losses could be allocated on the basis of banks' net credit *limits* with the failed bank at the time of failure. While the former is based on actual exposure and the latter on willingness to take on exposure, both would have similar incentives for receiving banks to monitor the creditworthiness of the banks from which they accept transfers.

Of all the parties to a wire transfer, the receiving bank is in the position to monitor the soundness of other banks at the lowest cost. Also, the receiving bank is in a position to refuse to accept a wire transfer if it suspects the sending bank will fail to settle. Finally, because the rule allows funds to be revoked from receivers, the rule allows risks to be shifted to receivers and ultimately, perhaps, to senders. In that the allocation of risks among receiving banks and their receiving customers is a matter that could be determined by private contract, the last consideration is consistent with the characterization of the cheapest-cost avoider as the party best able to contract with others to bear the risk. To the extent that receiving banks bear costs under an *ex post* finality rule, then, the rule does seek out the cheapest-cost avoider.

This rule has most of the advantages but not the disadvantages of the previous *ex post* settlement rule. That is, it restricts the option of a settlement unwind and motivates receiving banks to monitor banks for which they are net creditors. But because it allocates costs on the basis of exposure, it creates stronger monitoring incentives and therefore makes the possibility of a disruptive settlement failure less likely. If risk spreading is preferred as a criterion to risk reduction, however, using exposure to assign risks will not spread risk as widely as with the previous settlement finality rule.

Receiver Finality

This rule makes settlement irreversible and also requires that receivers be granted irrevocable credit when a payment message is accepted. In other words, there is no recourse to the receiver. Thus, risks are concentrated on the receiving bank.

A way in which a receiver finality rule could be implemented is to provide that when a receiving bank accepts a transfer it becomes liable to the receiver for the amount of the transfer. Further, when the receiving bank accepts the transfer, the sender's obligation to the receiver on the underlying transaction is discharged.[12] The principle is that the receiving bank's acceptance of the transfer is the determining event in establishing liability, and it is the receiving bank that is in the best position to determine the soundness of the sending bank.

As the cheapest-cost avoider with no ability to shift costs, the receiving bank would have far stronger incentives to monitor the soundness of other banks than would be the case in any of the other alternatives. The only obvious way costs could be shifted to others would be in transaction fees. Thus, the internalization of losses would be most complete under receiver finality. From the standpoint of behavior modification, then, receiver finality represents the most promising rule, since "receiving banks may be forced to examine the creditworthiness of each and every incoming payment" (Lee 1986, 2). In addition, it would provide the most certainty of how risks would be allocated if a settlement failure were to occur. Finally, because it does give banks incentives to monitor and thereby reduce credit risk, receiver finality should reduce systemic risk.

The major disadvantage of receiver finality derives from the substantial potential liability it imposes on receiving banks (Lee 1986, 7). It is possible that banks might judge their expected costs from receiver finality to be greater than their expected benefits from handling net settlement network transactions. If this were the case, banks might cease to participate in the network or else do so only at fees higher than the value of the service to many of their customers. While this would mean lower risks, it would also mean less of a valued service. Thus, while the receiving bank may at first appear to be the cheapest-cost avoider, a full consideration of the costs of receiver finality might tell otherwise.

Another objection to receiver finality is that it concentrates risk on certain individual banks and therefore might increase rather than decrease systemic risk (Association of Reserve City Bankers 1985, 18–19). That is, placing all the risks on the receiving bank makes it more likely that the receiving bank could fail if a sending bank defaulted.

Defenders of receiver finality might answer in two ways. First, the critics of receiver finality assume no behavior change among network participants. In other words, they assume that under receiver finality receiving banks will be fully responsible for the same level of failure costs as would have prevailed in the absence of receiver finality. But risk is in part a function of monitoring by receiving banks. If receiver finality makes banks pay more attention to banks from which they accept transfers, risk will fall and expected costs will be lower, since the receiving bank will be in a position to avoid the losses. While transaction volume might be somewhat lower, it should not fall to zero, since banks will balance monitoring costs against avoided failure costs at the margin.

A second answer to the criticism involves a thornier issue. The contention that banks will abandon net settlement networks in response to receiver finality and thereby deprive the public of a valued service assumes there are no substitutes available. This is not the case, since Fedwire would still be available. But, as has been pointed out by the Department of Justice, Fedwire provides receiver finality without extra charge while guaranteeing against settlement failure.[13] Thus, if receiver finality were to be considered for imposition by regulation, competitive equity might demand that pricing of Fedwire daylight overdrafts be considered at the same time. This also called into question the appropriateness of codifying receiver finality into law, since it might put the UCC into the position of favoring one network over the other.[14]

Summary

A comparison of the effects of finality rules is shown in table 4-1 under the assumptions outlined above. Each finality rule is ranked according to its ability to influence behavior, to spread risks, to increase risks to individual depository institutions, and its effect on systemic risk. As can be seen, the choice is ambiguous and would require a weighting of each characteristic. If one placed great weight on risk spreading, for example, then check finality or settlement finality II might be preferred, while a high weight on behavior modification would shift the balance toward receiver finality.

Qualifications to Finality Rules

Thus far the analysis of finality rules has assumed that banks have accurate information regarding the risks of other banks on their network and that

Table 4–1. Summary of the effects of finality rules

	Check Finality	Settlement Finality			
		I Ex Ante Sender Collateralization	*II* Ex Post Risks on Network	*III* Ex Post Risks on Creditors	Receiver Finality
Encourages risk reduction	Low	Least	Moderate	High	Most
Spread risk	Unclear, but possibly high	To deposit insurance funds and unsecured creditors	High	Moderate	Least
Risk to individual banks (potential liability)	Unclear, but possibly low	Least	Moderate	High	Most
Systemic risk	Most	None	Moderate	Low	Least

there is no intervention by parties outside the network. This section analyzes the effects of dropping each of these two assumptions.

Changing Informational Assumptions

As of this writing, a settlement failure on a large-dollar wire transfer network has never occurred. It is safe to say that the probability of one occurring, while finite, is exceedingly low. Yet if a settlement failure were to take place, the costs could be enormous. Analysis of such a low-probability, high-cost event suggests analogies with the economies of insurance against natural disasters.

For insurance against most losses, individuals purchase insurance on the basis of their estimate of expected losses. The expected losses are in turn the product of the probability of a loss occurring and the loss itself. In such areas as mortality, automobile accidents, and most other losses, the probabilities can be determined from actuarial data and the losses judged from experience.

In contrast, there is far less experience with disasters such as earthquakes or toxic spills from which to compute probabilities or actual losses. The situation is even worse for settlement failure, since there is no experience on which to base probabilities. Even subjective probability assessments are likely to be arbitrary, although it is conceivable that various "expert" judgments of probabilities could be combined into a consensus value (Sampson and Smith 1982).

In the literature on low-probability, high-cost events, there is a general finding that people misperceive risks in such cases.[15] Specifically, because the probability is so low, people appear to treat it as insignificant. The result is little interest in either insurance protection or other measures to lessen risk.

One explanation for systematic misperception of risks may be found in work by cognitive psychologists. Tversky and Kahneman (1974) have described various intuitive decision processes, known as heuristics, which people use in making actual decisions. While such devices are useful as means of economizing on information and processing costs, they can also lead to systematic biases. One heuristic, availability, has people judge probabilities of events according to the ease with which examples come to mind. This implies that rare events such as settlement failures are not easily imagined and as a result are not considered likely. While the event in question is already a low-probability event, availability tends to bias individuals' estimates still farther downward. Another heuristic, described by Slovic et al. (1977), has people ignore losses if the subjective probability estimate of their occurring is below a certain threshold. As with availability, the justification for this heuristic is economizing on information and processing costs, and the result, of course, is to further underestimate risks. Finally, Tversky and Kahneman (1986) point out that systematic errors can occur when decision makers face unique situations because there is no opportunity for feedback or learning.

If there is validity to the psychologists' contentions regarding low-probability high-cost risks, then there may be reason to question the efficacy of most of the finality rules described above. More important, the more a rule concentrates risk on the cheapest-cost avoider, the more critical accurate risk perceptions become. If risk perceptions are expected to be systematically biased downward, finality rules will not have the hoped-for behavior modification effects.

In order to determine the effect of alternative assumptions regarding risk perceptions, assume that network participants systemically underestimate the risks of settlement failure. The resulting unreliability of risk assessments would affect receiver finality and the two *ex post* settlement finality options but would have little effect on check finality or *ex ante* sender collateralization. Specifically, since receiving banks underestimate settlement failure probabilities, they do not engage in sufficient monitoring and do not reduce risks. Moreover, nothing increases the ability of these rules to spread risks. Thus, while risk is concentrated on either receiving banks or receiving banks and receivers, little happens to reduce risks. The result is that under risk misperception receiver finality could increase systemic risk.

Two alternatives are not greatly affected by risk misperception. For check finality, the uncertainty of the risk allocations and the rough potential for risk spreading remain the same as under the assumption of accurate risk perceptions. Similarly, *ex ante* sender collateralization would have the same effects under accurate or inaccurate perceptions, since it is simply a risk-spreading rule.

Thus, a tendency to underestimate risks of settlement failure would argue against any rule that attempts to create incentives for banks to reduce risks. Because both receiver finality and *ex post* settlement finality rules depend on accurate information, the preferred alternatives could be narrowed. If the uncertainty of check finality risk allocations lead to rejection of this alternative, then either *ex ante* sender collateralization, more stringent net debit caps, or any other alternative that does not require accurate risk assessments by network participants might be preferred to a finality rule that attempts to elicit monitoring from a cheapest-cost avoider.

There are at least four possible objections to considering the role of risk misperceptions. First, it may be objected that it attributes irrationality to people because they systematically fail to take account of information that it would be to their benefit to use. But in ignoring rare events, people may be acting rationally by economizing on information they do not expect to use. Second, one may point out that risk misperception is purely a short-run problem, since learning will take care of the misperception once a settlement failure occurs or almost occurs. This may well be true, but the question remains whether one wishes to wait for such a failure or, as a matter of policy, attempt to avoid such a disaster before it occurs.

A third objection is more difficult to answer. It is possible that risk misperceptions are a function of the low level of monitoring under current ambiguous risk assignments. That is, no party to a transaction now has incentives to incur the costs of developing reliable assessments of failure probabilities. Once receiver finality is instituted, however, the concentration of risks on receiving banks will give them incentives to form more accurate risk estimates and act accordingly. Unfortunately, this is an empirical matter, which could only be answered from observing behavior after adopting receiver finality. Perhaps monitoring would increase after risks were assigned to receiving banks, but it is also possible that misperceptions would continue as before. This is a chicken-egg question that cannot be answered a priori.

A final objection to taking its misperceptions into account is that they could just as easily lead to overestimates of risk as to underestimates. This possibility has been noted by Slovic, Fischhoff, and Lichtenstein (1982), who point to the effect of a movie like *The China Syndrome* on perceptions of nuclear power or of *Jaws* on swimming. Once a disaster becomes readily imaginable, the availability heuristic causes an upward bias to probability estimates. While it is unlikely that Hollywood will come out with a movie dramatizing the effects of a settlement failure, it is possible that concentrating on worst-case scenarios, as Humphrey (1986) did, without considering the plausibility of the assumptions on which such simulations are based could lead network participants to exaggerate the dangers involved. The answer to the objection depends on one's policy objectives. If the overriding aim is to avert the ill effects of a settlement failure, then there is little to fear from overestimates of risk. It must be conceded, however, that from an efficiency standpoint overestimates have little to recommend them over underestimates.

Settlement Failure Resolution Policy

Even if one accepts the informational assumptions necessary for the effectiveness of *ex post* finality rules, there is a more serious problem likely to undermine such rules under current policies. If, in the event of a settlement failure, regulators were expected to act to allow settlement by "bailing out" the failing bank, then neither receiver nor settlement finality would affect overall risk. That is, if banks do not expect they will actually bear the costs allocated to them by a finality rule, they have little reason to take the rule seriously.

If a bank does fail to settle, a bailout could occur in various ways.[16] For example, the bank itself might be rescued from failure. Alternatively, a line of credit could be made available. Finally, a discount window loan could be made to allow settlement to proceed. In all the examples, a party outside the network assumes the costs of the failure and relieves network participants of the risk.

Expectation of a bailout would lead to a moral hazard on the network, that is, a willingness for banks to take extra risks in the knowledge that they will be relieved of the costs if a failure does occur. The result would be a higher degree of credit risk. But at the same time, systemic risk would be eliminated, since the failure costs would be intercepted by the outside party rather than passed on to network participants. Thus, the risk allocation resulting from bailing out a settlement failure is similar to that of *ex ante* sender collateralization. In neither case do receiving banks bear risks. The disadvantage is that there are only weak incentives for receiving banks to monitor risks. Consequently the outside party bears more risk. The advantage, however, is that the potentially severe consequences of a settlement failure are averted, and that may be the paramount consideration in the minds of regulators.

The overriding concern for systemic stability may be seen in a recent Canadian bank failure. When Northland Bank failed in 1985, the Bank of Canada assumed the settlement risk by means of a $30 million "extraordinary entry" to Northland, which is the equivalent of a discount window advance. This relieved Northland's clearer of the risk, and was done under the belief that a clearing bank "should not be placed in a position of jeopardy on account of payments initiated by that other financial institution from an account at the Bank of Canada" (Bank of Canada 1985). In other words, there was a conscious decision that the integrity of the payment system demanded that the clearing bank should not have to bear the risk. While such a bailout may not be an attractive option, the alternative may be even less attractive.

It should be emphasized that discount window loans or bank lines of credit in connection with a settlement failure do not always lead to a moral hazard. Suppose that instead of making funds available to the bank failing to settle, credit were extended to receiving banks experiencing liquidity problems. That is, lending is only to solvent banks. Since the borrowing banks are obligated to repay the loan at interest and thereby to absorb the risk, the risk allocations of *ex post* finality rules would be imposed as intended. Such a loan would eliminate systemic risk by keeping liquidity problems from being transmitted from one bank to another but would not relieve banks of the credit risks.

Thus, if network participants know that all lending in response to a settlement failure would go to allay liquidity problems rather than to the failing bank, they will have reason to take account of the risk allocations in a finality rule. The problem is, given current government involvement in bank failures, is there a credible way to make a finality rule? The obstacle to be overcome is convincing network participants that they will be required to bear the risks specified in a rule if a settlement failure actually occurs. There are at least two reasons such credibility might be hard to achieve.

The first is the belief that certain banks are "too big to fail." Particularly after the Continential Illinois rescue in 1984, it is safe to say that there is some doubt as to the willingness of federal authorities to let a major bank fail. This belief has been more recently reinforced by the current experience with First RepublicBank Corp. and First City Bancorporation in Texas. While there is no analogous experience with a major participant in CHIPS, the reluctance of officials to sit back and watch while a failure causes a major disruption is understandable. While the Northland Bank example occurred in Canada, not in the United States, the incentives of regulators may be similar across countries.

A second problem is more general. Settlement failure policies are subject to the problem of making a credible commitment to enforce the cost allocations in *ex post* finality rules.[17] Given, say, a receiver finality rule, policymakers will declare that receiving banks will bear the costs if a settlement failure occurs. But if the failure actually does occur, there is the danger that receiving banks will be threatened by such severe liquidity problems that their own survival is threatened. At this point, the choice is between bailing out the bank failing to settle or letting the receiving banks fail along with the sending bank. Of the two unpleasant choices, the bailout is the less disruptive. But network participants know that authorities would choose a bailout if the only alternative were a chain of settlement failures, so they have little incentive to monitor risks before the failure occurs. Thus, they do little to control their risk exposures.

A simple example may help to illustrate the decision process involved.

Table 4–?   Bank Choices as Seen by Regulators

	Failure Occurs	No Failure Occurs
Banks limit risks	3	8
Banks do not limit risks	0	10

Table 4–3.   Bank and Regulator Choices as Seen by Banks

	Bailout	No Bailout
Banks limit risks	8	3
Banks do not limit risks	10	0

Assume a bank can earn profits equal to 10 from participating in a network. A settlement failure would wipe that entire amount out. If, however, the bank decides to monitor risks more carefully, the monitoring cost (including forgone income) is 2 but the losses from settlement failure are reduced from 10 to 5. Table 4–2 summarizes the possible outcomes, assuming no bailout. Regulatory authorities hope that their policies will induce banks to employ a maximin strategy. That is, they would like banks to choose to limit risks in order to avoid the worst possible outcome, which is complete ruin.

But banks see matters differently, as shown in table 4–3. Banks forgo income by limiting risks. And they know regulators have the option of a bailout, which would insulate banks from losses. So if a settlement failure occurs, regulators have to choose between a bailout and no bailout whether or not banks previously chose to limit risks. Thus, when failure occurs, regulators themselves end up pursuing the maximin course. In other words, they choose the bailout to avoid the worst possible consequence, namely, the settlement failure that wipes the banks out.

The full decision process is diagrammed in figure 4–3. Regulators (or the legislature) adopt an *ex post* finality rule with the aim of influencing the behavior of network participants. But the participants know that the actual sequence of decisions and events will proceed as in the diagram. First, the banks choose to limit or not to limit risks. Second, a settlement failure either occurs or does not. Third, if a failure occurs the authorities decide whether or not to bail out the bank. For banks, the best and worst outcomes are possible if they choose not to limit risks, but the best is far more probable. More important, they anticipate that regulators will choose a bailout in order to avoid the worst outcome. This is true even if re-

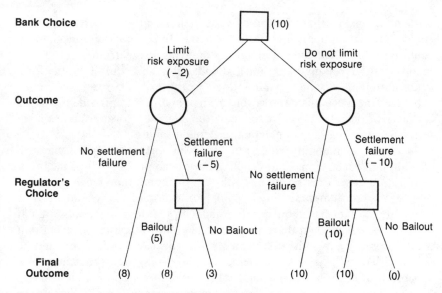

Figure 4–3.   The bank risk monitoring decision.

gulators attempt to deny they will go for a bailout if settlement does fail. The result is more risk in the system because of implicit insurance of settlement by regulatory authorities.

To summarize thus far, *ex post* finality rules, especially receiver finality, promise greater internalization of costs than do other rules. But in order to be effective, they must be credible. And there are strong reasons to believe the risk allocations in such rules might not be enforced in an actual settlement failure. How, then, could policymakers design a credible finality rule?

A credible finality rule requires some sort of precommitment on the part of authorities not to intervene to prevent a settlement failure. Otherwise, it seems likely that expectation of a bailout would influence banks' decisions. While authorities could issue verbal assurances that no bailout would be forthcoming in a settlement failure, these might not be believed. It is more likely that an automatic procedure that removes discretion from regulators would be credible as a risk allocation policy.

For example, suppose network participants were required to post collateral that would be used to cover receiving banks' losses in a settlement failure. For receiver finality or settlement finality based on exposure, collateral could be equal to a bank's highest net credit limit.[18] For

settlement finality that distributes losses among all members, collateral
could be based on the loss allocation scheme. In either case, a mechanism
could be established for automatically applying losses from a settlement
failure to the receiving banks' posted collateral. This could take the form
of an automatic discount window loan to the exposed receiving banks.
Whatever the mechanism, however, the main point is to provide increased
certainty of risk allocation by reducing the amount of discretion available
to regulators in handling an actual settlement failure.

In choosing a finality rule, then, it is important to ask if the risk
allocation in each rule is enforceable. If, for example, a credible means of
distributing losses over receiving banks can be found, then receiver finality
or an *ex post* settlement finality rule might be feasible. This would allow an
essentially market-based means of reducing risk. If loss allocations are not
credible, however, then there may be little point to such rules except that
they discourage unwinds of settlement. But this same objective could be
accomplished by an *ex ante* settlement finality rule, that is, sending bank
collateralization. While this would do little to reduce credit risk, it would at
least guarantee systemic stability and provide certainty to participants. In
fact, *ex ante* collateralization could be instituted along with receiver
finality, although in this case receiver finality would no longer serve a
risk reduction function. The job of reducing risk would for better or
worse be left to regulation by such means as net debit caps and more
intense supervision.

Conclusion: Legal or Regulatory Reform?

Given the above considerations regarding finality rules, the question
remains of whether finality rules should appropriately be codified in law or
left to agreements and regulation. There are at least three reasons for
writing a finality rule into law. First, writing a rule as law would inject a
higher element of certainty into commercial and financial relationships
than would result from relying on either administrative regulation or the
development of case law. Second, the rule contained in law would provide
a "backstop" rule for transactions not covered by private agreements
(Scott 1983, 1668). Finally, it could provide a model rule on which private
agreements could be based. In other words, if the UCC's draft committee
could agree on what constitutes an ideal rule, it would set the bounds
within which variations from the law would take place.

Unfortunately, as outlined previously, there are factors that may make
even the most stringent finality rule ineffective. First, misperception of

risks in the payment system may dull the effectiveness of receiver or *ex post* settlement finality rules as means of bringing about the internalization of risks. Second and more serious, expectation of a bailout of the settlement failure may make the risk allocation in a finality rule irrelevant, since participants do not expect it to be enforced. Thus, whatever a finality rule promises, it could be undermined by either informational or policy factors. But if this is true, such a rule should not be enshrined in law.

It is also possible that, despite the desideratum that provisions of the UCC be uniform across states, there could be differences in the provisions actually enacted (see Ballen 1986, 44–45). The result could be different finality rules for different states, which would seriously detract from the certainty and coherence one would hope to find in the legal environment.

Further, whatever rule is adopted, it could actually apply to few transactions. The UCC would not apply directly to Fedwire, since Regulation J effectively provides both guarantee of settlement and receiver finality. With regard to private networks, however, the result would depend on whether network participants could vary the finality rule by agreement. If, on the one hand, CHIPS participants were allowed to contract their way out of a finality rule by network agreement, then whatever rule is law could be left to apply only to a narrow class of transactions. If, on the other hand, the law does not allow participants to contract out of the rule, then it raises a new question: Should the right to vary the finality rule by agreement be restricted? Unless one were totally convinced of the absolute superiority of the rule in the law, the desirability of restricting the right to contract is questionable.

A final problem with writing a finality rule into law is complexity. The two polar cases of rules, check finality and receiver finality, would be fairly simple to codify. Check finality would make payment final and discharge the underlying obligation when the receiving bank has final settlement, although the resulting risk allocation would be anything but simple. Receiver finality would make payment final and discharge the sender's obligation when the receiving bank accepts the payment message. The three settlement finality alternatives, however, would be far more complex and might be better left to administrative regulation or system rules. But this would leave open the question of when the sender's obligation is discharged. The objective then becomes to determine an appropriate balance between law and regulation.

The final draft of Article 4A shows the problems with writing a finality rule into the law (National Conference of Commissioners on Uniform State Laws 1989). The draft provides receiver finality by making the receiving bank liable to the receiver for a payment message when it accepts it from a sending bank. Also, acceptance discharges the sender's obligation to the receiver. Importantly, receiving banks are not allowed to contract for conditionality with their customers, so receiving banks may not charge back settlement losses to receivers if a settlement failure occurs.

But the receiver finality in draft Article 4A may be a paper tiger. The reason is that it contains an exception for wire transfer systems that fail to arrive at a settlement under the terms of an existing loss sharing agreement.[19] In such an eventuality, the receiving bank's acceptance is reversed, the receiving bank may recover funds from the receiver, and the underlying obligation between sender and receiver is revived. In other words, the transaction is unwound.

Essentially, then, the draft provides for receiver finality under normal circumstances, but not when most needed. The rationale for writing a law this way is difficult to fathom, except that a loss sharing agreement would make such a failure unlikely. But that is like allowing ships to carry life preservers that dissolve when wet under the rationale that nowadays sinkings are unlikely. As emphasized throughout this chapter, for a finality rule to be effective banks must know they will be required to bear the costs of a failure. Under draft Article 4A, however, banks can attempt to evade the costs of a general settlement failure. Thus the primary justification for receiver finality is gone.

An alternative for a backstop finality rule would be to include in the new Code provisions forbidding settlement entries from being unwound. In other words, senders or sending banks could not revoke transfers,[20] nor could settlement entries between banks be reversed. The law would not have to go into further detail but would leave wire transfer networks or their regulators with a choice. They could require sending bank collateralization under an *ex ante* rule. Or they could develop a loss allocation scheme (probably with receiving bank collateralization) under an *ex post* settlement finality rule. They could even go all the way and institute receiver finality. The choice would hinge on whether an enforceable rule could be developed so that banks would know they will bear the risks as specified. Given that a credible rule is difficult to achieve, it appears that check finality is as far as the law can go in trying to control risks.

Given the difficulties in writing a finality rule into law, what should be the respective contributions of legal reform and regulatory reform? The comparative advantage of legal reform should be in areas of general principle that do not require detailed specification of actions to be taken in specific situations. For example, the law seems the appropriate place for clarifying the relationship between the sender and receiver whose transaction is the underlying reason for a wire transfer. Because the sender and receiver will not always have continuing relationships, they are unlikely to have incentives to contractually specify their rights and obligations. If the law does nothing more than make clear when the sender's obligation to the receiver is discharged, then it will remove much potential for uncertainty and litigation while saving the parties the cost of drawing up a detailed contract. And despite its disadvantages, a check finality rule would serve this purpose just as surely as would receiver finality.

In contrast, regulatory action or network agreement seem best suited for those risk reduction tasks that require both detailed specification and flexibility. For example, any rule requiring collateralization for its effective implementation will probably have to be spelled out in fairly minute detail. But such detail means more occasion for changes, which are slower and more difficult to attain by law than by administrative regulation. By its nature, the law is more difficult to change, especially if it requires the approval of each state legislature and that only after a lengthy process of drafting. While regulatory bodies might not be known for willingness to adjust to changes, at least they are capable of instituting, modifying, and revoking rules when the need arises.

Notes

1.   Wholesale wire transfer and the wholesale wire transfer networks are described in the appendix. Network payment volumes are for March 1988.

2.   *Evra Corp.* v. *Swiss Bank Corp.*, 673 F.2d 951, 955 (7th Cir. 1982). See Miller and Harrell (1985, 279–82).

3.   See National Conference of Commissioners on Uniform State Laws (1989). It should be emphasized that the final version of Article 4A could differ substantially from any of the alternatives described in this chapter.

4.   In contrast, gross settlement would involve actual exchange of funds between banks for each transaction.

5.   For further discussion, see Mengle (1985, 19–21).

6.   Lingl (1981) and Geva (1987) discuss the CHIPS rules and options for dealing with a settlement failure. For a simulated worst-case scenario of a chain of settlement failures, see Humphrey (1986, 100–111).

7.   There is an analogous problem with insurance against earthquakes: "...insurance is seen to some extent as a substitute for making...changes that would reduce risks." U.S. Congress (1987, 35).

8.   This framework is developed in more detail in Mengle, Humphrey, and Summers (1987).

9.   This alternative is based on the "good funds" theory of wire transfer described by Warren and Jordan (1986, 19–20, 27–32).

10.   Corrigan's (1987) proposed "liquidity balance" requirement for wire transfer networks is essentially a form of *ex ante* settlement finality.

11.   But it could affect the incentives of unsecured creditors or guarantors to reduce the

likelihood of a failure to settle.

12. Warren and Jordan (1986, 21–25) A pure receiver finality rule would not allow receiving banks to contract with receivers for provisionality.

13. U.S. Department of Justice (1984, 34–35). The same considerations apply to *ex post* settlement finality rules but not, interestingly, to *ex ante* net debit collateralization.

14. At least in the case of the Uniform New Payments Code, a specific guiding principle was that the law "should not distort user choices among different payment systems...". Scott (1983b, 1).

15. See, for example, Kunreuther et al. (1978). In a banking and finance context, Guttentag and Herring (1986) refer to this tendency as "disaster myopia."

16. For further discussion of how the Federal Reserve might handle a settlement failure, see Dudley (1986).

17. This phenomenon has been called "time inconsistency" in the economic policy literature. See Taylor (1985) for a nontechnical explanation.

18. This would also help prevent banks from walking away from their obligations and thereby necessitating a settlement unwind.

19. CHIPS has recently announced a loss sharing agreement (corresponding to settlement finality III in the text). New York City Clearing House (1989).

20. This is now part of CHIPS rules and the case law of electronic funds transfer. *Delbrueck & Co.* v. *Manufacturers Hanover Trust Co.* 609 F.2d 1047 (2d Cir. 1979).

21. This appendix is adapted from Mengle et al. (1987).

References

Association of Reserve City Bankers. 1985. *Finality in Private Payments Systems.* Payments System Committee. Finality of Payments Task Force.

Ballen, Robert G. 1986. "The Federalization of Articles 3 and 4." *Uniform Commercial Code Law Journal* 19 (Summer): 34–46.

Bank of Canada. 1985. "Matters Arising from Transactions of the Northland Bank with Its Clearing Agent The Royal Bank of Canada, and with the Bank of Canada, on August 30th, 1985." Press Statement (September 18).

Board of Governors of the Federal Reserve System. 1985. "Policy Statement Regarding Risks on Large-Dollar Wire Transfer Systems." *Federal Register* 50 (99, May 22): 21120–21130.

———. 1987. "Interim Policy Statement Regarding Risks on Large-Dollar Wire Transfer Systems." *Federal Register* 52 (151, August 6): 29255–29267.

Calabresi, Guido. 1970. *The Costs of Accidents: A Legal and Economic Analysis.* New Haven: Yale University Press.

Clarke, John J. 1969. "An Item Is an Item Is an Item: Article 4 of the U.C.C. and the Electronic Age." *Business Lawyer* 25 (November): 109–119.

Cooter, Robert D., and Edward L. Rubin. 1987. "A Theory of Loss Allocation for Consumer Payments." *Texas Law Review* 66 (November): 63–130.

Corrigan, E. Gerald, 1987. "Financial Market Structure: A Longer View." *Annual Report*, Federal Reserve Bank of New York.

Dudley, William C. 1986. "Controlling Risk on Large-Dollar Wire Transfer

Systems." In *Technology and the Regulation of Financial Markets*, 121–135, ed. Anthony Saunders and Lawrence J. White. Lexington, Mass.: D. C. Heath.

Geva, Benjamin. 1987. "CHIPS Transfers of Funds." *Journal of International Banking Law* 4: 208–221.

Guttentag, Jack M., and Richard J. Herring. 1966. *Disaster Myopia in International Banking.* No. 164, Essays in International Finance. Department of Economics, Princeton University.

Humphrey, David B. 1986. "Payments Finality and the Risk of Settlement Failure." In *Technology and the Regulation of Financial Markets*, 97–120, ed. Anthony Saunders and Lawrence J. White. Lexington, Mass.: D. C. Heath.

Humphrey, David B., David L. Mengle, Oliver Ireland, and Alisa Morgenthaler. 1987. "Pricing Fedwire Daylight Overdrafts." Staff Discussion Paper (January 13). Federal Reserve System.

Jordan, Robert L., and William D. Warren. 1986. Draft Article 4A. Memorandum to Drafting Committee on Amendments to Uniform Commercial Code— Current Payment Methods (August 21). School of Law, University of California, Los Angeles.

————. 1987. Revised Draft Article 4A. Memorandum to Drafting Committee on Amendments to Uniform Commercial Code—Current Payment Methods (September 25). School of Law, University of California, Los Angeles.

Kunreuther, Howard, Ralph Ginsberg, Louis Miller, Philip Sagi, Paul Slovic, Bradley Borkan, and Norman Katz. 1978. *Disaster Insurance Protection: Public Policy Lessons.* New York: Wiley.

Lee, John F. 1986. Letter to William D. Warren and Robert L. Jordan, New York Clearing House (July 14).

Lingl, Herbert F. 1981. "Risk Allocation in International Interbank Electronic Fund Transfers: CHIPS and SWIFT." *Harvard International Law Journal* 22 (3): 621–660.

Mengle, David L. 1985. "Daylight Overdrafts and Payments System Risks." *Economic Review* 71 (May–June): 14–27. Federal Reserve Bank of Richmond.

Mengle, David L., David B. Humphrey, and Bruce J. Summers. 1987. "Intraday Credit: Risk, Value, and Pricing." *Economic Review* 73 (January–February): 3–14. Federal Reserve Bank of Richmond.

Miller, Fred H. 1986. "Report on the New Payments Code." *Business Lawyer* 41 (May): 1007–1011.

Miller, Fred H., and Alvin C. Harrell. 1985. *The Law of Modern Payment Systems and Notes.* Norman. Oklahoma: University of Oklahoma Press.

National Conference of Commissioners on Uniform State Laws. 1989. Draft Amendments to Uniform Commercial Code. Article 4A—Funds Transfers.

New York City Clearing House. 1989. "Increased Assurance of Settlement Finality on CHIPS." Memorandum (April 28).

Penney, Norman, and Donald I. Baker. 1980. *The Law of Electronic Funds Transfer Systems.* Boston: Warren, Gorham, and Lamont. Cumulative Supplement 1987.

Sampson, Allan R., and Robert L. Smith. 1982. "Assessing Risks Through the Determination of Rare Event Probabilities." *Operations Research* 30 (September–October): 839–866.

Scott, Hal S. 1983a. "Corporate Wire Transfers and the Uniform New Payments Code." *Columbia Law Review* 83 (November): 1664–1716.

———. 1983b. "An Introduction to the Uniform New Payments Code." Memorandum to the National Conference of Commissioners on Uniform State Laws (June 15).

Slovic, Paul, Baruch Fischhoff, and Sarah Lichtenstein. 1982. "Fact Versus Fears: Understanding Perceived Risk." In *Judgment Under Uncertainty: Heuristics and Biases*, 463–489, ed. Daniel Kahneman, Paul Slovic, and Amos Tversky. New York: Cambridge University Press.

Slovic, Paul, Baruch Fischhoff, Sarah Lichtenstein, Bernard Corrigan, and Barbara Combs. 1977. "Preference for Insuring Against Probable Small Losses: Insurance Implications." *Journal of Risk and Insurance* 45 (June): 237–258.

Taylor, Herb. 1985. "Time Inconsistency: A Potential Problem for Policymakers." *Business Review* (March–April): 3–12. Federal Reserve Bank of Philadelphia.

Tversky, Amos, and Daniel Kahneman. 1974. "Judgment under Uncertainty: Heuristics and Biases," *Science* 185 (September): 1124–1131.

———. 1986. "Rational Choice and the Framing of Decisions." *Journal of Business* 59 (October): S251–S278.

U.S. Congress. 1987. *Earthquake Insurance: Problems and Options*, by David Cheney and David Whiteman. S. Print 99–220. Senate. 99th Congress, 2d Session.

U.S. Department of Justice. 1984. *In the Matter of Proposals to Reduce Risks on Large-Dollar Transfer Systems. Comments of the U.S. Department of Justice* (November 15). Docket No. R-0515.

Warren, William D., and Robert L. Jordan. 1986. Wholesale Wire Transfer. Memorandum to Drafting Committee on Amendments to Uniform Commercial Code—Current Payment Methods (March 25). School of Law, University of California, Los Angeles.

Appendix: Wholesale wire transfer networks[21]

Wholesale wire transfer

Also called large-dollar wire transfer, wholesale wire transfer refers to payment networks that electronically transfer payments between depository institutions. The payments may be for the depository institutions' own benefit or for the benefit of their corporate or government customers. Retail customers of depository institutions seldom have occasion to use wholesale wire transfer directly. In contrast, retail funds transfer includes automated teller machine networks, point-of-sale systems, bank credit card networks, and other consumer-oriented forms of funds transfer.

Fedwire

This is the wire transfer network operated by the Federal Reserve Banks. Currently, more than 220,000 Fedwire funds transfer transactions totaling over $638 billion occur on an average day. Mean transfer size is about $2.9 million. Transfers involving book-entry U.S. government securities number approximately 40,000 per day, for a total daily value of over $350 billion. Average securities transfer size is $8.7 million. Both funds and securities transfers have grown dramatically over the past decade. An important distinction between Fedwire and other networks is that settlement of transactions made over Fedwire is immediate, inasmuch as it occurs by means of credits and debits to depository institution reserve accounts on the books of the Federal Reserve Banks. Because the immediate settlement feature means that Fedwire transactions constitute "good" or final funds as soon as notification of payment is made, banks participating in Fedwire as receivers of payments are relieved of risk. The risk that the sending bank may not be able to fund its position is borne by the Federal Reserve when it accepts and settles a Fedwire transfer.

CHIPS

The Clearing House Interbank Payment System (CHIPS) is a privately operated wire funds transfer network associated with the New York Clearing House. About one-half of its transfers concern international dollar transactions involving U.S. depository institutions. As of March 1988 approximately 134,000 funds transfers amounting to almost $622 billion were transacted on CHIPS daily. The average transaction was approximately $4.6 million. CHIPS was started in 1970 to efficiently transfer interbank balances involving international transfer of dollars on the books of the New York Clearing House Association banks. This essentially eliminated the use of the paper draft to effect the transfers. While payment messages are sent over CHIPS throughout the business day, actual settlement of net debit and credit positions takes place at the end of the day through a special account at the Federal Reserve Bank of New York. CHIPS currently has 140 participating institutions, of which 21 settle directly with the network. Nonsettling participants must settle their CHIPS transfers on the books of one of the twelve New York Clearing House banks. (For a more detailed description of CHIPS, see Geva 1987).

Policies to Control Risks

In recognition of concerns about intraday credit risks, the Board of Governors of the Federal Reserve System in 1986 implemented a voluntary program to limit intraday credit and improve control over risk by users of all large-dollar wire transfer networks. The current program is voluntary and consists of three main elements.

1. Banks using any large-dollar wire transfer system are requested to perform a self-evaluation based on their operational and credit controls, policies, and procedures, as well as their creditworthiness or ability to fund themselves to cover unexpectedly large funds outflows or reduced inflows.
2. Based on the results of the self-evaluation, each participant adopts a total ratio of Fedwire daylight overdrafts plus CHIPS net debits to capital as its limit on how much a participant may send out in excess of what it receives across all networks. The ratio is called a cross-system *net debit cap* multiple.
3. Participants also establish network-specific sender net debit caps as well as *bilateral net credit limits* (limits on how much a receiving bank may be a creditor to a particular sending bank) on CHIPS to obtain net settlement services from the Federal Reserve.

Under the policy, CHIPS participants are required to compute two net debit caps. First, cross-system caps covering Fedwire and CHIPS together are calculated as a multiple of capital. Second, a network-specific cap for CHIPS is based on a formula that attempts to capture the market's assessment of other CHIPS participants' soundness. If a bank only uses Fedwire, then its cross-system cap and its network-specific cap are one and the same.

COMMENTARY
by Hal S. Scott

This commentary evaluates the case for mandating a receiver finality rule requiring banks to give customers unconditional credit at the time accounts are credited for incoming funds transfers but before settlement occurs. This rule would prevent banks from contracting with customers to make credits conditional on settlement. The commentary begins by showing that the importance of receiver finality depends on the degree of settlement finality. It then examines the basic economics of risk reduction in a funds transfer network and concludes that there is no need to displace contracts as to receiver finality under perfect market assumptions. It then examines whether there are market imperfections—externalities, misperceptions of risk, or the presence of a Fed settlement guarantee—which justify such displacement. It acknowledges that the presence of a widely perceived Fed guarantee gives inadequate incentives for risk reduction efforts by banks but concludes that mandated receiver finality is not the answer to this problem.

After discussing a zero cap proposal as an alternative way to deal with the Fed guarantee problem, the commentary reviews the receiver finality provisions of the current draft of Uniform Commercial Code Article 4A.

Introduction: Settlement and Receiver Finality

David Mengle's paper analyzes alternative finality rules for electronic transfers sent over a network like CHIPS (Clearing House Interbank Payment System) with end-of-day net settlement. Two of these rules deal with receiving customer finality. The check finality rule allows receiving banks to make the finality of customer credits conditional on the completion of settlement. The receiver finality rule prevents this. It requires that credits be final when posted to customer accounts. These are alternative rules governing the contractual relationship between the receiving bank and its customer. If the check finality rule is adopted, one must also deal with the rights of the receiving customer against other parties in the event a credit is revoked.

Three alternative settlement finality rules are discussed. Settlement finality I *ex ante* requires banks to collateralize their intraday net debit positions on the network. Settlement finality II *ex post* imposes the settlement risk on all network banks by some criterion unrelated to exposure. Settlement finality III *ex post* imposes the settlement risk on net creditors of the failed bank on the basis of their exposure to the failed bank. These are alternative rules governing the contractual relationship among banks participating in the network.

These settlement finality rules have implications for receiving customer finality, since they may limit risk to receiving banks. This in turn reduces risk to receiving customers under the check finality rule. Under settlement finality I, assuming adequate collateral, settlement would occur through the liquidation of collateral, and there would be no losses imposed on other participants. Absent loss, the issue of receiving customer finality is moot, as in Fedwire. But collateral may not be adequate, and there may be loss after all. Settlement finality rules II and III leave banks with losses, albeit different banks, so the issue of customer finality would still be relevant.

The discussion of both the customer and settlement finality rules envisions prohibition of freedom of contract. Adoption of the customer receiver finality rule is intended to prevent the customer and its bank from contracting for conditionality. Adoption of one of the settlement finality rules would presumably prohibit banks in a network from contracting for another alternative. This commentary examines the case for displacing freedom of contract as to customer finality. As indicated, customer finality will remain an issue under all versions of settlement finality, particularly under settlement finality II and III. A similar analysis could be done for displacing bank contracts for settlement finality, but I leave that to another day.

The Economics of Risk Reduction

Perfect Market Assumptions

Absent market imperfections, parties in privity will contract for the most efficient allocation of risk. Between receiving banks and their customers, the industry practice is that receivers contract for conditionality and not finality. In Mengle's terms, they contract for a check finality rule. Why does this occur? A simple numerical example illustrating some basic economic relations can serve as background for this inquiry.

Suppose receiving bank risk reduction cost was $1 (including profit) for every $100 transfer and that discounted losses on every $100 transfer (the amount of loss times the probability that the loss will occur) are $4 without risk reduction and $2 with it. Risk reduction may involve monitoring the riskiness of and exposure to a sending bank as well as adopting procedures to limit this risk by lowering bilateral credit limits. If there was receiver finality, the bank would engage in risk reduction activities, and the discounted value of each transfer would be $98. The bank would charge the customers $3 for each $100 received, $2 for the risk assumed, and $1 for risk reduction cost. Net discounted yield to the customer would be $97. If there was no receiver finality, no risk reduction would occur, and the net discounted yield to the customer would be $96 ($100 minus the $4 discount).

Clearly, the customer and the bank would be better off with risk reduction. The net discounted yield to the customer is greater and the bank makes a profit. Yet, as noted, banks and customers invariably agree that customers should bear the risk of settlement failure. Why do they do this?

It is conceivable that risk reduction costs exceed the value of risk reduction. This means one of two things. First, unlike the example, each dollar spent on risk reduction might produce less than a dollar of risk reduction. If this is so, it is inefficient to reduce risk, even though risk could be reduced. In short, it does not pay to spend $2 to save $1. This possibility is unaffected by the level of total losses. It would be inefficient to spend $2 to save $1 whatever the level of total loss. Second, banks may already be expending an amount equal to expected loss, $4 in the example. They will not spend $5, because they would be better off bearing a risk of $4 than spending $5 to avoid it.

Even if it is true that it is inefficient for banks to reduce risk, and there is thus no positive reason for the parties to agree that the banks will assume the risk, this does not necessarily mean that the parties will agree that customers should assume the residual risk. The question remains as to why this residual risk is not assumed by banks and priced to the customers. It is possible that the parties cannot arrive at satisfactory agreement about the price equivalent of the risk. Unlike the situation in the numerical example, the parties may not be able to estimate, with any confidence, the amount of potential loss or the probability that it will occur. While subjective estimates of the probability could be elicited, it is another matter as to whether anyone would be prepared to act on them.

There is reason to believe this holds true in the case of CHIPS settlement failure risk. Since there has never been a settlement failure, estimates of the probability of its occurring in the future would be somewhat arbitrary. It would be even more difficult to estimate, with any confidence, a particular bank's losses if a settlement failure were to occur. This would depend on which bank failed to settle and whether a particular bank was in a net credit position with the failing bank. Banks, like other parties entering into contracts, will be extremely reluctant to assume credit risk without compensation. Since banks will be unsure of what adequate compensation will be, they may not be willing to assume the credit risk, at least at a price that may appear reasonable to the customers.[1]

In light of this fact, the parties may agree that the assumption of risk by customers is a preferred alternative because this spreads the risk to parties who are better able to bear it. Humphrey (1986) has shown that, in a worst-case scenario, a settlement failure by one bank in CHIPS could bankrupt other banks, since the settlement shortfall may exceed the capital of those banks. Under a conditionality rule, the settlement shortfall will be spread to many customers rather than concentrated in one firm, a bank. Furthermore, many of these customers will be large industrial firms with substantially larger capital bases than a highly leveraged bank. Customers will be likely to prefer absorbing some prorated portion of the risk over paying the price the bank would demand for concentrating the risk in its hands, particularly where the risk, if it materialized, could threaten the solvency of the bank.

It is also important to understand that customers that have their conditional credits revoked may not wind up actually bearing the loss. The receiving customers have not been paid on the underlying obligations of the senders of the credits, and should have the right to recover back against these senders.[2] This puts funds transfer senders at risk for the settlement failures of their own banks, but the senders can monitor the solvency of their banks and avoid this risk by banking with comparably sounder banks. Thus, the conditionality rule may reduce settlement failure risk by providing for monitoring at the front end, by senders of sending banks. This might more efficiently reduce risk than would back-end monitoring, by receiving banks of sending banks.[3]

Absent the possibility of market imperfections, present contractual behavior can be understood in terms of risk spreading and assignment of ultimate legal risk to the customers of the bank that fails to settle. The question then becomes whether there are market imperfections that might point to other explanations and thus justify overriding freedom of contract.

Market Imperfections

Three possible market imperfections might suggest that contractual outcomes are inefficient: (1) externalities, (2) misperception of risk, and (3) the presence of an external Fed guarantee of settlement.

Externalities.   The case for the existence of an externality that justifies imposition of receiver finality is not strong. It is true that the net credit exposure accepted by bank A on bank B can affect other banks in the network. This is sometimes referred to as systemic risk. In the event that bank A's failure triggers bank B's failure, other banks with net credits to bank B can be put at risk. But these banks could protect themselves. They could monitor bank B's credit exposure to A and react to any increases in that exposure by lowering their credit limits on bank B. More complicated scenarios could be run on computers during the day.

At present, CHIPS does not allow a bank to monitor the bilateral positions between two other banks. Apparently this is done for reasons of confidentiality. This greatly impedes the ability of banks to protect themselves against systemic risk. But this prohibition could be easily changed; the information is available.

The classic case of an externality, where the activity of one party (a polluter) imposes harm (soot) on other parties with which it has no contractual relationship (farmers) or in which contractual costs are prohibitive (1000 farmers) does not exist. Network banks belong to a system and can adopt rules to minimize third-party effects.

Even if one believed that banks could not protect themselves against imprudent exposures accepted by one of their members, it would not follow that the imposition of a receiver finality rule was justified. Indeed, receiver finality would *ex post* make it harder for the net creditor of the failed bank to settle. Without the possibility to revoking customer credits, the possibility of a chain reaction effect would be increased.

Misperception.   The second argument for prohibiting freedom of contract is premised on misperception of risk. Mengle observes that there may be a tendency for people to underestimate low-probability events. Thus, it can be argued that if banks and customers accurately assessed the probability of a settlement failure, the probability would be high enough to provide an incentive for banks to contract for finality and engage in risk reduction.

The problem with this analysis is that there is no a priori reason to assume that people underestimate low-probability events. Indeed, the literature suggests that some low-probability events, like nuclear power plant accidents, are overestimated, not underestimated (Slovic, Fischhoff, and Lichtenstein 1985, 264). While it is true that others are underestimated, there is no basis for determining in which of these two categories settlement failure would fall. Furthermore, much of the relevant literature compares lay person estimates against a base line of actual statistical probabilities or expert judgments. In the case of settlement failure, experts are assessing the probabilities, and there is no statistical base line.

There is no way to prove that all transactors are systematically underestimating the probability of a settlement failure. If this affliction were not universal, and a correct estimation would produce risk reduction, some banks and customers would contract for finality. But this does not appear to be the case. The assumption, rather than the demonstration, that settlement failure is underestimated provides a weak basis for interfering with contract. Finally, the psychology of underestimation, even if applicable to this situation, will not be changed by imposing receiver finality. Banks will not change the way they underestimate the probability of a settlement failure just because a receiver finality rule is imposed.

The Fed Guarantee. The third argument for displacing contract as to receiver finality is based on the possible shared expectation of network banks that the Fed will not permit a settlement failure to occur because of its concern over the chain reaction effect. The argument reduces to the proposition that the imposition of receiver finality compensates for the distortion of incentives introduced by this expectation.

The Fed Guarantee Expectation May Not Affect Contractual Decisions on Receiver Finality. While there well may be an expectation of a Fed guarantee, this does not necessarily justify the imposition of receiver finality. If parties widely believed there was no real risk, they would be indifferent between a contract calling for conditionality and one calling for finality. Put another way, it is hard to see how the perception of Fed rescue would systematically lead banks and customers to contract for conditionality.

The Effect of the Fed Guarantee on Risk Reduction. The probability of a Fed rescue could affect the maximum expenditure that banks are willing to make in risk reduction efforts. Returning to our numerical example, banks will not expend more than $4 to reduce risk, the total amount of expected loss. A key variable in determining loss is the probability of a settlement failure. The probability of a settlement failure is a function of two component probabilities: the probability that the bank will be unable to settle with its own funds, and the probability that the Fed will not provide the funds. For example, if the probability of the bank being unable to settle with its own funds is .001 and the probability that the Fed will not provide the funds is .40, the actual probability of a settlement failure is .0004.

If the probability that the bank will be unable to settle with its own funds is sufficiently small, risk reduction efforts may be inefficient without regard to the Fed guarantee. For example, risk reduction efforts might not be justified at a .001 probability of a settlement failure, let alone at a .0004 probability level. On the other hand, it is conceivable that risk reduction efforts would be desirable at the .001 but not at the .0004 level. In that event, removal of the Fed guarantee would affect the maximum amount of risk reduction effort. Total expected losses would increase, and increased costs to avoid these losses would also be justified.

But for risk reduction efforts actually to be undertaken they must be efficient; more than $1 of reduced risk must be achieved from an additional expenditure of $1 on risk reduction. If it is not efficient to engage in risk reduction efforts, such efforts will not increase even if expected losses increase. Those asserting that removal of the Fed guarantee will inevitably induce risk reduction must also show that additional efficient expenditures on risk reduction can be made by receiving banks.

Receiver Finality as a Substitute for Removal of the Guarantee. Even if this were demonstrated, the preferred solution would be the credible removal of the Fed guarantee, not the imposition of a receiver finality rule. But, as Mengle's chapter ably shows, it will be difficult for the Fed to credibly remove the guarantee. Almost everyone believes that there is a very high probability that the Fed will guarantee settlement when the chips are down, whatever the Fed says now.[4]

The objective of removal of the guarantee is to increase perceived total losses to the point at which they would be without the guarantee so that increased risk reduction efforts could be undertaken. Perhaps the case for receiver finality is that it is another way of achieving the same result.

The effect of imposing a receiver finality rule is to increase the losses experienced by a net creditor of a failed bank. With conditionality, the expected loss is the portion of loss from the settlement failure, as determined by the settlement finality rule, less expected chargebacks or recoveries from customers. Under the receiver finality rule, the cost is purely the loss that results from settlement failure. By definition, no chargebacks or recoveries are permitted. The receiver finality rule increases the loss from settlement failure by the amount of the forgone chargebacks and recoveries. The increase will differ for each bank depending on how much the bank had expected to be able to recover from customers.

The problem with this approach is that it is far from clear what the relation is between the increase in total losses produced by a receiver finality rule and the total loss increase that would have been produced by a credible removal of the Fed guarantee. Any coincidence between these two amounts is unlikely. If total losses imposed by receiver finality exceed total losses that would have been produced by a credible removal of the Fed guarantee, the increased incentive for risk reduction is excessive. Imposition of the rule overcompensates for the imperfection introduced by the Fed guarantee. Conversely, it may undercompensate. In my view, this is likely to be the case. The small probability of the lack of a Fed guarantee has a much greater impact on expected losses than would the inability to recover from customers in the event of a settlement failure.

Possible Adverse Effects of a Receiver Finality Rule. The fact that total expected losses are increased by a receiver finality rule will not necessarily lead a net creditor to increase risk reduction efforts. A major constraint on risk reduction behavior is that it might be more expensive than the benefit achieved.

The imposition of the receiver finality rule could simply increase expected bank losses, and, as John Lee of CHIPS has suggested, might lead banks to refuse to take CHIPS-type transfers. Banks might consider increasing transaction charges to customers to cover their increased risk.[5] But, as Mengle points out, bank finality charges might lead customers to insist on Fedwire payments, where such additional charges are not imposed.

The result might be to add to Fed dominance of the payment system, a result that adversely effects the long-term efficiency of that system. This would not only be bad from the competitive perspective but would also increase Fed risk, since on Fedwire the Fed is directly exposed to and committed to assume the risk of a settlement failure. Given the situation, it is not surprising that the private sector is suspicious of the Fed's motives in pushing for receiver finality.

The Zero Cap Alternative

If a receiver finality rule is not the answer to the distortion of incentives that may be induced by a perceived Fed guarantee, what is? One would have to look toward significant limits on overdrafts, on CHIPS as well as Fedwire.

A first step in this direction has already been made through the requirement that net settlement networks like CHIPS adopt bilateral and net debit caps. System risk might be further reduced by prohibiting any bank participant from having an unfunded or uncollateralized (uncovered) net debit position on CHIPS or an overdraft on Fedwire.[6] This would be a zero cap rule. Some banks would have to borrow on an intraday basis, at a market price, to avoid uncovered positions on CHIPS or overdrafts on Fedwire. Funds covering CHIPS net debit positions and Fed overdrafts might be held in reserve accounts at the Fed, paying interest.

Payment of interest is justified because the Fed can earn profits from the level of increased balances. These profits should be passed on to the banks in the form of interest. The Fed's interest is served by having the balances and avoiding the risk of a settlement failure, not by profiting from the situation. The negative spread between interest paid by the Fed and interest paid to intraday creditors, plus administrative costs, would represent the costs to the banks from this alternative.

This proposal is very much like Corrigan's clearing balance idea and quite close to David Mengle's settlement finality I (*ex ante*) alternative. A zero cap solution produces settlement finality by eliminating the risk of a settlement failure. It thus moots the need for conditionality on private networks.

This alternative is preferable to receiver finality for CHIPS because it equalizes cost across both systems. The total cost to the banking system, however, might well be higher than under a receiver finality rule. Indeed this cost *should* be higher if I am correct in believing that total expected losses from a credible removal of the Fed guarantee would be higher than under a receiver finality rule. But it has the virtue of eliminating systemic risk and preserving competitive equality. It may well spur transaction netting as customers seek to avoid the increased transaction charges that a zero cap rule will generate, but that may be a good thing.[7]

From the banks' point of view, they would prefer neither receiver finality nor a zero cap. The Fed guarantee at no charge is preferable. If given the choice, they might divide depending on their view of (1) which rule produced higher costs; (2) whether additional efficient risk reduction expenditures could be made; (3) the importance of CHIPS remaining competitive with Fedwire; and (4) the impact on that competition from a receiver finality rule. For example, if a bank believed that the costs of a zero cap rule would be significantly higher than those of a receiver finality rule, and that these costs were more important than the competitiveness of

CHIPS with Fedwire, it would prefer the receiver finality rule. Support for a receiver finality rule might be seen as an attempt to fend off the more costly alternative of the zero cap.

Some at the Fed appear to resist a zero cap for CHIPS because a collateralization requirement gives legitimacy to the perception that there is a Fed guarantee. But this creates a Catch-22 situation. The distortion of incentives created by the perception, whether or not accurate, cannot be corrected without recognizing that there is a basis for the perception, or at least that the perception will not be changed.

Furthermore, if a zero cap were only adopted for Fedwire, total Fed risk would not be reduced. It would only be moved from Fedwire to CHIPS. From a competitive perspective, it could decrease Fed and increase CHIPS volume, the opposite effect that might be produced by a receiver finality rule.

CHIPS is reportedly giving consideration to adopting a new settlement finality rule in which net creditors would cover the settlement shortfall of a failed bank. Risk would be allocated to net creditors as a function of their credit line and actual credit position with the failed bank. But the promise of the net creditors to meet this obligation is only as good as their actual ability to do so. This could only be assured by requiring net creditors to collateralize their commitments. This would, in effect, lead to collateralization of net credit rather than net debit positions. In principle the amount of collateralization should be the same, since the net debit position of one bank is the same as the aggregate net credit position of its creditors.

A variation on this approach would require that only the position of the largest net debtor be collateralized, on the theory that no settlement failure could produce more loss than that amount. The virtue of this proposal is that it would be cheaper than my approach, which requires collateralization of all net debit positions rather than just the largest net debit position. Since the potential settlement shortfall cannot exceed the largest net debit position—assuming only one bank fails—this approach would ensure settlement finality at less cost to the banking system.

An initial problem with this approach is determining the allocation of the collateralization requirement to banks in the network. This could be done in a variety of ways, but suppose it was determined by the ratio of each bank's net debit position to the largest net debit position. Thus, if the largest net debit position was $500 million, and the total of the net debit positions of all banks was $5 billion, and bank X's net debit position was $5 million, bank X would have a collateral requirement of $500,000 ($500 million times $5 million/$5 billion).

But further suppose that a bank with a $400 million net debit position fails and that bank X is the only bank with either a bilateral credit line or an actual net credit position with the failed bank, i.e., the only bank whose collateral can be legitimately tapped to ensure settlement finality. If one used the collateral of other banks to ensure settlement finality, a method would have to be found for those banks to recover against bank X. It is unclear how that would occur, particularly given the possibility that bank X could not meet its reimbursement obligation.

The Approach to Finality of Proposed Article 4A of the Uniform Commercial Code

I will conclude with some brief comments on two aspects of proposed Article 4A's approach to finality: its position on receiver finality, and the rights of a customer whose credit is revoked as a result of a settlement failure (National Conference of Commissioners on Uniform State Laws 1988, June 1 Draft).

Receiver Finality

Article 4A now proposes that banks be free to contract for conditional credit. This represents a significant change from the prior draft, which only permitted conditionality where the credit came directly from the failed bank.

Under the prior draft, if customer A's bank, bank X, sent a CHIPS transfer to bank Z for customer B, and bank X failed to settle, bank Z could revoke the credit to B (February 1 Draft, 4A-409(3)). If, however, the credit originated at a bank prior to the failed bank, receiving banks could not contract for conditional credit; they were prohibited from revoking credits (February 1 Draft, 4A-405(1); (5); and 4A-409, comment 7). Conditionality was seen as inconsistent with the so-called skip rule, which applied in the latter case. If customer A's bank X had sent a transfer to bank Z through its correspondent bank Y, and bank Y had failed to settle with bank Z, bank Z could not revoke the credit, and bank X (the skipper) had to pay the amount of the transfer to bank Z (the skippee) (February 1 Draft, 4A-409(2)).

The skip rule approach made little sense. If it had been supposed that banks did not need conditionality because they would be made whole by the obligation of the skippers to pay them, this was mistaken. The skippee would have to come up with CHIPS settlement funds long before it reccived any money from the skippers. The prospect of being reimbursed would not help the short-term liquidity position of the bank; revoking credits would. Further, the skippee would not necessarily know whether the skip rule applied to a particular transfer, i.e., whether the transfer for its customer originated with a bank prior to the failed bank. Thus, the skippee would not know, at the time it mattered, which credits it could revoke and which it could not.

In many skip rule cases the skipper could have been a foreign bank that transferred funds through its U.S. correspondent. A high percentage of CHIPS transfers are of this kind. Article 4A could not force the foreign bank skipper to pay the domestic bank skippee. And given the fact that the skipper might not recover funds previously charged against its account by the correspondent, the skipper would have every incentive to resist the reach of United States law.[8]

The current draft provides that a bank can revoke a customer credit following a settlement failure in all cases, as long as its contract with the customer provides for this right (June 1 Draft, 4A-408). Article 4A thus rejects receiver finality and respects the result currently reached by private contract. One minor improvement might be made. Given that conditionality is currently the rule adopted in practice, it would be better to provide that credits are conditional absent contract to the contrary, rather than to provide that credits are final absent a contract specifying conditionality. Backstop rules should start by adopting the rules reflecting commercial practice. This is a minor quibble, however, given the ease of contracting for conditionality.

Upstream Consequences of Conditionality

Article 4A provides that a customer whose credit is revoked as a result of a settlement failure can claim the amount of the revoked credit from the failed bank (June 1 Draft, 4A-408(3)), but the customer's likelihood of any substantial recovery, as an unsecured creditor, would be small. Article 4A specifically precludes the customer from recovering back against the sender, absent a specific agreement between the sender and receiver allowing such a recovery (June 1 Draft, 4A-407). This is justified by analogizing a funds transfer to a cashier's check (June 1 Draft, 4A-407, comment 2). Under the Uniform Commercial Code, the obligor's underlying obligation is discharged when a cashier's check is "taken" for an underlying obligation (Article 3-802(1)(a)).

This represents a significant departure from the prior draft, which dealt with recovery back in cases where conditionality was allowed, i.e., where the skip rule was not applicable. The prior draft provided that the customer could, in such cases, have recovery back against the sender.[9]

Prevention of recovery back undercuts one of the virtues of a conditionality rule. As previously discussed, given conditionality *and* recovery back, ultimate loss from a settlement failure would fall on the customer of the failed bank. This customer is in the position to monitor the risk of its own bank failing and to change its bank of account if the risk of insolvency becomes too great. The customer of the failed bank is certainly in a better position to avert loss flowing from the failure of its own bank than the customer of the receiving bank.

The cashier's check analogy is entirely unpersuasive. An obligee can refuse to take the cashier's check of a bank and thus avoid taking its obligor off the hook on the obligor's underlying obligation. When the obligor tenders the check, the obligee just says no and returns the check. The receiver of a funds transfer is given no such opportunity. The transfer goes directly to its bank; the obligee has no chance to reject the transfer. Settlement failure can occur before the receiving customer even finds out the identity of the sending bank.

While Article 4A does provide that the receiver and sender can contract out of this result, significant transaction costs would be incurred to achieve this result. Millions of contracts would have to be struck between senders and receivers. This is far different than conditionality contracts between banks and their customers, where one contract can be struck as part of the basic account agreement.

In this case, Article 4A should return to the more sensible result provided for in the prior draft.

Notes

1. The situation is further complicated by the fact that the customer is being asked to pay a price for final, but not necessarily good, credit. Under a receiver finality contract, the customer would pay a price to be protected against the revocation of credits, but if its bank fails as a result of the settlement failure of another bank, it would stand to lose any funds on account—funds not withdrawn—over FDIC insured limits, even if the credits reflected in the deposit were final. Similarly, under a conditionality contract, the bank has the right to recover funds but is not assured it will actually be able to recover the funds. If the customer has withdrawn the funds by transferring them in payment on another transaction, return of the funds might jeopardize the customer's solvency.

2. This result was specified in the Uniform New Payments Code (NPC), Permanent Editorial Board Draft No. 3 (June 2, 1983), §100. I have discussed the rationale for this rule in Scott (1983).

3   The same rationale would apply in more complicated examples. Suppose bank Z revoked customer B's credit when bank Y, bank X's correspondent, failed to settle. Customer B would then sue customer A on its underlying obligation. Customer A would still be able to recover its payment from bank X. Bank X would be solvent and able to pay. This places the risk of loss on bank X, which is remitted to recovering what it can in bank Y's insolvency. This is justified if one assumes that bank X should be at risk for the insolvency of its correspondent, which it chose and whose solvency it can monitor. See Scott (1983, 1684–1689).

4.   Indeed, Gerald Corrigan insisted at this symposium that there is no Fed guarantee of settlement. While he is certainly correct that no formal guarantee exists, I doubt that he convinced the audience that the Fed would allow a major CHIPS settlement failure to occur.

5.   Another possibility is that the banks would attempt to circumvent a receiver finality rule. They might hold incoming customer credits in a suspense account to avoid a finality rule triggered by crediting customer accounts. Customers could get effective use of incoming funds by having a credit line for the amount of incoming credits. After settlement, the loan account balance would be extinguished by a credit to the customer's demand account. If there was a settlement failure, the loans, or some portion of them, would still be due.

6.   An exception might be made for the level of overdrafts that could be expected as a result of system malfunctions. Under this proposal, there would be no need for limiting total overdrafts, a cross-system cap, since no overdrafts would be permitted on Fedwire and all net debit positions on CHIPS would be collateralized.

7.   Banks might react to a zero cap for CHIPS by expanding the use of offshore net settlement dollar clearings. This would put the Fed in the awkward position of having to support settlement by American bank participants in foreign systems in order to avoid the chain reaction effect, while knowing it was relatively powerless to provide the same support to a foreign participant whose failure to settle could equally endanger other American banks and the world's banking system as a whole. This problem could only be solved through international cooperation in which the central bank of the country hosting the clearing required the same collateralization as was required for CHIPS.

8.   Given the obvious deficiencies of the skip rule it is puzzling why it was ever seriously contemplated. Perhaps this is explained by the fact that the New York Clearing House had advocated the rule. It may simply have seen the "skip rule" as a less costly alternative than a broader reaching receiver finality rule, or a zero cap. In any event, the Clearing House has now abandoned its support of the rule. See Lee (1988, p. 5).

9.   The February 1988 Draft provided that a sender only discharged its underlying obligation to a beneficiary when the receiving bank "accepted" a transfer order (4A-408(1)) and that revocation of a credit resulted in the transfer order "never having been accepted" (4A-409(4)).

References

Humphrey, David B. 1986. "Payments Finality and the Risk of Settlement Failure." In *Technology and the Regulation of Financial Markets*, 97–120, ed. Anthony Saundees and Laurence J. White, Lexington, Mass.! D. C. Heath.

Lee, John F. 1988. Letter to Carlyle C. Ring, Jr., New York Clearing House (April 12).

National Conference of Commissioners on Uniform State Laws. 1988. Draft Uniform Commercial Code (February 1; June 1). Articles 3 and 4A.

Scott, Hal S. 1983. "Corporate Wire transfers and the Uniform Payments Code," *Columbia Law Review* 83 (November): 1664–1716.
Slovic, Paul, Baruch Fischhoff, and Sarah Lichtenstein. 1985. "Regulation of Risk: A Psychological Perspective." In *Regulatory Policy and the Social Sciences*, ed. Roger Noll.

5 Payment Risk, Network Risk, and the Role of the Fed

Gerald R. Faulhaber, Almarin Phillips, and
Anthony M. Santomero

This chapter analyzes alternative policy approaches to managing payment and network risks in large-dollar payment and settlement systems. The focus is on systemic risk, that is, the risk that a failure by an individual institution to meet its commitments in funds transfers will generate a chain of failures among other institutions. It is clear that the risk of systemic failure is not independent of the risk of failure by individual participants in a payment network. Indeed, systemic failures derive from the failure of individual institutional participants. In turn, the payment failure of a participating financial institution may occur because one or more of its deposit or loan customers fail to meet their payment commitments (Smoot 1985; Stevens 1984; Rosborough and Urkowitz 1983; Mengle 1985; Mengle, Humphrey, and Summers 1987).

The perspectives we bring to this discussion derive from two fundamental insights. The first of these is that the current debate concerning bilateral caps and overdraft limits springs from a particular—even peculiar—view of the problem: a regulatory and, perhaps, industry perspective that quantity constraints rather than prices should be the main mechanism of risk control in the payment system. We find this view unfortunate. It results in a nonoptimal pattern of payments. It probably results as well in less innovation and fewer private-sector developments in this area than would occur if an appropriate pricing system were used (Humphrey et al. 1987).

The second insight concerns the wide set of risk control options available to the industry as alternatives to the current structure. The issue of network access and risk exposure is necessarily related to a fundamental information problem among the members of the industry with respect to the solvency of their clearing partners. In other industries and at other times, similar problems arising from asymmetric information have been handled privately and with joint liability. The present payment system handles the problem centrally and with regulatory liability. We argue that the Federal Reserve has some advantages in accepting this role, since that function complements and indeed is a central part of, its role as bank regulator. It ought not do so, however, to the exclusion of private, market-induced clearing systems.

We conclude with a call for adequate, accurate pricing of transactions, overdrafts, and balances, and simultaneously a firm recognition of the proper, but nonexclusive role of the Federal Reserve in the payment process.

Institutional Background of the Payment Risk Issue

There are two major large-dollar transfer systems in the United States, Fedwire and CHIPS (Clearing House Interbank Payment System). The former is operated by the 12 Federal Reserve Banks; the latter by the New York Clearing House Association. CHIPS specializes in funds transfers arising from international trade and foreign currency transactions. Two smaller systems had also been set up: Cashwire and CHESS (Clearing House Electronic Settlement System). Cashwire was established by the Payment and Administrative Communication Corporation, a consortium of U.S. banks, while CHESS was founded by the Chicago Clearing House Association for its Seventh Federal Reserve District member institutions. Both of these have since ceased operation.

There is, in addition, the large financial message system, SWIFT (Society for Worldwide Interbank Financial Telecommunications). This technologically sophisticated communications system serves as a funds transfer system when the affected accounts are at the same institution. When separate institutions are involved, the transfers of funds typically require the use of one of the other large-dollar payment systems even though SWIFT may fulfill related communications needs.

Fedwire effects payments among institutions with reserve or clearing accounts at the Federal Reserve Banks. Computerized communications send payments to and from these institutions, with the appropriate debits and credits to the institutions' reserve and clearing accounts. The participating institutions act in response to payment directions by their customers —typically large corporations and deposit and nondeposit financial institutions that do not keep Federal Reserve balances. The Fed levies transaction charges for Fedwire transfers.

Banks that settle through the CHIPS system also make and receive net settlement payments via Fedwire through accounts at the Federal Reserve Bank of New York. Securities underwriters and dealers are among the nondeposit financial institution customers of the Fedwire participants, including those involved in the underwriting of and trading in U.S. Treasury and federal agency issues, for which special transaction rules apply. Fedwire is also used for net settlement services for institutions participating in automated clearinghouses (ACH), automatic teller machine (ATM), and point-of-sale (POS) terminal networks and bank card clearing networks (Board of Governors of the Federal Reserve System 1987a).

In 1987, about 8000 institutions maintained direct access to Fedwire. These institutions made an average of about 200,000 funds transfers per day, with total payments amounting to over $500 billion. A typical participating organization sends and receives many transfers each day, each of which is reflected in a charge or a credit to its account at a Federal Reserve Bank.

Fedwire is a daylight (Eastern Time, U.S.) system, with the several Federal Reserve Banks opening no later than 9 a.m. and closing at 5 p.m. The actual funds transfers are made as the payment orders occur, rather than being batched to an announced net settlement hour. Payments by Fedwire are final to the receiving institution at the time it is notified of the payment by its Federal Reserve Bank.

Daylight overdrafts occur on Fedwire when, at any point in time, payments by an institution exceed that institution's Fedwire receipts in an amount so great that the institution's reserve or clearing account is insufficient to cover its payment obligations. An institution in an overdraft position at one moment may, of course, have a substantial positive balance a moment later.

The differences between the accumulated amounts indicated at any time as due from and due to particular institutions on CHIPS are also referred to as overdrafts, although CHIPS net settlements occur only at the close of business each day. In late 1987, it was estimated that, with both CHIPS and Fedwire included, about 1,100 institutions got into an overdraft position each day, with the aggregate amount of these overdrafts reaching as much as $80 billion. (An additional $60 billion in overdrafts occurred each day under the transfer system for government securities. See Board of Governors 1987a.)

Regulatory Concern over Payment System Risk

The Federal Reserve has been concerned with the risk exposure of the Federal Reserve from the combined Fedwire and CHIPS overdrafts. This concern arises because it is assumed that the failure of a Fedwire participant to meet its overdraft payment obligations would result in the Federal Reserve's absorbing any resulting loss. The risk of systemic failure on Fedwire is not great, however, since Fedwire assures immediate payments to each of the recipients. On the other hand, the possibility of systemic failure due to the failure of a particular institution on CHIPS does exist, since the ability of each member to pay its CHIPS obligations depends on its receiving the credit from the payment obligations incurred by the other members over the course of a clearing day. A chain of defaults may follow the failure of one participant to settle, which would lead to the unwinding of what had been regarded as settled transactions among all of the affected banks in the system.

The current policy of the Federal Reserve seeks to limit these risks through the application of four general rules: (1) The transfer networks that obtain Fedwire net settlement services—CHIPS and others—are required to establish limits for each member's net credit positions with respect to each of the other members of the system. (2) Each of these networks must set a limit on the net debit position of each member with respect to all other members of the network. (2) Each institution must establish a limit on its combined overdraft position on all large-dollar networks, including Fedwire. (4) A $50 million limit has been set on each transfer of U.S. government and agency securities payments that are processed on its book entry, Fedwire sytem.

The Nature of the Regulation Currently in Place

Some observations are in order concerning the direction taken by current policies and regulatons. First, the present risk-reducing rules depend on quantity constraints rather than explicit or implicit prices. Second, the rules are applied on top of other central bank policies that do not employ market prices: no interest is permitted on the positive balances in reserve and clearing accounts, and there are no interest charges on daylight overdrafts. Interest is, of course, charged for borrowings made through the Federal Reserve Banks' discount windows, although even here the applicable rates are ordinarily below market rates. Only overnight (i.e., between clearing periods) interbank borrowings of Federal Funds carry market rates of interest. It should be no surprise that banks find daylight overdrafts and minimal positive net balances could be mitigated by the payment of interest on these balances and interest charges for intraday overdrafts.

Third, the Fed's present pricing structure is focused only on transaction charges with either a zero or below-market price for the use of money. Such inefficient pricing inhibits entry into the wire transfer business. With the existing pricing, entry against the Fed as a competitor is unprofitable. This could be because of economies of scale: the Fed may be so efficient that even full-cost prices will not attract entry. It seems unlikely however, that the existing transactions-based fees cover the cost of the system as a whole. In this context, the requirement that all institutions that issue transactions accounts must hold non-interest-bearing reserves and the absence of interest costs on overdrafts make the setting of efficient transactions prices all but impossible in any case. Related to the apparent absence of price allocation attempts is a concomitant absence of "value-dated" transactions—transactions that provide a final (or collected) balance at a specified future time.

Fourth, it must be recognized that this issue is unique to the United States market, at least in scale. Because of legal restrictions on the geographic and product markets of institutions, there are far more individual banks than would be present in an efficiently organized structure. If banks were integrated into larger systems, what are now interbank transactions would become intrabank transactions. Rationalization of this sort would result in a very substantial reduction of the number of institutions that have direct access to Fedwire and an even greater reduction in the volume of interbank transactions. Curiously, even though the risks associated with banks' customers' meeting their payment obligations would be the same, the dollar volume of daylight overdrafts would, in all likelihood, fall. Note that these results from internalization through common ownership—that is, through consolidations among banks—could be achieved through contracted, nonownership arrangements as well. Banks that are independently owned could avail themselves to a greater extent in correspondent clearing networks or create consortia for more extensive internal clearing, with the use of Fedwire for external payments. But, as noted, no price (or cost) incentive apparently exists to bring such reorganizations into effect.

Finally, although presentations by the Federal Reserve refer to the risk it assumes in assuring immediate and final payment to all Fedwire funds transfer recipients, this risk when carried by a central bank is not very great. The Federal Reserve can costlessly create the funds necessary to meet such obligations. The problem is not that the risk may be costly in the usual sense, but rather that undesirable Federal Reserve credit may thereby be created. Indeed, if no penalties apply, the bank that fails to cover overdrafts would be granted the equivalent of an interest-free loan from the discount window, a result that is hardly desirable.

Efficiency Characteristics of the Present System

The above notwithstanding, the Federal Reserve and affiliated banks have addressed payment system risks by setting caps to limit the exposure of any one bank and the system to a failure by any other. How efficient is such a system? Perhaps of more interest, how can one derive appropriate limits within such a system?

To address these issues, think of the current system as a networking problem. We have at present a communications network between agents that are members of the Fedwire system and the CHIPS system. Figure 5–1 illustrates a primitive view of these two networks for a group of four participants. Each network operates separately, with immediate settlement on Fedwire and end-of-day settlement on CHIPS, through Fedwire. Denote the net balances on Fedwire and CHIPS for institution i as f_i and c_i, respectively. Denote the bilateral position between agents i and j on CHIPS as c_{ij}, which designates the credit balance of i with respect to j. Since all transactions on Fedwire are with the Fed, there is no counterpart to c_{ij} for that system. Current policies and regulations on the clearing system impose limits on an institution, denoted as $\bar{f}_i$, $\bar{c}_i$ and $\bar{t}_i$, with obvious definitions. These regulations put the following constraints on bank balances:

1.   Bilateral limits on CHIPS require that $c_{ij} \geqslant \bar{c}_{ij}$.
2.   Bank limits require that $f_i \geqslant \bar{f}_i$ and $c_i \geqslant \bar{c}_i$.
3.   Combined limits require that $\bar{f}_i + \bar{c}_i \geqslant \bar{t}_i$.

Each of these constraints is imposed to limit the exposure of the system to default by one of its members. However, as noted, there is currently no

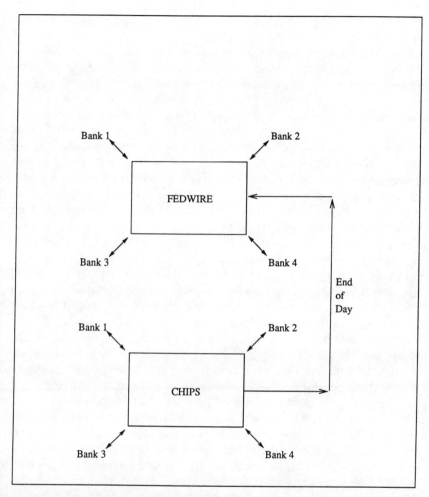

Figure 5–1.   Schematic of fedwire and chips.

incentive to economize on such (negative) balances or to reduce the number of transactions. The lack of an explicit charge by the Fed for debit balances and its per-item charge on each transaction do not foster contracts governing bilateral balances between agents or subsystem pooling to minimize network transactions. Further, the Fed's recognition of its regulatory role of lender of last resort, at least in the Fedwire system, negates the need for agents to plan realistically for either bilateral or system-wide exposure limits. Put another way, banks have no need to be concerned with the risk of exposure when the Fed insures the risk completely and without cost to the banks.

How, then, can the current system's limits be evaluated by an observer who is interested in their inherent efficiency and appropriate level? How can one evaluate the relative desirability of one value of $\bar{c}_{ij}$, $\bar{c}_i$, or $\bar{f}_i$, for example, relative to another? One way to seek an answer to this problem is to compare the resultant social welfare loss of the current system of discrete limits to the system's solution when it is allowed to achieve its unconstrained fully efficient network solution. The latter would be the result of the imposition of full marginal costs per transaction and interest payments per dollar of balances held over time on the current and potential networks of clearing systems. That is, the appropriate benchmark to compare the current system of discrete (arbitrary) limits is the optimal payment structure that would result in the absence of regulatory and cartel pricing of transfers and average intraday balances. From this benchmark one can evaluate the cost of discrete limits as the cost of the ad hoc second-best structure currently in place. However, to develop such a system would require considerably more information than is currently available. Such an evaluation would require the full array of marginal costs and bank responses to the current clearing system.

Without developing such an elaborate system, can some insights into the appropriate values for $\bar{c}_{ij}$, $\bar{c}_i$, $\bar{f}_i$, and $\bar{t}_i$ be gleaned? Perhaps yes. First, it should be apparent that the existence of $\bar{f}_i$ and $\bar{c}_i$ are redundant limits for credit risk control and add inefficiency to any system that contains $\bar{t}_i$ constraints. Unless the covariance of Fedwire and CHIPS transfers is exactly 1, the resultant loss from diverting payments over time or across systems is Pareto-inferior to a single limit per member of the joint networks. Even in the case where the covariance is 1, the solution to the network results in no better behavior of the clearing system, but the constraints become redundant.

Second, due to the arbitrary nature of the pricing of transactions and balance credits, it is not clear where the appropriate limits lie, relative to the current ones. Specifically, given that balances currently pay no interest (but do have economic value, which is being garnered by the Fed), there is a natural bias to increase negative balances (overdrafts). Given the conditional nature of CHIPS clearing, this is feasible systemwide. On the other hand, the true marginal cost of transfer clearly does not correspond to the current price charged users of the clearing system. This feature of the system tends artificially to increase the volume of transactions on the network. Accordingly, while the combined effect of underpricing for balances and underpricing of transactions leads to balances varying systematically from optimal levels, even the direction of movement toward the optimal from the current values for $\bar{c}_{ij}$, $\bar{c}_i$, $\bar{f}_i$, and $\bar{t}_i$ is unclear a priori.

In the absence of a more accurate pricing of clearing services, there is no solution to this problem. It is to this issue of appropriate pricing we now turn.

Alternative Solutions to the Payment System Risk Problem

Pricing Issues

Central to the controversy over payment system risk is the inappropriate pricing currently in place. This pricing has led the Fed to impose quantity constraints to offset the inherent tendencies of the system to respond to the pricing structure when determining profit-maximizing clearing behavior. To redress this result, the entire set of products that encompass the clearing process needs to be repriced, or at least evaluated. The latter includes three discrete pricing areas:

1. The per-unit price for various transfers
2. The intraday value of money for balances, either credit balances or overdrafts
3. The premium for possible default on overdrafts accumulated intraday

The current system includes a price for transfers that does not represent true marginal transfer costs. This leads to an excessive amount of transfers throughout the day, many of which are offsetting. The current system does not discourage this practice; banks are granted free overdrafts because of the peculiar institutional nature of borrowing and lending practice. Banks are forced to "settle" at the close of the day. This requires net transfers and end-of-day finality on CHIPS and a book entry recording of balances for reserve and accounting purposes. During the day, entries and balances proceed without reference to value, subject only to the regulatory caps imposed by the banks with Fed approval. At the end of the day, funds are borrowed through the Federal Funds market or the discount window to support the bank's balance sheet from the close of one day to the opening of the next.

In essence, the system charges a full day's interest for a fraction of the business day and charges nothing for borrowings limited to the trading day. This results in a neglect of intraday balances and an overemphasis of end-of-day figures. It seems obvious that the solution to this problem is to

extend credit and credit charges in a uniform manner throughout the day
(Humphrey et al. 1987). This could be achieved by computing average
intraday balances in the Fedwire clearing account, charging those institutions that have debit balances, and crediting those with balances. While
computational costs and breakdowns might limit this approach, it would
encourage the internal management of intraday float, just as the system
currently requires interday float management. In all likelihood, it would
also be considerably less expensive and less subject to technical problems
than some critics now claim. Many of the payments would net to near zero
by day's end, with banks that are chronic debtors paying others that are
consistent creditors in the system. Most of the payments made will be
intra-industry and offsetting.

Of course, charging for intraday borrowing raises the question of what
price should be charged. As the above list indicates, this appears to involve three separate issues. The first is straightforward: If one were to
neglect default risk, the cost of intraday borrowing is nearly risk-free
and is exactly comparable to interday borrowings between banks. The
appropriate rate, therefore, appears to be the average Fed funds rate for
high-quality institutions.

However, the essence of the payment risk issue lies in the default risk
issue or, in financial terms, the risk premium to assess banks in intraday
overdraft positions. What premium should the Fed charge banks needing
intraday funds in their clearing balances? To answer this question, one
must be willing to explain why this question should elicit an answer that
is different from that of a similar question: What rate should the Fed
charge banks to borrow interday balances? Obviously these questions are
essentially identical. Interday borrowing between banks occurs at the Federal Funds rate, and central bank borrowing is priced at the discount rate.
The latter moves with, but is not exactly equal to, the former. Therefore,
it would seem that the Fed already has a mechanism to price intraday borrowing within the clearing system.

The third issue concerns the time during the day and the period of time
for which intraday loans are made. The present system induces peak demands for loans as the settlement time approaches, with interest charged
for a full day for borrowings that cannot be repaid by settlement. Explicit
pricing—even average pricing—will tend to reduce the peaking that now
occurs, but there is no reason to believe that it would be eliminated. Similarly, unlike the current system, an institution may require large intraday
borrowings for a limited period. This period need not, and typically will
not, extend for a full day. This suggests that the Federal Funds market
ought to develop loans of shorter, intraday duration.

The Fed may not like this solution, which suggests that its current system of quantity constraints be replaced by real marginal cost pricing and the standardization of lending practices that extend around the clock. It may be argued that such procedures would still result in large overdrafts and the potential for financial instability. However, this is not all obvious. Specifically, without adequate and cost-based pricing, there is no way of determining appropriate intraday clearing balance positions. In addition, and very important, there is no way of knowing that other institutional arrangements and clearing houses would be established by the private sector in response to the accurate pricing of Fedwire and clearing accounts. Indeed, the present structure virtually excludes more efficient privatization of the clearing process because of its apparent subsidization through a (non)pricing policy.

Privatization

Some would argue that an alternative way of handling payment system risk is to move more explicitly to the private sector, expanding its role in the payment process. It should be noted that there is clear precedent for doing so. In fact, the current clearinghouse arrangements in the securities and options markets are private partnerships with unlimited joint liability; Cox and Rubenstein (1983) provide a description. So, too, in the banking industry there is a long history of private clearinghouses, as Gorton and Mullineaux (1988) and others report. An alternative mechanism to resolve the clearing needs of the banking system, therefore, is the privatization of the activity, essentially extending the CHIPS experience to domestic clearing that currently uses Fedwire.

Private clearing introduces a number of complexities into the payment risk problem. In comparison to today's system, banks could no longer rely on the Fed to certify solvency or guarantee "goodness" of each clearing transaction. In principle, each bank (and possibly each depositor of each bank) would have to make a bilateral credit decision with respect to every other bank regarding the default risk it takes on when it clears with that bank. In order for such a highly decentralized system to work, the creditworthiness of each bank's balance sheet would have to known to all participants. Each bank's liabilities would be discounted to reflect the risk that the holders of its liabilities would bear. A bank's promise to redeem an instrument for, say, $50 may be worth very little to the bearer if it were judged that the bank were likely to fail before the instrument could be redeemed. In such a system, however, there are no surprises; if a bank were to fail because its assets turned bad, depositors and other banks would know this and liquidation of assets could be arranged without contagion and without other banks becoming suspect, as illustrated by Gorton (1987).

The information requirements for such a highly decentralized system would be immense, particularly if, as today, banks were to clear with some 8000 other banks domestically (on the Fedwire system) and even more internationally. If the number of banks with which each bank clears is defined as n, then the number of bilateral credit decisions needed is $n(n - 1)$. Clearly, there are efficiency gains to centralizing the information, as pointed out by Diamond (1984) in another context.

One solution to this problem is the establishment of a delegated monitoring system by which the industry establishes a credit evaluation role for the private clearinghouse. Such a solution increases the efficiency characteristics of the clearing system over its bilateral counterparts. In such a "clearinghouse coalition" (Gorton 1987), the member banks delegate the central clearinghouse to monitor each bank's solvency, and to co-insure banks and depositors against the default of any member bank, with the combined credit of all banks in the coalition. Depositors and member banks need no longer individually monitor the creditworthiness of their clearing partners; the coinsurance contract assures them that a bank's liabilities would be made good by the system as a whole. Gorton (1987) shows theoretically that such a contract is incentive compatible if the clearinghouse controls the debt-equity ratio of its members, in which case it is also a Nash equilibrium and Pareto-superior to the decentralized clearing system. Information is produced efficiently and coinsurance assures depositors and banks alike that they need not expend resources on duplicating relevant information. While such a system looks very much like today's Fedwire, theory suggests that it may not be necessary for the clearing system to be controlled by government.

History has shown how such a system might evolve. During the period of the Free Banking Era (1837–1863) in the United States banks printed their own notes, with a promise to pay in specie upon presentation. These banknotes were traded by note brokers, usually at a discount that reflected the costs of presentation and the uncertainty and risk of payment by the issuing bank. These brokers had an interest in informing themselves about the condition of banks, and that information and other transactions costs were reflected in the discount at which a particular bank note traded. Clearinghouses had limited use in these circumstances.

The National Banking Era (1863–1914) was one in which private clearinghouses emerged. Checks came into wide use and state bank notes (and note brokers) disappeared. After 1863, under the National Banking Act, national bank notes became essentially uniform in value. Gorton (1987) argues that the private clearinghouse then constituted a contractual substitute for the Fed's "transactor and guarantor" role in clearing.

These counterparts notwithstanding, it should be clear that a privatized payment system would not be equivalent to the current central bank model. How might such a private clearinghouse system compare with the existing arrangement? Many differences of both a positive and negative nature are likely to exist. The most likely of these, listed from most to least desirable, are the following:

1. A private system would more likely be priced efficiently, as subsidies for its activity would not exist.
2. While a private system could insure banks, even depositors, against payment risk, it would have neither the interest nor the capability of guaranteeing institutions themselves. Only a sovereign central bank would support an entire institution or class of institutions that are "too big to fail."
3. A private system could establish any clearing rules that a sovereign central bank could, but its ability to enforce such rules is less clear. The latter depends upon its ability and member willingness to impose penalties and expel member banks for rule infractions. The Fed's ability to enforce clearing rules derives from the coercive power of the state, subject only to possible bureaucratic lobbying efforts. Governance structures, therefore, are quite different.
4. In a private system, member banks would have to monitor the clearinghouse organization to ensure that it was enforcing the clearing rules vigorously and impartially. With a central bank, member banks also have an interest in tracking its activities and possibly influencing its actions, but its control is less likely to be seized by subgroups within the industry.
5. A private system could monitor the quality of member banks' balance sheets but would have less power than a sovereign central bank to compel the complete and accurate revelation of information.
6. Finally, a private system has a potentially serious monopoly problem. Those banks that establish a dominant role in clearing and within the clearinghouse have an incentive to exclude others or charge such high entry fees as to expropriate all rents. This is particularly true since the only alternative to membership is to clear through an existing member.

These differences in the two systems are substantial, yet difficult to quantify. Nonetheless, judgment suggests that, on balance, the central bank approach is likely to be superior to a fully private system, at least for the domestic market. The enforceability issue, coupled with data quality improvements, favors this conclusion. In addition, the private monopoly issue looms in the background. However, both insurability of payment risk and economies of scale of monitoring could be realized by either system.

On the international level, too, the feasibility of a private-sector clearing system, divorced from central bank control, is unclear (Padoa-Schioppa 1988). One could not only imagine such a system, but CHIPS has some of its salient features. Such an international clearinghouse organization could monitor the risk of its member banks in various countries, which is a current feature of the CHIPS system. In the event of some form of payment failure, the suspect bank could borrow the needed funds from the clearinghouse to complete its transactions. This might involve the member bank producing acceptable collateral for the loan, which would demonstrate to the clearinghouse the underlying health of the bank's balance sheet. In any case, it would require a substantial broadening of the mandate given to CHIPS by its member banks.

However, such a model is unlikely to come to pass. It requires that member banks have appropriate financial incentives to monitor and enforce the clearinghouse agreement. In the current system, any losses that appear in international transactions between banks may be recoverable (at least for depositors) from some form of domestic insurance, the Herstadt experience notwithstanding. Therefore, the incentives for member banks to monitor and enforce an endogenous international clearinghouse agreement, *in the presence of domestic insurance*, may be quite low. Paraloxically, the very presence of a central bank in each country, willing to insure banks and depositors against untoward events via the discount window, the FDIC, and their foreign equivalents, militates against a private cooperative solution in the international arena.

We are left, then with an odd asymmetry in the clearing process. We argue that the current system of sovereign central bank control of the domestic clearing system is a likely preferred solution. For the international side of the clearing process, however, such a solution is not feasible, and some form of a cooperative private arrangement is the only alternative. This results in large measure from the fact that central banks implicitly insure their domestic institutions and the fact that there is no international counterpart for the global economy.

At present CHIPS serves the role of the international clearing system. In the future, some form of consortium of central banks, acting as transactors and guarantors might emerge. Such a system would be private in the sense that it lacks the sovereign power over its members, but public in that each of its members have such control regionally. Potentially, a global private system could emerge, which would be both transactor and guarantor, as it did on the domestic scene at the end of the nineteenth century. In the presence of domestic insurance, however, any global system has an inherent "beggar my neighbor" incentive. Given the backdrop of domestic central banks, if one bank fails to settle with another, the domestic central bank of the injured party will have the guarantor responsibility to make its domestic bank whole.

As Karekan and Wallace (1978) observe, it is the guarantor function of the central bank that creates the need for sovereign control. In the current and foreseeable international systems, each nation's central bank fulfills its guarantor role against a backdrop of the progressive loss of sovereign control as the volume of international clearing increases. In the absence of a solution to this dilemma, central banks will find it increasingly difficult to fulfill this role. The international clearinghouse system, then, will move toward de jure privatization, while its implicit guarantees may find the system more and more de facto public.

Summary and Conclusions

The present system of payment clearings has received considerable scrutiny recently, at least in part because of the Federal Reserve's concern about payment system risk. Under regulatory pressure, the members of Fedwire and CHIPS have developed a series of limits to overdraft exposure that serve to reduce the efficiency of the system and its exposure to systemic default risk.

An evaluation of this trend suggests that the quantitative constraints imposed upon the system are the result of inappropriate pricing within the payment process, and not a needed part of it. Such limits cannot be described as optimal, no matter what their amount. Prices should largely replace quantity constraints. More specifically, we recommended a relatively quick phasing-in to achieve the following:

1. Interest payments on reserve and clearing balances held at the Fed
2. Marginal cost pricing of Fedwire transactions
3. Charges for intraday overdrafts at the going Federal Funds rate

As such pricing arrangements are put in place, private-sector alternatives and private, complementary clearing subsystems are likely to arise. These should be welcomed as moves toward greater efficiency, not viewed as causes for alarm. Similarly, the development of explicit pricing will make existing caps increasingly irrelevant. Indeed, as long as caps were nonredundant, incentives would exist for additional clearing credit through private systems—even at a rate premium relative to that charged by the Fed. In turn, however, the caps would tend to become redundant.

The above notwithstanding, the current system is not likely to be replaced by a purely private network. A sovereign central bank appears to have advantages over a private clearinghouse system in both monitoring members and guaranteeing transactions (though not without cost). However, the inability to extend coercive regulatory power to international clearing results in a substantially different prognosis for the international environment. Here, the presence of local central banks, but absence of a global counterpart, leaves the door open for many kinds of clearing arrangements, with no single one appearing to be dominant.

References

Association of Reserve City Bankers. 1983. *Risks in Electronic Payments Systems.* Risk Task Force.

Board of Governors of the Federal Reserve System, 1981. "Federal Reserve and the Payment System: Upgrading Electronic Capabilities for the 1980s," by George W. Mitchell. *Federal Reserve Bulletin* (February): 109.

———. 1984a. "Measures to Reduce Risk in Large Electronic Fund Transfers." *Federal Reserve Bulletin* (April): 329–330.

———. 1984b. "System's Wire Network: Revised Schedule." *Federal Reserve Bulletin* (January): 26.

———. 1985a. "Policy on Large-Dollar Wire Transfer Systems." *Federal Reserve Bulletin* (July): 533–534.

———. 1985b. "Policy Statement on Large-Dollar Wire Transfer Systems: Interpretation." *Federal Reserve Bulletin* (October): 778.

———. 1986. "Changes to the Operating Schedule for Fedwire." *Federal Reserve Bulletin* (January): 28.

———. 1987a. "Daylight Overdrafts and Payments System Risks," by Terrence M. Belton, Matthew D, Gelfand, David B. Humphrey, and Jeffrey C. Marguardt. *Federal Reserve Bulletin* (November): 839–852.

———. 1987b. "Interim Statement on Reducing Risks on Large-Dollar Transfer Systems." *Federal Reserve Bulletin* (September).

———. 1987c. "Proposed Actions." *Federal Reserve Bulletin* (March): 210.

———. 1987d. "Proposed Actions." *Federal Reserve Bulletin* (April): 296–297.

Cox, John C., and Mark Rubenstein 1983. "A Survey of Alternative Option-Pricing Models." *Option-Pricing: Theory and Applications*, 3–33, ed. Menachem Brenner. Lexington Books, Lexington, MA.

DeGennaro, Roman Paul. 1984. "The Effect of Settlement and Payment Procedures on Asset Pricing." Ph.D. Dissertation, Ohio State University, Columbus, Ohio.

Diamond, Douglas. 1984. "Financial Intermediation and Delegated Monitoring." *Review of Economic Studies* (August).

Diamond, Douglas W., and Phillip H. Dybvig. 1983. "Bank Runs, Deposit Insurance, and Liquidity." *Journal of Political Economy* 91 (3).

Gale, Douglas. 1987. "The Core of Monetary Economy Without Trust." *Journal of Economic Theory* 19: 456–491.

Gorton, Gary. 1985. "Clearinghouses and the Origin of Central Banking in the U.S." *Journal of Economic History* 45 (2).

———. 1987. "Incomplete Markets and the Endogeneity of Central Banking." Mimeograph, University of Pennsylvania.

Gorton, Gary, and Donald J. Mullineaux. 1987. "The Joint Production of Confidence: Endogenous Regulation and Nineteenth-Century Commercial-Bank Clearing Houses." *Journal of Money, Credit, and Banking* 19 (November): 457–468.

Humphrey, David B. 1982. *Costs, Scale Economies, Competition, and Product Mix in the U.S. Payments Mechanism.* Washington, D.C.: Board of Governors of the Federal Reserve System.

———. 1984. *The U.S. Payment System: Costs, Pricing, Competition, and Risk.* Monograph 1984–1/2, Salomon Brothers Center for the Study of Financial Institutions, Graduate School of Business Administration, New York University, New York, N.Y.

Humphrey, David B., David L. Mengle, Oliver Ireland, and Alisa Morgenthaler. 1987. "Pricing Fedwire Daylight Overdrafts." Staff Discussion Paper (January 13), Federal Reserve System.

Kareken, John H., and Neil Wallace. 1978. "Deposit Insurance and Bank Regulation: A Partial Equilibrium Exposition." *Journal of Business* (July).

Lingl, Herbert F. 1981. "Risk Allocaton in International Interbank Electronic Fund Transfers: CHIPS and SWIFT." *Harvard International Law Journal* 22 (3): 621–660.

Mengle, David L. 1985. "Daylight Overdrafts and Payment System Risks." *Economic Review* 71 (May–June): 14–27. Federal Reserve Bank of Richmond.

Mengle, David L., David B. Humphrey, and Bruce J. Summers. 1987. "Intraday Credit: Risk, Value, and Pricing." *Economic Review* 73 (January–February): 3–14. Federal Reserve Bank of Richmond.

Padoa-Schioppa, Tommaso. 1988. "Credit Risks in Payment Systems: The Role of Central Banks." *Economic Bulletin* (February): 64–69. Banca d'Italia.

Rosborough, Bruce, and Michael Urkowitz. 1983. "Meeting the Challenges of Risk Management." *Journal of Commercial Bank Lending* (September): 2–9.

Smoot, Richard L. 1985. "Billion-Dollar Overdrafts: A Payments Risk Challenge." *Business Review* (January–February): 2–12. Federal Reserve Bank of Philadelphia.

Stevens. E. J. 1984. "Risk in Large-Dollar Transfer Systems." *Economic Review* (Fall). Federal Reserve Bank of Cleveland.

White, Lawrence. 1984. *Free Banking in Britain.* New York: Cambridge University Press.

COMMENTARY

by Robert E. Litan

I must warn you at the outset that I am a relative neophyte on payment systems issues. Accordingly, my comments will reflect what amount to "man from Mars" views on the excellent chapter by Professors Faulhaber, Phillips and Santomero.

My first impression is that the authors are certainly not the first to call for some type of pricing mechanism to minimize systemic risks from daylight overdrafts. Many others, both inside and outside the Federal Reserve System, have been urging similar action. But the authors do succeed in giving us a cogent well-made case for pricing.

Their arguments are straightforward; current net debit caps are likely to be inefficient, although we can't know for sure by how much. And because of informational advantages and concerns about private monopoly, a central bank approach to payment clearing is likely to be superior to a fully private system. The authors conclude by urging the Fed to adopt a three-part pricing system, one that would pay interest on reserves, price Fedwire transactions at marginal cost, and charge banks for average daylight overdrafts at the prevailing Federal Funds rate.

Before briefly addressing certain of these suggestions, I want to ask a simple question: Why hasn't the Fed adopted a pricing mechanism before?

While this may appear to some to be a naive question, I think it points

214

to some fundamental issues. The question is perplexing to me because, unlike most other federal agencies, the Fed is filled with economists—arguably the best economists, taken as a group, in the federal government. And as we all know, virtually every well-trained economist has learned to love the virtues of the price system as a mechanism for efficiently allocating resources. When I was working in the federal government, I learned to my dismay that many noneconomists in most other federal agencies did not share this outlook. In the ten years since, it appears much has changed, largely because of the vigorous efforts by the Office of Management and Budget to oversee federal regulatory programs. Why, then, has the federal agency staffed with the most well-trained economists seemingly lagged behind by refusing to embrace a pricing mechanism for minimizing the payment system risks to which it claims to be exposed?

Part of the answer, I believe, lies in the nature of the risks that the Fed assumes in assuring finality on all Fedwire transactions. As the authors point out, if a participating institution is left with an overdraft position at the end of the day, the Fed will be called upon to extend a risk-free loan from the discount window, which can lead to an undesirable—although almost certainly temporary—increase in Federal Reserve credit. Many of us, I suspect, will disagree over whether this is something Federal Reserve officials should lose sleep over.[1] But whatever our attitudes, I think we would all agree that *if* this is a risk worth worrying about, it is likely to be a lot more dangerous if the total overdraft at the end of the day is quite large—say, $5 billion or more—than if it is small.

Of course, it is highly unlikely that the Fed will have to cover a very large systemwide overdraft. But if this event arises, it is more likely to happen because *one bank* has fallen into a substantial net debit position than because *many banks* at the same time have run lesser end-of-day overdrafts. Then one must ask whether *any* pricing system is going to deter the kind of mega-overdraft the Fed fears most. I doubt it. Even if it has to pay a penalty, a bank otherwise likely to end up with a big overdraft at the close of the business day for legitimate or nefarious reasons is still likely to end up with an overdraft unless it is constrained by a quantitative limit.

Of course, the Fed may also be worried about being bled to death by the monetary equivalent of a thousand cuts—many small to medium sized overdrafts run at the same time by numerous institutions. This kind of behavior *could* and probably *would* be efficiently deterred by a pricing system.

Perhaps there is some room for compromise. Why not take advantage of the benefits of *both* a cap system and a pricing mechanism? In brief, why shouldn't the Fed consider implementing a pricing procedure while *at the same time* retaining some level of sender caps? The Faulhaber-Phillips-

Santomero chapter implies that this is desirable, but I would be more explicit. The Fed could start with the existing caps and then either lower them (as it has been doing) or even raise them. Good arguments can be made for movements in both directions. The key point, however, is that the Fed can decide to set the caps at a level low enough to prevent a mega-overdraft but also high enough to allow prices to work their magic under the ceilings.

Now, I want to turn briefly to two of the suggestions advanced in the chapter. First, the authors suggest that the Fed pay interest on reserves. Although they do not discuss this extensively, the argument for paying interest is that it would give banks stronger incentives to avoid daylight overdrafts. The authors do not clearly distinguish, however, between required reserves and clearing balances. Clearly, paying interest on the first is more ambitious than paying interest on the second. That distinction should be noted.

But even if interest were to be paid only on clearing balances, it is useful to keep in mind that a pricing system can work with sticks as well as with carrots. That is, if the Fed were to charge banks for running daylight over-drafts, it is not clear how much additional risk reduction would be achieved by paying banks interest on their clearing balances as well. Put another way, just because the Fed may decide to charge interest for intraday credit does not automatically mean that it must pay interest on positive credit balances, although doing so would certainly ease any bank opposition to a pricing mechanism.

The payment of interest on required reserves raises much larger issues. Clearly, by paying interest on reserves the Fed would lose most, if not all, of the profit it earns and returns to the Treasury each year. Indeed, it might even need an annual appropriation from Congress to operate. And if this were to happen, I suspect Congress might try to exert greater control over the Fed than it does now. I doubt whether many in the Fed would say that the benefits of reducing payment risk by paying interest on reserves is worth any loss in the agency's independence that such a change in Fed policy might entail.

Second, the authors suggest that the Fed charge banks the federal funds rate on their average daily overdrafts. Since federal funds are currently extended for about 16 hours—from 5 p.m. at the end of one day until 9 a.m. until the following morning—this proposal effectively trans-lates into charging banks one-half the daily federal funds rate on the average daily overdrafts (since Fedwire is open for eight hours).[2]

This solution clearly has the virtue of simplicity. And because it is based on the market-determined federal funds rate for overnight borrowing, it very closely resembles what a market would charge for intraday credit.

However, a noteworthy problem the authors do not discuss concerns the practical difficulties of implementing a pricing mechanism. As Humphrey and Dowden (1988) have noted, there is a 9 percent risk that at any time one of the Federal Reserve banks could experience a computer outage. Such a problem, if it arises, can delay the receipt of payments and hence artificially increase measured overdrafts at some banks. As a result, any system that charges the hourly equivalent of the daily federal funds rate is likely to end up overcharging many banks.

Since computer systems are unlikely ever to be perfect, one way to meet this problem is to compromise by agreeing to adopt a somewhat lower price for all overdrafts. The Fed could do so experimentally. That is, why not start with a price method that yields an average price at the lower end of a plausible range and then be prepared to ratchet the rate higher if the reaction of bank participants warrants? For example, suppose that the Fed were to start with the existing rate on day loans used by broker and dealers to purchase securities prior to delivery and payment by customers. Say that rate is 100 basis points. Then observe how that rate affects the volume of overdrafts. If there is no perceptible change, the rate is likely to be too low. Then use a method yielding a somewhat higher rate. I can't tell you when to stop increasing the rate; that depends on the Fed's tolerance for overdrafts. But, at a minimum, the experimentation approach would allow the Fed to see how overdrafts react to price signals.

It might be objected, of course, that a commitment to experimentation would lead to uncertainty among Fedwire participants; the reaction of these participants to any price or debit ceiling would therefore not reflect equilibrium behavior. There is something to this objection. However, given the rapid changes that are occuring with technology, banks and other financial institutions should already be accustomed to changing their practices and strategies. In this environment, any changes by the Fed in its prices or ceilings on intraday credit should fall within the noise level of other changes that are now affecting bank behavior.

Finally, while I tend to agree with the authors that a fully private clearing system poses a potential problem of monopoly, I think readers would like to see a more thorough discussion of why the monopoly problem would be so much more serious in the banking sphere than it is in the securities and options markets, where clearing now is fully private.

Notes

1. If the bank running the overdraft is merely illiquid, then it can be counted upon to repay the discount window loan the next day or soon thereafter. If the borrowing bank turns

out to be insolvent, then at worst the Federal Reserve will suffer a loss (assuming that its collateral is not perfected), which will be reflected in a temporary inflation of total bank reserves. This addition to reserves, however, can be gradually offset later.

2. Mengle, Humphrey, and Summers (1987) have proposed a similar pricing solution. Under one of their options, they suggest that the Fed charge one-eighth of the Federal Funds rate on any particular overdraft, on the grounds that the average overdraft lasts about three hours.

References

Humphrey, David B., and Pat Dowden. 1988. "Risk Management Techniques." Draft manuscript.

Mengle, David L., David B. Humphrey, and Bruce J. Summers. 1987. "Intraday credit: Risk, Value, and Pricing." *Economic Review* 73 (January–February: 3–14. Federal Reserve Bank of Richmond.

III PRIVATE AND PUBLIC ROLES IN THE PAYMENT MECHANISM

The chapters in part III focus on the role of the Federal Reserve in the payment system. The first, by Donald Tucker, concerns the public policy and competitive implications of the Federal Reserve serving as both regulator and competitive supplier of payment services. The second, by Marvin Goodfriend, concerns how these roles, along with the provision of deposit insurance by the FDIC, have been used to justify regulatory intervention in banking over time. While such a dual role has existed since the inception of the Federal Reserve System in 1914, the past relationship between the Federal Reserve and private banks was more benign. Initially, payment services were provided free to Federal Reserve member banks, partly to compensate banks for holding idle reserve balances and partly to promote the demise of nonpar checking. Nonpar checking involved paying less than the face value of check, ostensibly to pay for collection costs.

With the advent of priced payment services in the early 1980s, the Federal Reserve and large correspondent banks both competed fui the payment business of smaller institutions. Their payment market shares came under increased pressure as new local check clearinghouses came into being. Consequently, some in the banking industry have suggested that provision of payment services has no place in a quasigovernment agency, particularly one that also regulates many private-sector suppliers of these services. Tucker does not endorse this view, although he cautions that the potential for abuse is real. On balance, he feels that the competition can provide important efficiency and accessibility benefits for payment system participants but emphasizes that this should be done in as open and fair a manner as possible.

Commentary on the Tucker paper is provided by Robert List-field, who presents a different view of Federal Reserve involvement in the payment system. To Listfield, the goals of maintaining efficiency and providing open access for a diverse set of payment users may largely be obtained through regulatory oversight as opposed to active involvement as a service supplier. While there are some public goods aspects to Federal Reserve involvement, these would appear to justify only a small amount of direct involvement rather than the high level of participation that exists today.

Additional commentary is provided by Gerald Faulhaber. He raises the issue of how regulatory and legal oversight has worked to ensure efficiency and open access in telephone communications market after the breakup of AT&T. Given the experience in this area, he suggests (contrary to a suggestion made by Listfield) direct Federal Reserve involvement as a payment supplier is likely the preferred method to achieve certain social goals.

The chapter by Marvin Goodfriend traces the historical development of banking and payment systems in terms of trade-offs between accepting some credit risk in return for obtaining greater economic efficiency. He suggests that this trade-off was behind the substitution of banknotes for commodity money, the evolution of institutions providing credit to facilitate exchange, and the development of private multilateral clearing arrangements among banks. All of these cost-reducing institutional changes necessarily led to some absorption of credit risk by the general public and those entities supplying payment services. With the establishment of the Federal Reserve, and especially the FDIC and its nonactuarially priced deposit insurance, the credit risks previously faced by the public have been greatly reduced. However, this comes with a different type of cost, namely the ability or need for these agencies to regulate or intervene in banking and financial markets to protect themselves and the public from the risks inherent in the system. In this manner, there is an important public policy link between bank and payment system regulation and the conduct of certain aspects of monetary policy by the Federal Reserve.

Commentary on the Goodfriend paper is provided by Clifford Smith. He endorses the view that contract theory can provide a useful framework to understand the trade-offs involved in the historical development of money and banking in the United States. However, he feels that banks are not necessarily different from other types of institutions and ascribes the differences we do see to a history of regulation that has served to reduce risks previously taken on by the public at large in order to obtain certain efficiencies from the payment system.

The final chapter in this book, the Conference Summary, is by Manuel Johnson. He highlights the Federal Reserve's concern with improving payment system efficiency while continuing to reduce systemic risk. In the efficiency area, something of a dilemma exists. For many applications, it appears that electronic payments can be cheaper than continued reliance on checks. Yet because checks are the preferred payment instrument (after cash), the public and Congress have exerted continued pressure to improve the check system even though it is unlikely to ever achieve the cost efficiency of most electronic applications.

With respect to payment risk, specifically daylight overdrafts on large-dollar wire transfer networks, it is likely that further efforts in this area will be forthcoming. There is support for arrangements, such as pricing of Fedwire overdrafts and settlement finality on CHIPS, that shift more of these risks to the private-sector beneficiaries of the payment system. If the risks can be more clearly assigned to participants, the presumption is that behavior will be altered and risk will be reduced to more manageable levels.

6 THE CONFLICTING ROLES OF THE FEDERAL RESERVE AS REGULATOR AND SERVICES PROVIDER IN THE U.S. PAYMENT SYSTEM

Donald P. Tucker

I want to talk on a fairly abstract level about the mix of public policy objectives in the payment system and about conflict of interest at the Fed. I think the Fed has some major rethinking to do on both a policy level and a procedural level to come to grips with the fundamental conflict it has over the issue of private-sector competition in payment services.

Private Competition as a Goal

The Monetary Control Act of 1980 set the requirement that the Fed must charge prices for its payment services based on the full direct and indirect costs of providing those services and must make these services available to all depository institutions. That language is now incorporated into the Federal Reserve Act, and it has virtually revolutionized the delivery of payment system services.

The legislation has been widely interpreted as expressing Congress's intent that private-sector providers of payment services should have an opportunity to compete directly with the Fed, an opportunity that would

223

not be available if the Fed were to charge less than full cost for certain services in order to suppress competition.

The Federal Reserve also understood this as one of the objectives, as indicated by the testimony of Chairman G. William Miller before the House Banking Committee in 1978.

> Our proposal on pricing is to price competitively, but not to undercut the market. Our view is that it is healthy to have the Federal Reserve provide services so as to insure a secure system of payments and the basic services that are essential to a safe central bank. But we also look with favor upon the growth of optional, innovative, cost-effective, techniques for handling services. And we think pricing would bring about that trend and would probably increase participation in the private sector in the performance of the services.

It is important to note, however, that Congress did not mention private competition explicitly in the 1980 Act. The Fed, consequently, does not have a clear legislative mandate to encourage or foster private competition in payment services. It is thus possible to suggest a different interpretation—that perhaps Congress was mostly concerned with cutting the public subsidy of payment services and leveling the playing field between Fed member institutions and nonmembers, and that perhaps it did not care so much about private competition.

In view of this ambiguity, what should be the fundamental policy objectives of the Fed in the payments area, and where should private competition fit in?

The first objective, of course, is the *absolute reliability* of the system, so that the private sector can count on its payments going through without concern about the risk of breakdowns in the system. The second objective, I would presume, is maintaining and continually advancing the *efficiency* of the system, in order to minimize the resource costs of carrying out payment transactions, and closely related to this is promptness, so that paying and receiving parties can go about their business with minimum delay from waiting for the completion of funds transfers. The third objective, broadly speaking, is *fairness*, or *equity*. Access to the payments networks should be open to all qualified parties on an equal basis.

Competition, per se, does not stand alone as another objective in this list. It is merely a means to an end, but it is a critically important means to achieving the efficiency objective.

The reason competition is so important is that the Fed has no monopoly on technical proficiency in the payment area, nor is it immune from the laziness and insensitivity that set in when a producer enjoys a monopoly without serious threat of competitors. Fostering and accommodating private competition that would challenge and potentially displace the Fed's own payment services should therefore be a fundamental element of the Fed's policy strategy for achieving maximum efficiency in the payment system.

I do not mean to suggest that the Fed should step aside for private competitors. The Fed's operational role is sound and deserves to be developed to its maximum potential. I am not advocating an ideological trip into the fantasy realm where the public sector can never do things right. In fact, the public sector—in this case the Fed—does many things very well indeed, but the optimum for achieving efficiency in payment services is a mix of public and private, with open competition between them.

Private Alternatives to Enhance System Reliability

Private-sector participation, firmly regulated by the Fed, also deserves to be regarded as enhancing the reliability of the system in important respects, because it contributes both *decoupled operational redundancy* and a competitive spur to achieving higher standards of reliability at the Fed.

The Fed is just as fallible in achieving system reliability as it is in achieving maximum efficiency, and it needs that competitive spur. Anecdotal reports suggest, in fact, that the Fed has a serious problem of recurring breakdowns on Fedwire and a significant vulnerability to prolonged and possibly disastrous outages. I would be very surprised, moreover, if the Fed did not also have its share of breakdown problems in processing checks and automated clearinghouse (ACH) transactions.

The Fed can obviously enhance its service reliability to some degree by backing up its own facilities with surplus operational capability, if it chooses, but that is not what I would call decoupled redundancy. Extra phone lines, backup computer facilities and power supplies, and so on don't do any good if something happens that takes the whole system down—a software glitch, for example, or a facilities fire—because the extra capacity is still all coupled into the same system.

For this reason, the overall reliability of interconnected networks is substantially enhanced by the availability of alternative processing units that function independently of each other—that are decoupled, in other words. Private processors competing with the Fed naturally provide the kind of decoupled redundancy that is needed.

This is in addition, of course, to the obvious incentive effects of competition to improve service reliability so as to attract customers. Customers—particularly in payment services—want reliability and predictability and will go to the processor that stands out in that regard. Look at what has happened in the delivery services where the Post Office has had competition, in packages and overnight parcels, and compare that with the reliability of first-class letter mail, where the Post Office keeps its monopoly. The first-class mail service is unreliable because of no competition.

I am sure the Fed, for its own reasons, does not want to fall into the Post Office morass. The most important thing the Fed can do to avoid that over the long run is to include private-sector competition within its vision of the ideal market structure in priced services.

The Fed's Anticompetitive Mindset

The Fed has not in the past exhibited this attitude, however. In fact, the Fed has tended toward a marked anticompetitive mindset, which has generated a very ambivalent attitude toward private competitors.

This was evident in 1983 when hearings were held to examine some of the correspondent banks' complaints about their difficulties competing with the Fed in check processing. At no time did Fed officials speak positively about the role of private competition in contributing innovation and a spur to increased efficiency. The attitude at that time appeared to be that private competitors must be tolerated so as to keep Congress happy but that the Fed would take no initiative, beyond the bare cost recovery requirements of the Monetary Control Act, to encourage private processors.

Had the Fed felt supportive of the role of private processors, the 1984 policy statement on "The Federal Reserve in the Payment System" would have been the natural place to have expressed this formally. No such support is expressed, however. This statement identifies as one of the Fed's responsibilities "a fundamental commitment to competitive fairness," but it offers no elaboration as to what this means or how it is to be carried out. At best, the Fed is saying it will try to be good and not to throw its weight around to drive competitors out of business, but that certainly does not represent any kind of ringing endorsement of the idea that active private participation serves the broader public interest.

I see encouraging signs that this attitude may be changing, but it is still very deep-rooted at the Fed because it is so inextricably bound up with the issue of systemic risk.

The Fed is very risk-averse, which is entirely proper, given its mission of stabilizing financial markets and the economy generally. But the problem is that pursuing this goal of controlling systemic risk also provides a wonderful cloak for hiding a strong anticompetitive bias. It is such a good disguise that I think many Fed people really believe their own rhetoric about how dangerous it would be for the financial system if we accommodate this or that demand of the private sector.

A particularly good example of this was the strong efforts of the Federal

Reserve Board a couple of years ago to prevent commercial firms from gaining access to Fedwire through nonbank banks. The rhetoric was all about the dangers to the financial system, but that risk argument never did ring true. From a congressional perspective, it looked like the Fed's dismay over a bunch of new competitors moving into some key banking markets.

Another illustration that shows the breadth of the anticompetitive policy attitudes at the Fed over the years has been the Fed's hostility to public disclosure of adverse facts about banking corporations. Statistics on overdue and problem loans, which the regulators get routinely, should not be revealed for individual banks, since the public could misinterpret such information—or so the Fed has always argued. And heaven forbid that the public should know about disciplinary actions or adverse supervisory steps against individual banks! And just think of the dangers to financial markets if banks had to mark their long-term fixed-rate assets to market to reflect current interest rates.

Such information would be the raw material for keener competition among banks, and keen competition in a crowded and heavily regulated market may cause casualties. The Fed, for this reason, has always tended to be ambivalent at best toward competition in banking markets, and thus the anticompetitive mindset I mentioned extends far beyond the priced services area.

Conflict of Interest

It is also extremely important in this context for the Fed to be open in acknowledging the direct and serious internal conflict of interest it faces. I refer, of course, to the conflict between pursuing the safety and efficiency goals wherever they may lead, on the one hand, and protecting the Fed's own operations in the Reserve Banks from competitive pressures, on the other. It is very convenient and tempting to argue that the overriding importance of safety and stability requires that the Fed retain operating control of the principal payment services itself, especially electronic wire transfer services, but internally, behind its closed doors, the Fed needs to be honest enough to continually question whether its policy judgment is being swayed by a narrower self-interest in protecting its existing Reserve Bank operations.

In my judgment, the Fed's 1984 policy statement on "Standards Related to Priced-Service Activities of the Federal Reserve Banks" does not reflect the honesty that is needed. This document states that the Fed "has exercised care to avoid actual or apparent conflict" between its role as a provider of services and its role as a regulator of the payment mechanism.

This is a fiction. The Fed cannot avoid that conflict. It is inherent in the dual role of the System

Conflicts of interest, per se, need not be destructive, and acknowledging the existence of this conflict in the Fed system does not imply that anything improper is going on. It is only a warning signal, but it is a warning that if ignored or dismissed as irrelevant may in fact seriously corrupt the policy process.

What Should the Fed Do?—Procedural Reforms

What should the Fed do to clean up its act? How can the Fed enlist the full potential of private competition for enhancing efficiency in the payment networks while still fulfilling its equally important responsibilities for safety and open access?

The most important things the Fed can do, I think, are procedural in nature. First, the Fed should issue a clear public commitment—and should adopt a formal policy statement expressing the commitment—to maintaining a regulatory environment that is consciously supportive of competition in payment services and that seeks to encourage the availability of private-sector alternatives. Any such public commitment and policy statement should place the Fed squarely behind the idea that active private participation in payment services serves the broader public interest.

Procedurally, the job is not done just by issuing a policy statement, however. Any such policy statement is effectively a dead letter unless the commitment is carried out internally by making it part of the Board and Reserve Bank culture, a part of the commonly understood framework for addressing all policy questions related to payment services.

How do you do that? That's tough, and I can't give a complete answer, but it clearly needs to start with senior officials both at the Board and in the Reserve Banks speaking out, especially internally, about the positive contribution of private-sector involvement, even when it seriously challenges existing Reserve Bank operations.

A second procedural step the Fed needs to take is to establish formal rules for coping with its internal conflict of interest in payment services, perhaps something akin to "Chinese Wall" procedures. In particular, operations and regulatory policy for priced services need to be handled by totally separate staffs. Moreover, the policy staff should be required, when preparing background and briefing papers for policy decisions, to state explicitly the nature of the conflicts posed by each issue.

In a sense, what is needed is a "sunshine" approach. The most insidious danger, I think, is pretending there is no conflict and ignoring the issue. The best way to enable balanced decisions to be made is a formal policy of bringing conflicts into the open, so that senior policy officials and Board members are continually forced to confront them.

Let me also say a word here about the idea of a separate autonomous payment corporation, for I see this as a possible procedural response to the conflict-of-interest problem. Setting up a separate corporation would, in effect, be an extreme form of the "Chinese Wall."

At present, I don't think it is necessary for the Fed to go that far. Internal conflict situations can be handled adequately by responsible organizations without such drastic measures. Nevertheless, it is important to continue to think of the payment corporation as a useful conceptual model, because it delineates cleanly the procedural objective of keeping the payment operations totally separate from policy making.

Substantive Issues Affecting Private Competition

There are also important substantive issues facing the Fed that come down ultimately to issues of what climate the Fed will establish toward private competition.

First, the Fed needs to take a fresh look, in light of its prospective new commitment to be open to private-sector competition, at whether it is still subsidizing its own service offerings in subtle ways, contrary to the congressional mandate in the Monetary Control Act.

For example, is there an implicit subsidy—possibly a substantial one— in the fact that the Fed absorbs all the risk of settlement failure in Fedwire by guaranteeing payment finality? There is no direct operating cost of providing this guarantee, but implicitly the Fed has committed substantial capital as backing for this guarantee, to cover its cost for any settlement losses, just as a competing private network would have to commit substantial capital to provide a credible private guarantee, and I do not believe this element of implicit capital is reflected in the Fed's PSAF (private sector adjustment factor) at present.

Similarly, the Fed needs to reconsider what subsidies are implicit in its internalization of risk in ACH settlement and whether this constitutes unfair competition against private ACH providers.

Another longstanding subsidy issue that continues to trouble me has to do with the absence of any provision in the PSAF computation for capital required for cash items in the process of collection, comparable to what the private sector has to maintain. The regulators' present capital standards for banks include cash items as a component of assets against which adequate capital must be maintained, and thus any private institution competing with the Fed in check processing has a cost for the capital maintained against cash items in the process of collection (CIPC) assets arising from its processing operations. The failure of the Fed to make a corresponding provision for capital in its PSAF would thus appear to represent an improper subsidy, contrary to the requirements of the Monetary Control Act.

Moreover, the joint agency proposal on risk-based capital guidelines for commercial banks also provides that cash items in process of collection would be part of the risk-adjusted assets against which capital would have to be maintained. They would be assigned to category 3, with a risk weight of 20 percent. Accordingly, even if the currently proposed risk-based standards should become the primary or sole capital standard, private institutions will still be required to bear a certain cost for the capital that will be required in proportion to their CIPC assets.

Another PSAF issue has to do with the fact that the Fed, to the best of my knowledge, has never responded substantively to the 1983 criticism of the National Payments System Coalition concerning the methodology for computing the rate of return on capital in the PSAF computation. The coalition argued persuasively that the implicit rate of return in the Fed's PSAF should be a "required" rate of return, based on what the financial markets require private-sector investments to yield, and not merely the actual accounting return on book capital obtained by some model firms.

There are difficult conceptual issues involved in determining which approach represents the more appropriate way to compute the Fed's PSAF, but the fact that the coalition's approach would yield higher prices for Fed services certainly does not make it wrong. If the required-return methodology is the correct one, then the present approach continues to represent a significant Fed subsidy to all its priced services, and so the Fed owes the public and Congress a coherent and balanced analysis on that issue. Better later than never!

Finally, the Fed's attitude of supportiveness toward private-sector competition is beginning to undergo a wholesale test in the ACH arena. I do not want to comment on how the negotiations over interdistrict net settlement should come out, or what terms the Fed should set for delivery and availability deadlines for private ACH processors; I simply cannot absorb all the technical issues at this point to have any recommendations. It is clear, however, that this may become the most active area of what could be called "creative tension" between the Fed and the private sector in payment services, and it will be a major testing ground of whether the Fed intends to implement the principle of encouraging private-sector service providers whose presence will improve the efficiency of the system.

Cautions, Conclusions, and the Role of Congress

As I have said, I am not looking for the Fed to step aside and adopt the opposite attitude that the private sector can do it better than the Fed, nor do I want the Fed to downgrade the priority it has always placed on safety, reliability, and open access. Those are absolutely essential objectives, and the Fed needs to continue to regulate both its own operations and all private service providers with a firm hand to ensure their compliance with necessary reliability and fairness standards.

Moreover, the Fed's effort to meet those other objectives will necessarily limit the opportunities for private participants to some degree, and that is a regulatory judgment that Congress has always intended the Fed to exercise, I believe. The objective is not more private participation for its own sake but rather a scrupulous pursuit of efficiency and innovation from all sources, public and private.

What role should the Fed expect Congress to play in delineating the proper role of the private sector in payment services? Not a large one, I think. In fact, it would be a cop-out for the Fed to say that more direction is needed from Congress at this point.

Why? Because the objectives discussed here should be the Fed's own objectives for the payment system. I am not talking about how the Fed should behave so as to implement some congressional whim or explicit congressional policy. I am talking about responsible public management of a unique responsibility where the ultimate objectives are not in dispute.

There is great talent in the Fed system at this point, and enormous Fed energy has gone into bringing the payment system to its present state of operational capability. It is an impressive accomplishment. But the time has come to bite the bullet on private competition, which is something the Fed has not effectively done before now. For a good public agency, which the Fed is, that should be an interesting and inviting challenge—and I hope the Fed will always view it in that light.

COMMENTARY
by Robert J. Listfield

In providing comments on the chapter by Don Tucker, I believe it is necessary to depart somewhat from the chapter itself and to provide an understanding of why there is Federal Reserve competition with the private sector and what steps can be taken to ensure fair competition. It is fundamental to the discussion of the role of the Federal Reserve in the payment system to understand why the Fed has an operational role in the first place. Tucker's chapter appears to start with the premise that the Fed should have an operational role (or at least he does not argue against such a role). Indeed, there are very few examples in the United States outside of banking where such direct private-sector versus public-sector competition exists. Furthermore, many foreign central banks have little, if any, direct competitive involvement in their countries' payment system operations, other than to facilitate settlement.

Tucker notes that the Fed's fundamental policy objectives in the payment system are to ensure reliability, efficiency, fairness, and equitable access to the payment system. While I do not disagree with these objectives, it strikes me that such objectives differ little from the Fed's policy objectives in all areas of banking, yet the Fed does not compete directly

232

with the private sector in making loans or taking deposits. Rather, the Fed uses its regulatory authority in general banking matters to ensure safety and soundness, while using both regulatory and operational means to achieve the same objectives for payment services. Without a clear understanding of why such an operational presence is (or is not) necessary, it is difficult to address adequately the issue of the proper role of the Federal Reserve.

The Need for the Federal Reserve in the Provision of Payment Services

I believe that the large number of depository institutions (commercial banks, savings banks, savings and loans, and credit unions), coupled with the expansive geography of the United States, makes it virtually impossible to have an efficient and equitable payment system without either public-sector participation or heavy regulation. Further, without the Federal Reserve's presence in the payment system, small remotely located depository institutions would not have affordable or efficient access to the nation's bank collection system, and as a consequence, trade in these areas would suffer. Most other countries lack the geographical breadth or the fragmented banking system to require a public-sector operations provider.

The Fed's part is vital in the payment system for the following reasons:

1. The Fed's maintenance of reserve accounts, which provides the basis for payment system settlement. Because of the large number of banking entities, national settlement via correspondent banking is probably unworkable.
2. The Fed's nationwide presence, which is unavailable to the private sector because of current regulatory restrictions on geographical presence.
3. The Fed's economies of scale (owing in part to the settlement capability and nationwide presence) that make the centralized provision of fixed-cost functions, such as check transportation or data communications, more cost-efficient.
4. The perception among many banks that the Fed, more than a private-sector supplier would, operate fairly and equitably and is a "trusted intermediary."

One can add the Fed's roles as regulator and competitor to this list of reasons for Fed involvement. I do not believe the Fed must be an active participant in the payment system in order to regulate it, but there are advantages: if a regulator is a participant, it will better understand the functions it regulates.

The Private Sector's Role in the Provision of Payment Services

Considering all these advantages, some might conclude that the payment system represents a "natural monopoly" like the postal service and that, there should be *no* private-sector competition. While the payment mechanism exhibits certain characteristics of a natural monopoly, most observers would agree, as Don Tucker stresses, that payment system efficiency is enhanced by having private-sector competition, not only because active competition almost always spurs greater efficiency than a monopoly but also because the private sector provides a much needed augmentation to Federal Reserve services.

What the private sector provides that the Fed cannot is the customized and individualized local service often needed by payment participants. The Fed's large size, limited locations (e.g., 48 check-processing offices), and need to provide equitable access to all users precludes it from being as flexible as the private sector.

Thus, in many respects, the Fed operates as the major nationwide wholesaler of payment services, with some retail-type trade (smaller banks). The private sector tends to act as a retail provider, offering more localized and flexible services. Larger correspondents offer both retail- and wholesale-type services, particularly with respect to check clearing. Other private-sector, firms, such as CHIPS (Clearing House Interbank Payment System), SWIFT (Society for Worldwide Interbank Financial Telecommunications), and private-sector automated clearinghouse (ACH) operators, also compete with the Fed with wholesale-type services, although not with as comprehensive a market coverage.

Thus, I start with the premise that the most efficient payment system for the United States is one that involves both the private sector and the Federal Reserve. This duality will inevitably cause tension, when one party ventures into the other's primary territory and because the motivations of the two competitors are, or at least should be, different.

Motivations and Objectives in Payment System Services

For the private sector, the motivation for taking part in the payment system is profit. Thus, problems arise with a dominant competitor like the

Fed, which has no real profit motive and which enjoys the previously noted advantages of size, settlement, scale economies, and so on.

The Fed's major motivation for being in the payment system should be, as Tucker noted, efficiency. Any other motivations, such as maximizing profit or market share, are inconsistent with the duality I talked about, because if the Fed were driven purely by profit or market share, there would be no justification for public-sector involvement as there are plenty of private-sector firms with the same objectives.

Because of the Monetary Control Act requirement that the Fed match costs and revenues, the Fed does have some profit and market share goals. It is if and when these goals take precedence over the efficiency goal that the rationale for the Fed's involvement can and should be questioned. The very reasons why I believe the Fed must be active in the payment system—settlement capability, nationwide presence, economies of scale, and trusted intermediary—provide such a huge competitive advantage that abusing such advantages for the sake of profits or market share could wipe out any potential private-sector competitor and, in the long term, do damage to the efficiency of the payment system.

Does this mean that the Fed has to bend over backwards to avoid using its natural advantages so as to artificially prop up private-sector competition? In my opinion that would not be in the best interest of payment system efficiency either. However, I feel very strongly that the Fed should in no way abuse its natural advantages to the detriment of its sole justification for being in the payment system—to promote efficiency.

In his chapter, Tucker argues that one reason for the Fed to encourage private-sector participation in the payment system is to ensure reliability by providing operational redundancy. While actual or potential private-sector competition provides the Federal Reserve with the incentive to maintain highly reliable payment services, I do not believe that the Fed should promote private-sector competition simply in order to enhance "decoupled operational redundancy."

The provision of payment services includes three distinct components: a transaction-processing component; a delivery component, such as air or ground couriers for checks and data communications for ACH and wire transfer; and a settlement component. In the case of check processing, some transaction processing for which the Fed has no real natural advantage and some delivery components can be decoupled from settlement (via some form of net settlement or correspondent settlement arrangement). In the case of wire transfer and, to a certain extent, ACH, it is very difficult to separate the settlement function from the entire process. Thus, it has always been difficult for the private sector to provide the type of real-time funds transfer capability offered by the Fed.

Any inability to access the Federal Reserve for settlement would have major adverse consequences on the payment system, particularly for wire transfer because of the enormous dollar values. Thus, while the private sector augments Federal Reserve services, it does not and cannot duplicate all Federal Reserve services, for all payment participants. Therefore, I do not believe the private sector can provide sufficient "decoupled redundancy" to enable the Fed to provide any lesser standard of reliability and service than would be required if it were the sole provider.

Federal Reserve Performance in Carrying Out Its Role

Has the Fed abused its natural advantages? In my opinion, the Fed has done a good job of restraining a natural impulse of every good manager to seek expanded market share. However, there have been what I would consider examples of overaggressive pursuit of market share. These actions are perhaps no more serious than what a typical private-sector supplier considers routine, but that is not the standard by which the Fed should be judged. The Fed, given its natural advantages, must take exceedingly great pains not to use such advantages to promote its competitive posture. Some examples are perhaps in order.

Two of the Fed's largest natural advantages are its settlement capabilities and its transportation scale economies. Many Fed offices' check collection fine-sort service (a service often used by large correspondents to compete with the Fed for retail business) appear to be priced well above the true cost for these services. If the Fed were totally interested in payment system efficiency, such services would be priced closer to their actual average costs.

Another example is the pricing of the Fed's mixed cash letter product, which is clearly a retail-type product that competes with private correspondents. Many Fed offices price this produce at margins clearly below those of other, more wholesale-type products. These pricing techniques can be justified from a market share perspective but are questionable from an efficiency standpoint.

The two examples cited are situations in which the Fed has used "market sensitive" pricing rather than pricing based on average cost. It is, of course, very difficult to know the true average cost of services that utilize shared resources, such as space, equipment, transportation, and settlement capabilities. Therefore, the Fed could probably provide good rationale for its allocations. I bring these examples up not because an abuse can be proved but because it appears to reflect an attitude at some

Federal Reserve Banks that being competitive in the delivery of services is a more important goal than is promoting efficiency. Certainly, to many outside observers, the perception of the Fed is that it is more concerned with market share than it is with promoting efficiency. This probably cannot be proved or disproved, but the perception is, I believe, based upon some degree of reality.

The Private-Sector Adjustment Factor

Tucker discussed in his chapter the perceived inadequacies of the private sector adjustment factor (PSAF), which is designed to capture the profits that would be required by private-sector firms, thereby placing the competition on an equitable basis. Generally, I would concur with his observations regarding the provision of an implied cost of capital to support cash items in the process of collection and the need for adequate return for the risk associated with providing settlement finality (although imputing a cost for such risk is an impossible task).

I would, however, like to approach the PSAF from a different viewpoint. The Fed's PSAF model attempts to build a PSAF based upon a return on equity. One can find many flaws with what is included and not included, but in the private sector there is a general belief that PSAF is too low. I do not think that minor adjustments in the required rate of return rather than the actual accounting rate of return will change this view.

My concern over the PSAF results from the relatively low profit margin implied by the PSAF. The Federal Reserve's 1987 priced services report shows a target return on equity of $29.3 million on a pre-tax cost base (production expenses and imputed costs) of $559.5 million. Adjusting for taxes, the target profit margin (or markup on costs) is only 7.9 percent. Other than supermarkets, there are very few firms that price with a pre-tax sales margin of less than 8 percent, especially considering the risks inherent in the payment services business. To put this in perspective, my review of several manufacturing and service firms showed a margin of 11–15 percent. A review of money center and regional banks shows a pre-tax income to total noninterest expenses in the range of 20–45 percent. *I believe that a markup-over-cost model is a more realistic model* for payment services than the inputed return-on-equity model used by the Fed, and certainly one more often used by private-sector correspondents. Indeed, when correspondent banks price payment services, they tend to do so based upon cost markup, not upon return on equity.

Even if the return-on-equity model were to be used, certain modifications should be made. I agree with Don Tucker that adequate capital should be imputed for cash items in the process of collection, especially in light of the risk-based capital standards. I also question whether adequate costs are being imputed for account maintenance, as, I believe, some accounting costs are considered part of the cost base for nonpriced central bank services rather than priced services (a luxury that private-sector firms do not have). Also, there should be (if it is not present) an imputed FDIC insurance cost, reserve cost, cost of funds, and capital cost for the value of balances that would have to be held between Federal Reserve Banks for interdistrict settlement purposes to equalize for how such transactions take place by private-sector firms.

Social Engineering

I would classify social engineering as an attempt to produce "desirable" social behavior. The Federal Reserve, from time to time, tinkers with this notion, particularly as it relates to encouraging the conversion from paper forms of payment to electronic forms. Many studies have been performed to show how electronic payments have lower costs to society than paper-based systems and therefore should be encouraged. While the lower social cost conclusions may be valid, there is little evidence that either the banking industry or the ultimate payment users (primarily corporations and consumers) wish to convert many of their payments from paper to electronics.

It seems to me that the Federal Reserve should proceed with caution when and if it attempts to artificially raise or restrict payment system demand in order to bring about a desired social change in payment behavior. Although this issue was not really addressed by Don Tucker, it seems that the role of the Fed as an agent for change is one that needs some of resolution.

Certainly, the Fed has served as a catalyst for many desirable changes in payment practices, such as the elimination of non-par banking and the promotion of MICR. Thus, it would be unfair and perhaps unwise to attempt to restrict the Fed totally from attempts at social engineering. However, given the Fed's awesome power in the payment area, and the competitive environment that it is now in, it might be useful to provide certain limits on the Fed as an active change agent (when such change is inconsistent with prevailing market forces). Certainly, I believe, an appropriate limit would be to require the Fed to work openly with private-sector industry leaders when contemplating such changes and to make such changes only when there is a clear industry consensus for such actions.

Conclusions

There are several conclusions I have reached regarding the Fed's role in the payment system. Some I have tried to justify in this chapter. Others, because of space considerations, I will merely assert.

1.   The dual system of public- and private-sector payment system activities is vital to maintaining efficiency in the United States, which means an ongoing role for the Fed (or substitute public-sector entity) in the payment system.

2.   Like it or not, the Monetary Control Act, which required the Fed to recover costs plus margin, placed the Fed and the private sector in competitive roles. Prior to the Act, the roles were at least as much supportive as competitive.

3.   It is inevitable that Federal Reserve payment system managers would tend to concern themselves with market share, growth, and profitability goals because it would be impossible to attract and maintain good managers without these or other tangible goals, and because with certain fixed costs in the provision of payment services, overall cost efficiency may be enhanced by attracting more volume.

4.   The Fed has certain natural advantages that not only justify its having a role in the payment system but also would allow it to dominate the system if abused. (To be fair, the private sector also has advantages, such as its ability to offer different prices and service levels to different customers and its ability to "skim the cream" and leave the Fed, which must handle everything, with the more expensive business. For example, some years ago, there was talk of large, automated banks forming an ACH for items between themselves, relying on the Fed to handle the low-volume, nonautomated receivers. Clearly, this would have raised the Fed's average cost and perhaps eliminated the ACH as a cost-effective vehicle for reaching small banks.)

5.   The existence of the Federal Reserve's natural advantages should *only* be used to promote payment system efficiency and not market share, growth, profitability, or other motives more commonly identified with the private sector.

6.   A separate public-sector corporation, as mentioned by Don Tucker, Gerald Corrigan, and others, is not, in my opinion, the answer. If

the separation between the corporation and the Fed were too great, some of the logical reasons for having a public-sector presence in the first place would be removed. If the separation were not great enough, the same problems that the proposal aims to correct would still exist. It is the existence of the reserve balances, more than anything else, that justifies the Fed's role in the payment system. In my view, to separate the balances from the provider will not work. Similarly, separating the payment system regulators from operating staff, as suggested by Tucker, is not, in my view, desirable, as it is beneficial to have regulators knowledgeable about the function they regulate.

7.   It should not be up to the Fed to *promote* private-sector competition. In my view, there is no way to do so without intentionally impairing payment system efficiency. For example, if the Fed can provide something more efficiently, why should it arbitrarily raise prices or reduce service simply to let the private sector do it less efficiently? Similarly, if the private sector can perform a function at the same cost, but with more risk or at lower service levels, why should the Fed withdraw? Furthermore, I do not believe the private sector needs nor even particularly wants such *preferential* treatment. What it wants is not to be handed the business but a *fair* chance to earn it. Finally, I do not think one can establish a procompetitive standard of measurement for the Fed. It is far more easy and desirable to establish a standard for the Fed that says it cannot be anticompetitive in using its natural advantages.

8.   The Fed has not, on the whole, done a bad job of adapting to the post Monetary control Act environment, especially considering the enormousness of the task of going from a supplier of free services to member banks to a market price supplier to all banks. Some Reserve Banks may have been overly aggressive in utilizing natural advantages to seek market share, but, given the revenue match pressures, that was somewhat understandable. It is useful to review the early days of pricing to draw inferences for future directions. In the initial pricing/service level efforts, guidance was sought within the Fed about how aggressive the Fed should be in seeking revenue match by attracting revenue as opposed to reducing cost. At that time, it was stated that there was a line that should not be crossed. The line could not be defined, but people would recognize it when it was crossed.

9.   In the five or so years since pricing, the Fed has not, to the best of my knowledge, further attempted to define the line, establish procedures for monitoring performance relative to that line, or set penalties for crossing that line.

In the early days of pricing, when revenue matching was a distant goal and services and prices changed frequently, it was understandable that little line drawing was done. Now that things are much more stable, I believe the time has come to better define the line. Indeed, I would argue that there are really two lines, which divide decisions up to three sectors: a clearly acceptable sector, a clearly unacceptable sector, and a "neutral zone." I would contend that this neutral zone has grown since pricing, not contracted as it should have.

10.   If it is accepted that drawing this line is a good idea, then somebody must draw it. Since this is my proposal, let me be the first to propose some definition with respect to lines for pricing, service levels, and marketing:

- *Pricing Line.* No price should deviate from a full average cost price (e.g., no "market sensitive" pricing) unless it can be demonstrated that to do so is in the best interest of payment system efficiency. The private sector adjustment factor should be reviewed to ensure the adequacy of imputed and other costs and returns that would be necessary for private-sector providers.
- *Service Level Line.* No service should be offered unless it can be demonstrated that it contributes to the efficiency of the payment mechanism, and that it has not been and arguably cannot be offered as efficiently by private-sector suppliers. (Efficiency includes, but is not limited to, cost, risk, quality, and accessibility of potential users. For example, if the private sector offers the service, but not fairly to all who wish to access it, the Fed could offer it as well.)
- *Marketing.* The Fed's marketing activities should be limited to education, and such education should be provided fairly, both with respect to the Fed's services and those of competitors. For example, it is not education to sell Fed services on price if the Fed's price is less but funds availability so much worse that the effective cost of Fed services is higher.

11.   I concur with Tucker that there is no need or even desire for further congressional action with respect to the Fed's payment system role. The only purpose for congressional action would be if each of the two parties somehow did not understand its role in the payment system. I believe the respective roles are clear; now it is time for adequate safeguards to ensure that those roles are properly carried out.

Possible Federal Reserve Actions

First, the Federal Reserve Board should clearly reaffirm its priorities in the payment system and communicate these to each Reserve Bank and the public as a whole. These priorities should be first, an efficient payment system with tolerable risk and equitable access, and second, to recover costs (plus reasonable private-sector adjustment).

Second, because efficiency is the primary objective, all current services and prices, as well as future services and prices, should be examined to determine what their contribution is to the efficiency of the payment system. The efficiency justification cannot be based solely upon the fact that the more providers, the better. Rather, the efficiency justification must be based upon the Fed's ability to provide a truly more efficient service than is done by the private sector. With respect to market sensitive pricing, the Fed should show that all prices based upon other than full average cost can be justified because they make a positive contribution or do not negatively contribute toward payment system efficiency. Market sensitive pricing and service justification should not be based upon market share consideration. To ensure that such justifications are reasonable and can be understood by current or potential private-sector competitors, such justifications should be reviewed by the Board of Governors or a designated high-level substitute, such as the Fed's pricing policy committee, and should be made available to the public.

My third suggestion would be to appoint a high-level and highly visible ombudsman at the Federal Reserve Board or Senior Board staff level who would be responsible for reviewing all claims of unfair competition made by the private sector or other interested parties. The ombudsman's role would be to thoroughly examine each complaint and report: (1) whether the allegations in the complaint are true, (2) if true, whether the actions constitute a violation of the principle that all Fed payment activities should further the efficiency of the payment system or at least not diminish it, and (3) if the actions are in violation of the efficiency guideline, what can be done to remedy the problem.

Finally, to emphasize the importance of the efficiency goal, any individual or Reserve Bank that violates the objectives should receive appropriate sanctions, including but not limited to termination.

Summary

Given the highly unusual nature of private-sector versus public-sector competition, I strongly believe that there must be some nonprofit justification (e.g., public good) for keeping a public-sector presence. I also believe that in the case of the payment system such justification exists, as few would argue that the Fed, because of its network of reserve accounts, nationwide presence, and scale economies is not critical to providing at least some check, wire transfer, and ACH services.

However, if the Fed merely acted as another competitor (e.g., sought only greater profits or market share) it would forfeit its right to compete directly with the private sector. The Fed has not, in my opinion, done so, but the potential exists without strong controls.

COMMENTARY

by Gerald R. Faulhaber

With regard to Don Tucker's chapter and the commentary by Robert Listfield, I am struck by the quite amazing similarities between this policy debate about the Federal Reserve's roles as regulator and service provider and the policy debate of the 1970s involving the Bell System's role in telecommunications.

These similarities may not be immediately evident to the casual observer in either field. However, having spent ten years of my professional life deeply immersed in the economics of telecommunications, and having been a (somewhat tangential) party to the policy debates, I must admit to a strong sense of *déjà vu*. Let me review some of the policy problems that were raised today about the Fed and relate them to the *identical* policy problems raised about the old Bell System back in the 1970s.

- The Fed (Bell System) is a dominant supplier that sets price and can punish/control competitors through its market power.
- The Fed (Bell System) is necessary because of economies of scale in its network operations.
- It is socially necessary for the Fed (Bell System) to provide its services to all who want them, at nondiscriminatory rates, including rural areas ("universal service").

- The Fed (Bell System) must be a supplier of last resort of credit (telephone service).
- The Fed's (Bell System's) prices for services should cover a "fair" rate of return but no more.
- The Fed (Bell System) is most likely subsidizing its activities in potentially competitive markets to discourage potential competitors.
- The Fed (Bell System) is using its regulatory powers (control over local access and distribution) to inhibit competition in certain markets.
- In order to control the Fed's (Bell System's) presumed predilection for this type of anticompetitive behavior, it is good public policy to regulate prices for services to cover accounting costs, including allocated overheads; establish service boundaries, within which the Fed (Bell System) may operate and outside of which it may not; establish a "Chinese Wall" (separate subsidiary) within the Fed (Bell System) to seal off its regulatory (monopoly) side from its service provider (competitive) side.
- If all else fails, a separate corporation (divestiture of local access and distribution) is a "possible procedural response."

As you can see, the parallels are quite exact and cover just about all the points raised in this conference as well as the telecommunications debates of the 1970s.

What is sobering about this close analogy is that we all know where the telecommunications debate ended up: with a ham-handed court-dictated divestiture that has been suboptimal, to say the least.

What was the problem? How did the Bell System get itself into the mess of divestiture? To shorthand a very complex process, federal regulators found that firms were clamoring to gain access to Bell's protected markets and that any response Bell made to aggressive entry was labeled predatory and anticompetitive by its new rivals. As the regulatory process once kept these new firms out, this same process now served as a means for the entrants to seek handicaps on the ability of the giant monopolist to abuse its market power. This situation gave rise to the policy dilemmas listed above, and there was no lack of "help": regulators, Congress, and the courts vied with each other for the right to fail to solve *any* of them.

Unfortunately, the policy atmosphere of the 1970s was highly adversarial, in large measure because that was Bell's strategy. By 1972, the Chairman of AT&T had made the decision not to accommodate entry but to fight it at every step, to "dig in his heels" to defend the regulated monopoly. Result: the Bell System was run over.

It is interesting to speculate whether a more cooperative posture by the old Bell System would have yielded different results. Of course, this counterfactual hypothesis cannot be subject to empirical test. Yet I am inclined to think so; a Bell System willing to give its potential competitors at least some of what they wanted, turning them into business partners rather than regulatory adversaries, might have had the flexibility and savvy to adapt to the newly competitive telecommunications marketplace while maintaining its national systems integrity.

What are the lessons for the Federal Reserve System in all this? My highly personal reading of this dolorous history suggests two lessons:

- The Fed has the opportunity to dodge a bullet here before it is even fired. The *last* thing the Fed needs is help from Congress in resolving the conflict that Dr. Tucker sees. In the late 1970s, Congress was by far the most destabilizing element in the telecommunications debate. Get this problem under control yourself.
- Adopt a strategy of accommodation with your customers/potential competitors. As long as those who can make some money from payment clearing see you as helpful to them, they will work with you. If they see you as blocking them at every turn, they will collectively find a way, probably political, to go around you. Or even worse, over you.

We seldom have the benefit of hindsight that tells us when a little problem can grow to overwhelm an institution. I believe this is such an opportunity; the lessons of telecommunications policy seem to teach much about the grim potential of Dr. Tucker's conflict problems. The combination of bad strategy on the part of the principal and a public policy process run amok was bad enough for our telephone system; let's not let it happen to our banking system.

7 MONEY, CREDIT, BANKING, AND PAYMENT SYSTEM POLICY

Marvin S. Goodfriend

The modern payment system is a complex set of arrangements involving such diverse institutions as currency, the banking system, clearinghouses, the central bank, and government deposit insurance. While there is an enormous literature about its constituent parts, there is little unifying analysis. Monetary economists have long pursued deeper understanding of currency as the medium of exchange. But they have generally ignored the banking system and clearinghouses, even when focusing on monetary policy. Financial economists, on the other hand, have been keenly interested in banks as financial intermediaries and in government deposit insurance. But, by and large, they have ignored the payment system aspects of these institutions; and they have tended to treat medium of exchange and monetary policy issues only peripherally.

To fully understand the payment system, including the evolution and

Mike Bordo, Mike Dotsey, Motoo Haruta, Bob King, Tony Kuprianov, Ben McCallum, and Cliff Smith provided helpful comments. The views are solely those of the author and do not necessarily reflect those of the Federal Reserve Bank of Richmond or the Federal Reserve System.

247

structure of its constituent institutions, it is necessary to appreciate both its monetary and financial aspects. This chapter presents a unified treatment by showing how the evolution of the payment system has been driven by efficiency gains from substituting credit (claims on particular institutions) for commodity money. The discussion emphasizes that the substitution of credit for commodity money was accompanied by arrangements to monitor and enforce restrictions on credit-issuing institutions. Among other things, it suggests alternative answers to some longstanding questions about banking. For example, it suggests why payment services and information-intensive lending have been provided jointly by the same set of institutions (banks); and it explains why maintaining the value of bank deposits at par has been efficient, that is, why banks have not been set up as mutual funds.

Insights developed by explaining the private payment system are subsequently employed to evaluate public payment system policy. I focus on the need for public protection of the payment system. One can imagine a payment system not in need of protection, namely, one using only government currency or perhaps a postal money-order system. However, the public has apparently been willing to accept some credit risk for the substantial efficiency gains that the use of credit instruments in place of cash has afforded. The public's willingness to accept purely private measures for controlling credit risk prior to the Federal Reserve and government deposit insurance indicates that private protection of the payment system was largely effective.

I explore whether the development of the payment system by private decentralized competitive forces was deficient, however, by evaluating three prominent public payment system policies: monetary policy, central bank lending, and deposit insurance. Briefly, although valuing deposits at par and holding fractional reserves is efficient for individual banks, it had the potential for generating destabilizing systemwide bank runs that could only be remedied efficiently by central bank monetary policy. In contrast to monetary policy, fully collateralized discount window lending as practiced by the Federal Reserve matters only because the rules for pledging bank assets favor the Federal Reserve over private lenders. The provision of payment finality by private clearinghouses prior to the establishment of the Federal Reserve, however, suggests that some Fed lending in the process of making payments may be efficient. Moreover, it also suggests that Fed limits on direct access to the payment system are also efficient, both to protect Fed lending and to protect the interbank credit market.

In contrast to safe discount window lending as practiced by the Fed, deposit insurance is a liability whose potential cost bank managers can increase by their choice of assets. Hence, deposit insurance must be supported by extensive supervision and regulation to protect the insurer's funds. My discussion points out some pitfalls of current protective provisions. It then uses insights developed in the discussion of private payment arrangements to suggest a tough exclusion principle as a potential remedy and to critique an alternative proposal, narrow banking.

The plan of the chapter is as follows. The first section outlines the fundamental efficiencies of monetized exchange, and the next section discusses the basic benefits and costs of substituting credit for commodity money. Then I treat the role of banks in the payment system, suggesting how the four characteristic features distinguishing banks from other financial intermediaries flow from the role of banks in providing efficient medium of exchange services. Further efficiencies made possible by the development of private multilateral arrangements among banks are examined, with two historically important examples: the Suffolk Bank System and the check clearinghouses. Finally, the chapter evaluates the three public payment system policies mentioned above.

The Medium of Exchange

As the medium of exchange, money overcomes inconveniences associated with barter, most notably the double coincidence of wants and commodity indivisibilities.[1] Money also naturally serves as the medium of account. Having high purchasing power to weight, money economizes on the cost of carrying or transporting assets to make payments. Equally important, money is easily recognized, saving costly verification of its authenticity and value. Needless to say, money must also be a reasonably durable store of value.

In the early hunting societies, skins served as money.[2] Such items as corn, tobacco, and olive oil served as money in agricultural societies. Of course, the precious metals silver and gold emerged as the most widely used commodity monies in the modern world. Their relatively great value in non-monetary uses, for example, for ornamentation and jewelry, has given them considerable purchasing power portability. When properly alloyed, their durability is also very high. Both metals are readily divisible, although silver's lower purchasing power to weight has made it more convenient than gold for fractional coinage. And both metals are easily recognizable. Beyond their color and metallic ring, simple tests like specific gravity and acid tests for gold identify them cheaply. Their coinability has made possible a further economization of verification costs in everyday exchange. A coin stamp certifies the original weight and fineness of the metal and, along with milling on the edges, makes evident any subsequent alteration.

The exclusive use of commodity money in making payments would mean that each transfer of goods was accompanied simultaneously by a transfer from the buyer to the seller of a quantity of commodity money of equal value. From the modern point of view, making payments exclusively with commodity money seems highly restrictive. Yet if it were impossible to judge or guarantee individual reliability, for instance, if individual identities were private information, other arrangements for making payments would be infeasible.[3] Settlement in paper claims on real assets would be ruled out because their value could not be verified. Similarly, individuals could not credibly precommit to settle in the commodity money itself, even in the near future. Since precommitment would not be enforceable, deferred settlement would not be feasible.[4] Although it has been possible, of course, to develop systems for enforcing settlement in terms of paper claims or even book entry claims, it is costly to manage them efficiently. Hence, it has remained efficient for society to finance the majority of its transactions with cash (government currency and coin).[5]

The need to employ cash gives rise to an inventory demand for it. The reason is that the cost of using cash is minimized by keeping an inventory on hand and replenishing it only infrequently. The average efficient cash inventory (the demand for cash) is smaller the lower is the replenishment cost. In addition, the efficient stock demand is lower the greater is the opportunity cost of holding it (the higher is the nominal rate of interest). It is, of course, the real value of cash demanded that is determined according to the above considerations. Other things being equal, the nominal demand for cash moves proportionally with the price level. The real demand, of course, is related to the real flow of cash purchases.

Credit in the Exchange Process

As a commodity, paper has all the attributes of an efficient medium of exchange except one. Paper is highly divisible and portable, and it can be made durable with the proper processing. But its purchasing power to weight ratio is far too low for it to be an efficient pure commodity money. However, if there is a technologically feasible means of information production and a means of enforcement that allows verification of the value of paper claims on real assets, then it becomes efficient for paper claims (warehouse receipts) to circulate in place of commodity money itself.[6] The efficiency stems from the fact that the purchasing power to weight of paper claims exceeds that for commodity money. In addition, leaving commodity money in a central location yields economies of scale in storage. These factors, in turn, reduce the cost of replenishing money balances, now paper claims, and thereby reduce the efficient inventory of money to have on hand. At the social level the reduced stock demand for money provides a benefit by freeing some of the money commodity for nonmonetary uses.

The abovementioned efficiencies are purchased at the cost of maintaining systems for monitoring and enforcement of the promise to honor the warehouse receipts. To understand the nature of these costs, it is useful to view the leaving of commodity money at a warehouse as lending.[7] The receipt, entitling its holder to reclaim the commodity money on demand, may be viewed as evidence of commodity money credit extended to the warehouse. Because the circulation of warehouse receipts in place of commodity money itself involves lending, it must be accompanied by rules and restrictions to protect the lender (claim check holder) against the possibility that the borrower (warehouse) will not repay the loan (will not honor its claim checks).

Efficient loan design involves the costly accumulation of detailed information about borrowers. To economize on the expense of acquiring information, lending is typically undertaken in the context of long-term relationships. In addition to establishing the borrower's reliability, there is usually an agreement to restrict the borrower's range of actions to reduce the risk of default. Typically the borrower agrees to collateralize the loan. That is, the borrower accepts a set of restrictions on the use or transfer of an asset designated as security. In order to enforce compliance with such restrictions, loan agreements contain provisions for the lender to monitor the borrower.[8]

Warehouse receipts, like claim checks for laundries, entitle the holder to reclaim the exact items left there. Moreover, such claims restrict their issuers from using or renting the items. In effect, then, commodity monies left with a warehouse (commodity money loans to the warehouse) are perfectly collateralized. They would be safe as long as someone representing the borrowers monitored the warehouse. Note that even though each unit of commodity money in storage, in effect, collateralized a specific claim check, the claim checks could circulate interchangeably if the commodity money collateral were homogeneous. They would, however, have to be transferable. But this could be arranged either by allowing an initial depositor to endorse the claim over to another, or by having the claim simply promise to pay the presenter.

Because fool-proof monitoring of the warehouse would be very costly, it would be useful to put in place other safeguards to protect the loan collateral (the warehoused commodity money) (see Jensen and Meckling 1976, sec. 4.2). An efficient means of doing so would be for a wealthy person of longstanding reputation in the community to run the warehouse. Default would be known to be costly for such a person in terms of reputational capital. Equally important, he or she could pledge fixed property to further collateralize the loans in case of a misappropriation of the commodity money and, in effect, would provide capital to protect the customers of the warehouse against loss.

All the costs of running the warehouse, including rent for the building, management fees, the cost of printing warehouse receipts, fees for monitoring and enforcing protective restrictions, and a return to the owner for putting up capital, would be built into the warehouse storage charge. If these costs were smaller than the benefits discussed above of using warehouse receipts as the circulating medium, then it would be more efficient for paper claims on commodity money to circulate in place of commodity money itself. Of course, a gain might only obtain for some transactions. If a wareshouse were only known locally, for example, then commodity money would still be used for traveling.

In fact, the evolution of the payment system has been, in large part, driven by efficiency gains from substituting credit (claims on particular institutions) for commodity money. The substitution of warehouse receipts for commodity money was only the first in a series of substitutions that have been found to be efficient. For reasons that will be discussed later, warehousing developed into banking relatively quickly. But the discussion of warehousing is conceptually valuable because it makes particularly clear the efficiency gains as well as the costs incurred in substituting credit for circulating commodity money. To reiterate, such substitution has been efficient because the costs of enforcing restrictions on and monitoring institutions that issue credit money have been less than the cost of using commodity money directly. In other words, the drive for greater efficiency, which has dictated a continuing substitution of credit for commodity money in making payments, has brought with it a need to make arrangements to protect the payment system.

The Role of Banks

Banks have been distinguished from other financial intermediaries by four characteristics. First, prior to the nationalization of currency, banks issued liabilities in the form of circulating banknotes. Second, bank deposits have normally been valued at par in terms of currency.[9] Third, banks have provided checking services for their depositors. Fourth, banks have specialized in information-intensive lending.[10] That is, a large portion of bank assets have been loans that are not traded on secondary markets and hence must be valued and managed entirely by individual banks themselves.[11] A longstanding puzzle in understanding banking is why payment services and information-intensive lending have both been offered by the same set of institutions, namely, banks. This section explains the mix of services distinguishing banks from other financial intermediaries as an efficient outcome of a further substitution of credit for commodity money in the payment system.

Once the commodity money warehouses were set up, there was relatively little need for circulating claims to be cashed in. Claims might be made for travel, for payments to distant locations where the warehouse was unknown, in response to changes in the nonmonetary demand for the money commodity, or in response to changes in commodity money demand itself. But for the most part claims could simply circulate, the average inventory per person being determined efficiently as outlined above. Claims could retain their value indefinitely, with systems in place to monitor and safeguard the commodity money collateral in the warehouse.

The payment system could be run even more economically, however, if the warehoused commodity money were invested at interest, leaving just enough to manage efficiently any claims that might be made. Keeping too small an inventory of commodity money would lead to excessively costly stockouts. Too large an inventory would be costly in terms of interest income forgone. Hence, a fractional reserve of commodity money was optimal. At the individual level interest earnings could defray some of the fee for leaving commodity money at the warehouse. If large enough, they could provide net interest to claim check holders. The social value of fractional reserves was to free the money commodity for nonmonetary uses. By reducing the opportunity cost of money (lowering the implicit rental rate on money) fractional reserves also raised the efficient stock demand for money and reduced the cost of managing money balances.

The efficiency gains of fractional reserves could not be had, however, without changing the character of the warehouse claim check. As discussed, a conventional warehouse receipt specifies a perfect collateral interest in the particular units of commodity money left in a warehouse, implicitly restricting the warehouse to hold 100 percent reserves of commodity money, or getting permission from the specific customer who owns the collateral every time it is moved around. Hence, to get the efficiency gains of fractional reserve banking, depositors had to give up perfected collateral interest and become general creditors.[12] This point about the character of the deposit contract will be important when I evaluate Federal Reserve discount window lending.

A bank free to invest in interest-earning assets but without any expertise in information-intensive lending would lend on the basis of easily verified safe collateral, that is, on real bills; or it could lend to entities well known to have good credit, such as blue-chip firms or governments. Being based on publicly available information, such loans could take the form of traded securities. So although the incentive to hold fractional reserves explains why commodity money warehouses evolved into financial intermediaries, it does not explain the emergence of other distinctive features of banking, in particular, information-intensive lending. The following argument, however, suggests such an explanation.

Having developed arrangements to support the efficient issue of notes, banks were positioned to further economize on the use of resources in making payments: they could offer checkable deposits and check collection services. Checks allowed individuals to make payments in person without carrying currency.[13] Because checkable deposits provided banks with loanable funds, they could pay a competitive return either as explicit interest or by defraying the cost of check-clearing services. Of course banknotes similarly represented a source of loanable funds for banks and could, in principle, pay interest to their owner periodically. Such interest payments, however, would cause the value of notes to rise as the interest payment date approached and to fall sharply immediately after. Moreover, their value would fluctuate with the nominal interest rate that converts the future interest payment into a present value. Individuals using currency would thereby have to agree on its value before an exchange could take place. Such inconveniences have apparently made it inefficient to pay interest on currency.

Hence, the primary efficiency gain made possible by checks was to allow society, in part, to substitute interest-earning checkable deposits for non-interest-earning currency. In addition, checks made payments through the mail more convenient and reliable. A further saving was achieved because checks could be deposited directly and collected in bulk through the banking system.

With no further arrangements among banks, checks would require immediate payment in commodity money when received by the paying bank. Once again, however, an efficiency gain was achieved by using credit in place of immediate settlement in commodity money, this time in the form of interbank balances. In general, checks sent for collection from one bank to another tend to net out, so if payment were always made as checks were received, commodity money would simply be shipped back and forth with neither bank accumulating or disbursing any, on average. Banks could therefore economize on such shipping costs by simply holding credit balances on each other instead of requiring immediate settlement in commodity money. For example, instead of triggering immediate shipment of commodity money from bank A to bank B, checks sent for payment by bank B to bank A could result in bank A giving bank B a deposit. Bank B would then be said to have an interbank deposit at bank A. When the flow of collections reversed, bank A could acquire a deposit at bank B. To economize on commodity money shipping costs, banks agreed to make temporary loans to each other on demand as dictated by developments in the payment system.[14]

Just as noteholders made arrangements to protect commodity money deposited with more primitive banks, banks employing interbank balances developed systems and expertise in monitoring and managing loans to each other. In contrast to individual depositors with relatively small deposits at a single bank, banks themselves needed numerous interbank relationships to provide efficient payment services to their customers. Moreover, such relationships were geographically spread out. In addition, payment system efficiency dictated that banks grant possibly large loans, by accepting balances at another bank, on very short notice, without the safety of specific collateral. In effect, banks offered lines of credit to their correspondent banks. Hence, banks had to be particularly careful about the correspondents through which they collected checks. Equally important, they had to devote resources to continually evaluate the creditworthiness of those banks with which they chose to have collection relationships. In other words, banks specialized in information-intensive lending to support efficient payment services for their customers.

There are two important implications of this point. First, because banks had an incentive to monitor each other in the process of collecting checks, they could provide an economical indirect means for depositors to monitor their own banks. Depositors could check what interbank collection relationships their own banks could arrange. Since good banks had an incentive to publicize such arrangements, depositors would have little trouble monitoring interbank relationships. A substantial number of relationship terminations would be taken as evidence that a particular bank had become a bad credit risk. Depriving a weak bank of the ability to have its checks accepted for collection at other banks would also greatly reduce its ability to successfully market checkable deposits. Alternatively, banks might continue to accept for collection checks drawn on a bank perceived to be a bad credit risk but announce that they would no longer hold deposits at the weak bank. Though it could still have its checks collected by other banks, the weak bank would be forced to hold larger reserves to manage its checkable deposits, forcing it to be less competitive in that respect.

Second, the holding of interbank deposits rather than publicly traded securities by banks made it much more difficult for depositors to continually evaluate bank solvency. This led banks to devote more resources to monitoring each other and reinforced the need for additional safeguards, such as more capital to back nontraded loans.[15]

I am finally in a position to suggest why payment services and information-intensive loans to nonfinancial firms have been provided jointly by the same set of institutions. Imagine a set of finance companies satisfying the nonfinancial demand for information-intensive loans. They would develop the same expertise currently used by banks to manage their loans. Moreover, one would expect such finance companies to organize a network to allocate credit to the best prospects and to help diversify their loan portfolios. Intercompany balances would be managed with the same systems used to manage information-intensive loans to nonfinancial borrowers. Intercompany borrowing and lending would exist even if finance companies offered no payment services.

Now, one can imagine a separate network of mutual funds offering payment services. Would it be efficient for the finance and payment companies to exist independently? It would not seem so. Finance companies would have in place much of the network, systems, and expertise to run a reliable and efficient payment system. They would merely need to accept demand deposits and set up facilities for handling payment flows. The point is that systems to evaluate credit, monitor and enforce loan agreements, and extend credit on short notice are productive both in originating loans to nonfinancial borrowers *and* in managing lending to support an efficient provision of payment services. This, I am arguing, helps explain why institutions specializing in information-intensive lending have applied their expertise jointly to the production of payment services and nontraded loans.

Moreover, nonfinancial lines of credit involve long-term relationships in which the finance company and the borrower each have an incentive to ensure that the other has staying power. A finance company requires information about a borrower. But borrowers who pay an ongoing fee for their credit line similarly need assurances of the finance company's staying power. Other things being equal, then, finance companies will offer checkable deposits more efficiently than pure payment companies, because potential depositors will already have acquired information about the reliability of finance companies as depositories. Independent payment companies could, of course, assure their reliability by holding publicly traded securities; but the low cost of verifying the value of traded securities would be reflected in a yield below that on nontraded loans. I am suggesting that, on net, using the same information to ensure the reliability of both credit lines and deposits allows payment services to be provided at lower cost by firms also offering line-of-credit services.

The joint product efficiencies of combining information-intensive lending with the provision of payment services also explains why bank deposits have been valued at par, that is, why banks have not been set up as mutual funds. Of course, practically speaking, this would have required banks to hold securities valued continually in the market. Yet restricting assets this way would certainly have been feasible, especially in modern times, and it would have made banks easier to monitor. As Fama and Jensen (1983, 337–410) point out, however, institutions specializing in nontraded loans are not run efficiently as mutual funds. The incentive for such institutions to employ par-value deposits whose yield is independent of the fortunes of the firm may be understood as part of a widespread use of bonds together with equity in the financing of firms in general. Jensen and Meckling (1976) have emphasized that, from the point of view of claimants, bonds are an optimal part of a financial package to monitor management and ensure an efficient choice of assets. In other words, bank deposits have been par-valued because it has been efficient for banks to use them to fund nontraded loans.[16]

The Payment System

To this point, I have discussed efficiencies in the means of making payments that involved bilateral relationships among banks. Here I discuss further efficiencies made possible by the development of private multilateral cooperative arrangements. I consider two historically important examples: the Suffolk Bank System, and the clearinghouses. The Suffolk System emerged as a more efficient means of redeeming banknotes. The clearinghouses economized on the collection of checks.

The Suffolk Bank System

The Suffolk Bank System arose in early nineteenth-century New England (see Whitney 1878). At that time, country banknotes made up the bulk of the regional circulating currency, although residents of Boston also used local checkable bank deposits to make payments. As pointed out, normally there would be little reason for banknotes to be redeemed. In the process of circulating, however, banknotes could flow some distance from the banks that issued them. During this period, the balance of payments within the region favored Boston, and country banknotes generally flowed in that direction.

Because banknotes entitled the holder to commodity money (by this time, gold or silver coin) at their issuing bank only, notes bore ever-greater discounts in terms of coin the farther they traveled from their bank of issue. The discount reflected both the transport and time costs of carrying the notes to the bank for payment and returning with the coin. If information on creditworthiness were difficult to obtain at a distance or if solvency were in doubt, the discount could include a risk premium. The cost of authenticating notes to detect counterfeits increased the discount even further.

Under such conditions, it became profitable for individuals known as notebrokers to buy notes with coin in Boston and return them to their banks of issue for payment. By buying up and returning notes in bulk, notebrokers could reduce the per-item transport cost. Competition among notebrokers thereby reduced the discounts on country banknotes in Boston. Carrying potentially large positions in notes of particular banks, brokers also had incentive to specialize in authenticating notes and evaluating bank credit risk. The economization on information production achieved by brokers probably also reduced the risk premium on notes.

Of course, competition would remove any abnormal arbitrage profit, as brokers bid the discount down to the point where it just covered the cost of redemption. In effect, notebrokering forced the country banks and the rural areas as a whole to finance their balance-of-payments deficit vis-à-vis Boston with coin instead of with paper credit (banknotes). Country banks and their customers deplored notebrokering because it forced banks to call in loans in order to accumulate coin, which then went to Boston.

It was in this environment that the Suffolk Bank System was organized. The Suffolk System was an arrangement by which the Suffolk Bank in Boston redeemed a country bank's notes with coin, provided that the country bank deposited coin at the Suffolk to cover the redemption. Initially, the system was set up on a purely bilateral basis and amounted to little more than centralized notebrokering with further economies of scale. Since country banks had to redeem their notes as before, the Suffolk System was unpopular outside of Boston. But because the Suffolk redeemed notes at a discount while nonmembers had to redeem theirs at par, country banks were given an incentive to participate.

After a while, the Suffolk System introduced a kind of collective net settlement, an important multilateral clearing procedure that was a precursor to that used in clearinghouses (Mullineaux 1987, 890). To make this possible, the Suffolk ruled that it would accept, as required deposits, the notes of any participating banks in good standing. This ruling allowed a bank to redeem its notes by swapping them for excess coin in another account. In effect, the procedure allowed interbank borrowing, which made more efficient use of coin on deposit and reduced the average inventory of coin that each bank had to keep on hand. Collective net settlement should be recognized as yet another example of the substitution of credit for the use of commodity money in the payment system. As in the earlier examples, the innovative use of credit was due to the saving it afforded in reduced commodity money shipping costs and smaller commodity money reserves. Here too the use of credit was supported by extensive safeguards on all the participants, including the Suffolk Bank itself, and especially by continual monitoring of the country banks by the Suffolk. One important control was the power to expel from the system a bank judged to be excessively weak.

The Clearinghouses

Clearinghouses emerged in various cities around the United States in the middle of the nineteenth century as private cooperative arrangements among banks to economize on check collection.[17] In part, clearinghouses did for check collecting what the Suffolk Bank System did for the payment of coin against notes.[18] The best-known clearinghouse innovation was the replacement of bilateral collection procedures with collective net settlement. Each morning, clearinghouse member banks took checks to a central house for clearing. There the checks were netted out or offset against each other and a net credit or debit position against "the clearinghouse" was computed for each member bank. Later in the day, banks covered any net debit positions with government currency or coin. Funds so received paid off the net creditor banks from that morning's clearing.

The basic efficiency gains were these. Instead of making collections individually, each bank could take its checks to a central location for collection. Thus, centralized collection itself saved significantly on transport costs. Netting out provided an additional saving by greatly reducing the volume of currency and coin that was transported in the settlement process. Moreover, to further economize on shipments of currency and coin, clearinghouse members kept the bulk of their reserves in the vaults of the clearinghouse, receiving in return claims to their reserves known as clearinghouse certificates (Westerfield 1921, 634–639). Then, instead of shipping currency and coin to settle, member banks could simply pass around clearinghouse certificates. The keeping of reserves at the clearinghouse, in turn, facilitated an interbank market that made possible a more efficient distribution of reserves among banks. These measures all contributed to reducing the efficient quantity of reserves that banks had to hold. By reducing checking fees, they also led to more intensive use of checks relative to currency on the part of the public.

Along with the set of benefits just described, clearinghouses eventually provided payment finality (*Constitution of the New York Clearing House Association* 1903). In the absence of finality, a check deposited for collection might not be paid if either the bank against which it was written failed or the deposit account against which it was written had insufficient funds. Obviously, neither the paying bank nor the clearinghouse would pay a check where there was insufficient funds, unless the drawer of the check had a prearranged line of credit at the bank. But with finality, a check deposited for collection in the same town was given immediate credit. In other words, finality ensured the check depositor against failure of the paying bank. In order to provide finality, clearinghouse member banks agreed to assess themselves if a member bank failed to cover its position with the clearinghouse later that day. The assessments were then used to pay the failing bank's checks in return for a lien against the receiver of the failed bank. Making use of their cooperative nature, then, clearinghouses provided a kind of check insurance to the depositors of their member banks. If checks could be deposited quickly, finality allowed a check's reliability to depend entirely on the individual issuing it. Hence, finality further enhanced the convenience of checks as means of payment.

The clearinghouse represents a highly sophisticated example of efficiencies in the payment system achieved by substituting private credit for commodity money. The uses of private credit were numerous. The daily clearing and collection process routinely generated credit against the clearinghouse. Member banks held currency and coin in its vault. Extensive interbank lending and borrowing of reserves was carried out under its auspices. And the clearinghouse managed an important contingent liability in the form of mutual insurance of checks in the process of collection.

As we would expect, the clearinghouse imposed numerous rules and regulations on its member banks and engaged in supervision and enforcement as well. There were minimum capital requirements. Coin and currency reserves at the clearinghouse partly collateralized the debit positions of clearing banks. There were relatively frequent examinations of member banks by a clearinghouse committee. And clearinghouses reserved the right to exclude, by vote, members shown to be weak.[19] The threat of expulsion was a powerful management tool because public expulsion would represent an adverse signal to depositors and cause a bank to lose the ability to have its checks accepted for collection at other banks. It was apparently efficient to restrict membership in the clearinghouse itself to a core of well-managed and highly-reliable banks. Other banks cleared their checks through the clearinghouse by retaining a member as an agent. But clearinghouses held agents liable for checks against their clients authorized for collection through clearinghouse member banks (*Constitution of the New York Clearing House Association* 1903). Thus, agents were given a powerful incentive to choose and monitor their client banks carefully. Agents thereby imposed a useful discipline on client banks.[20]

Public Payment System Policies

Previous sections explained the evolution of the payment system in terms of the efficiency gains had by substituting private credit for commodity money in the settlement process. Two insights were stressed. First, the shipping and inventory costs of settling in commodity money could be significantly reduced by making use of ever more sophisticated borrowing and lending arrangements. Second, these economies had to be purchased by setting up and managing evermore complicated safeguards to protect the institutional lending that supported the efficiency gains. One can imagine a payment system not in need of protection, namely, one using only government currency or coin, and perhaps a postal money-order system. With the proper controls, however, users of payment services have apparently been willing to accept some credit risk for the substantial reduction in costs that the use of credit in place of cash has afforded. Here, however, I explore whether the development of the payment system by private decentralized competitive forces was deficient from the macroeconomic point of view by evaluating three prominent public payment system policies: monetary policy, central bank lending, and deposit insurance.[21]

Monetary Policy

Monetary policy made possible two distinct efficiency gains. First, national paper currency replaced gold coin as the interregional means of settlement. Second, the power of the Federal Reserve to create currency provided better protection against systemic bank runs. I discuss each benefit in turn.

Prior to the Civil War, interbank balances were settled in gold coin. During and following the war, however, the national government created paper currency substitutes for gold that could be used for settlement. The greenbacks, unbacked notes issued during the war, were one such paper currency. National bank notes, authorized by the National Bank Act to be issued by banks with the backing of Treasury bonds, were another. The Treasury also issued gold and silver certificates, which were warehouse receipts for the respective metals held in the Treasury. Because these currencies were liabilities of the national Treasury, they were accepted throughout the country. Though the use of gold in the settlement process had been greatly reduced locally by clearinghouses, the appearance of Treasury currency significantly reduced the shipping costs of settlement among different regions of the country (see Garbade and Silber 1979). The Federal Reserve further reduced costs by settling interbank balances via book entry telegraphic messages rather than by physical transportation of gold or currency. It is worth noting that clearinghouse efficiencies provided by the Federal Reserve at the national level might have been provided privately had interstate banking not effectively been prohibited.

At any rate, management of high-powered money (currency plus bank reserves) by the Federal Reserve after 1914 provided another important benefit, which we can understand as follows.[22] We have interpreted the banking system together with clearinghouses as a set of credit arrangements that increased the efficiency of commodity money in providing payment services. In particular, we saw that it was efficient for checkable deposits to be valued at par and for banks to keep fractional reserves. Obviously, a widespread demand to convert deposits into currency could not be satisfied by such a system without a central bank. The clearinghouses, however, could protect the banking system against a run by temporarily restricting the conversion of deposits into currency. But restricting cash payments would tend to cause deposits to depreciate in terms of currency. Hence, the system was potentially unstable. Even minor banking problems that made a restriction possible could make forward-looking depositors seek to protect themselves against (or profit from) a potential depreciation by immediately attempting to convert deposits into currency. In aggregate, of course, such behavior could make a restriction inevitable.

In fact, between the end of the Civil War and the establishment of the Federal Reserve there were numerous banking crises, which involved the actual or expected restriction of the conversion of deposits into currency.

Though these episodes were violent and disruptive, the evidence suggests that their aggregate insolvency effects were relatively small.[23] In other words, the pre-Fed banking crises appear to have arisen from the inherent monetary instability described above.

Being able to create currency through open-market security purchases, Federal Reserve monetary policy could guarantee the exchange rate between bank deposits and currency against systemwide runs. Monetary policy is effective in this regard precisely because it protects the banking system by creating the currency it needs, so depositors otherwise confident in the solvency of their banks need not worry about a depreciation in the value of their deposits in terms of currency. Hence, with a central bank "lender of last resort," widespread runs need not develop, at least in the absence of real systemwide insolvencies.[24] Hence, monetary policy protects the payment system in a way that the private market cannot.

Central Bank Lending

In contrast to monetary policy, central bank lending involves making loans to individual banks with funds acquired by selling off other assets, usually government bonds. In other words, I am defining central bank lending to be analogous to private financial intermediation in that it neither creates nor destroys high-powered money. Obviously, because it involves making loans, central bank lending must be accompanied by provisions to monitor and enforce compliance with certain restrictions on potential borrowers. In the public sector, these are known as supervision and regulation.

The three major categories of Federal Reserve lending are all importantly related to payment system policy. Although discount window credit is not generated in the payment system proper, it is valued in large part for the assistance it provides to individual banks in order to protect the payment system.[25] In fact, the Fed's discount window is often cited as a comparative advantage for Federal Reserve management of the payment system (see, for example, Flannery 1988). Daylight overdrafts constitute a second category of Fed lending. They are intraday credits, granted by the Federal Reserve to depository institutions making payments over Fedwire, the Fed's electronic funds transfer network.[26] Though quantitatively less significant, Federal Reserve lending also takes the form of float generated in the process of clearing checks.[27] I evaluate, in turn, discount window lending and credit extended in the process of making payments.

While open-market operations are seen as capable of handling aggregate monetary conditions, the discount window is valued for its ability to direct potentially large quantities of funds, on very short notice, to individually troubled banks. No one argues that the discount window should be used to rescue insolvent banks, only that it be used to aid temporarily illiquid banks. While the distinction between the two is crucial for evaluating central bank discount window lending more generally, we can sidestep it here.[28] The reason is that, in practice, the Federal Reserve fully collateralizes its discount window lending with high-grade assets. Hence, discount window lending has involved little risk for the Fed. But what then explains the widespread use of discount window loans by banks in trouble? After all, private lenders should be eager to lend on the same terms as the Fed. Moreover, the Fed does not appear to charge a below-market rate for its emergency credit assistance.

The answer appears to be that banks cannot legally pledge specific assets against privately borrowed funds, that is, private lenders cannot perfect a collateral interest in specific assets of a borrowing bank. In case of insolvency then, private lenders must become general creditors. Government agencies, however, such as the U.S. Treasury and the Federal Reserve, are allowed to perfect a collateral interest in specific assets of a bank to which they lend funds.[29]

The pledging of particular assets to borrow funds is similar, in principle, to selling them for cash. If the need for funds is expected to be temporary, however, borrowing on the basis of pledged assets is more economical. It avoids the greater transaction cost of a sale, including for loan sales the cost of restructuring a loan servicing relationship. Hence, borrowing from the Fed on pledged assets dominates selling those assets.

The effect of fully collateralized discount window lending, then, turns on the pledging rules. If the rules were the same for the Fed and private lenders, discount window lending would make no difference, as long as no subsidy were involved in Fed lending. It is beyond the scope of this chapter to analyze the socially optimal configuration of pledging rules. But allowing the Fed to select good collateral to back its loans permits weak banks to obtain funds more cheaply to continue operating, possibly pledging their best collateral at the discount window to pay out uninsured depositors (the hot money) prior to a bank's being closed. Currently, then, the discount window can delay the declaration of insolvency while effectively moving uninsured depositors from last to first in line. This, of course, is at the expense of the deposit insurance fund. On the other hand, under current pledging rules the discount window is better able to save temporarily illiquid but solvent banks from bankruptcy, which is a social benefit. However, if it is socially efficient for the Fed to have pledging privileges, shouldn't such privileges be given to private lenders as well? As mentioned, the efficiency gains of fractional reserve banking could not be had unless depositors gave up perfected collateral interest. But couldn't private bank debt such as certificates of deposit be made eligible for perfected collateral? The point is that whatever pledging rule is judged to be socially optimal, it is difficult to see why the Fed and private lenders should not both the subject to it, in which case unsubsidized fully collateralized discount window lending would make no difference.

My evaluation of Federal Reserve credit extended in the process of making payments is considerably different than that for discount window lending. First of all, daylight overdrafts and float generated in the process of making payments are not perfectly collateralized as are discount window loans. Moreover, daylight overdrafts are conceptually related to the credit generated by clearinghouses in connection with the provision of finality. The fact that it was efficient for private clearinghouses to accept the generation of credit in that regard suggests that some portion of daylight overdrafts may be efficient. Since it is essentially feasible for the Fed to electronically monitor reserve accounts on a real-time basis, it would also be feasible to eliminate daylight overdrafts.[30] However, to do so would make it costlier for banks to manage their reserve flows during the day. Banks would likely respond with a combination of increased use of correspondent balances for clearing purposes, increased effort to coordinate inflows and outflows of funds, and larger reserve accounts. So daylight overdrafts should be reduced only to the extent found efficient based on proper pricing policy and the absence of subsidies.

Of course, the price of Federal Reserve credit generated in the payment system should also cover the cost of the supervisory and regulatory controls that the Fed must administer to protect its loans. In other words, the Fed should be careful to allocate such management costs efficiently as well, just as private clearinghouses had to allocate their costs. It has been said that the Fed's discount window gives it an advantage in managing the payment system. It should be clear that this makes little sense, given the way the Fed runs the discount window. However, in the sense that it is efficient for a national clearinghouse to oversee the payment system, it is efficient for an institution like the Federal Reserve to do so, although in the absence of restrictions on interstate branching, a national clearinghouse might easily have been organized by a group of private nationwide banks.[31]

On the basis of this discussion, one can appreciate the concerns of some policymakers for maintaining a separation between banking on one hand, and finance and commerce on the other, and for limiting direct access to the payment system (see Corrigan 1987). The separation of banking from finance and commerce would maintain a degree of homogeneity that would facilitate the monitoring and enforcement of safeguards in the interbank credit market. Moreover, it was efficient for private clearinghouses before the Fed to limit their membership to a relatively exclusive core of banks, allowing other banks access to the clearing system through agent member banks. This suggests that it is efficient for the Fed to restrict direct access to its national clearing system as well, both to protect Fed lending generated in the payment system and to protect the interbank credit market.[32]

Deposit Insurance

Deposit insurance is a promise to make good the value of covered deposits, in return for a bank's assets, in the event of a failure. The guarantee is essentially a put option on the assets of the bank, which gives management the right to sell those assets to the guarantor for the value of the covered deposits (see Merton 1977). Because deposit insurance is a potentially costly contingent liability whose value is influenced by a bank manager's choice of assets, the guarantor must protect its funds by monitoring insured banks and enforcing restrictions on their behavior. Uninsured deposits and minimum capital requirements are two key provisions for protecting the deposit insurer's funds. The discussion of deposit insurance that follows points out some pitfalls of these provisions. It then uses insights from the discussion of private payment arrangements to suggest a tough exclusion principle as a potential remedy and to critique an alternative proposal, narrow banking. First, however, it points out a deficiency in the payment system that deposit insurance helps to correct.

As it is organized in the United States, deposit insurance is financed by assessments on participating banks. Because it does not involve the creation or destruction of currency, deposit insurance is neither necessary nor sufficient to protect the banking system against monetary instabilities. It is not designed, as central bank lending is, to provide line of credit assistance to temporarily illiquid but solvent banks; nor does deposit insurance have anything to do with providing finality in the settlement process.

If deposit insurance has a role, it is a means of allowing depositors to better pool the risk of individual bank failures. Individual banks have an incentive to diversify to the point where the marginal benefit is just offset by the higher agency costs due to the reduced stake in the loans originated.[33] Nontraded loan portfolios are most efficiently diversified among those institutions specializing in information-intensive lending themselves (banks). Branching is probably the most important means of diversification, though interbank deposits, purchases and sales of loans, and loan syndications can provide the same benefits. The U.S. political system has, however, greatly restricted branching. The risk pooling made possible by deposit insurance may be useful as an additional means of diversifying bank assets in the presence of branching restrictions.[34] In other words, deposit insurance may be viewed as overcoming a deficiency in the payment system arising not from a private market failure but from inefficient political interference in the market for corporate control in banking.[35]

While deposit insurance probably substitutes to some extent for diversification through free branching, it is beyond the scope of this chapter to say how well it does so, especially relative to the alternatives mentioned. It is possible, however, to point out some weaknesses in the means of protecting the insurance fund that tend to make deposit insurance inefficient. Consider uninsured deposits. These provide a cushion for the insurance fund by making it more likely that bank assets will cover insured deposits in the event of a failure. In practice, however, uninsured deposits may not be a reliable cushion, for two reasons. First, as mentioned above, discount window lending makes it easier for uninsured deposits to be withdrawn from a weak bank before it becomes insolvent. Second, it is difficult for a public authority subject to political pressure to successfully precommit to not bailing out uninsured depositors *ex post*, especially in large bank insolvencies. In principle, bank capital also provides a cushion to protect the insurance fund. However, without the power to reorganize or recapitalize a weak bank before its net worth goes to zero, capital cannot provide a reliable cushion either.

Given that uninsured deposits and bank capital are an unreliable cushion, an attractive alternative suggested by the behavior of the pre-Fed clearinghouses is to use the power to exclude. The insurer could reserve the right to exclude a bank from participating in the deposit insurance program if its capital falls below minimum requirements, or if it is perceived to be weak and mismanaged.[36] As was the case for the clearinghouses, the threat of explusion would be a powerful disciplinary device because its announcement would represent an adverse signal. If society wished to protect the depositors of an expelled bank, it could offer deposit insurance briefly following the announcement. Such a guarantee, though, would require higher minimum capital requirements and tougher participation standards to protect the insurer. But it might be necessary to make the exclusion principle politically viable. Roughly speaking, an efficient exclusion criterion would fix the marginal cost of being tough (the compliance, monitoring, and enforcement costs) at the point where it equaled the declining expected marginal utility cost of claims on the insurer. Such a criterion could leave the insurer open to some risk, though it would provide the optimal degree of protection.

A well-known proposed alternative to deposit insurance is the fail-safe or narrow bank (see, for example, Litan 1986). This proposal involves restricting the assets backing checkable deposits to short-term marketable securities with little chance of declining in value due to credit or interest rate risk. One might imagine the Fed imposing such restrictions on banks in the payment system. It appears that narrow banking could, in principle, provide near-perfect protection of the payment system with relatively little monitoring and enforcement costs.

It would do so, however, by destroying the efficient joint application of information-intensive lending to payment services and loans, reducing the rate banks could offer on checkable deposits. One of the themes of this chapter, however, is that it has always been possible for individuals to employ perfectly safe means of making payments, but with proper controls the public has accepted credit risk for the reduction in cost it has afforded. Moreover, since narrow banking would do nothing to provide a better diversification of nontraded loans to help overcome branching restrictions, it should not be viewed as an alternative means of risk pooling or insurance.

Narrow banking could protect the checkable deposit guarantee against abuse by bank managers. But checkable deposits are only a small part of total deposits, and their share is likely to shrink under narrow banking because of the lower checkable deposit interest rate. Unless the government could precommit to not guaranteeing other deposits, narrow banking would provide only marginal protection against abuses. By establishing the principle that a portion of deposits ought to be perfectly safe, narrow banking might even raise the expectation of a government guarantee for other deposits. Closing the deposit insurance agencies might lower expectations of such a guarantee, but weakening government controls on bank asset choice could lead to more severe problems if banks continued to expect a government guarantee. On net, narrow banking would appear to offer little relative to deposit insurance augmented with a tough exclusion principle.

Summary

This chapter has analyzed the evolution and structure of the key components of the payment system: currency, the banking system, clearinghouses, the central bank, and deposit insurance. It began by pointing out efficiencies, such as recognizability and portability, that led particular commodities to be used as money. It explained the evolution of the payment system as driven by efficiency gains from substituting credit (claims on particular institutions) for commodity money. Two insights were stressed. Shipping and inventory costs of settling in commodity money were significantly reduced by making use of evermore sophisticated borrowing and lending arrangements. And these economies were accompanied by evermore elaborate safeguards to protect the institutional lending that supported the efficiency gains.

Fractional reserve banking, banknotes, demand deposits, and checks were all explained as economizing on the use of commodity money. Systems to evaluate credit, monitor and enforce loan agreements, and extend credit on short notice are productive both in originating loans to nonfinancial borrowers *and* in managing lending to support an efficient provision of payment services. This, I argued, explains why it has been efficient for payment services and information-intensive loans to be provided by the same set of institututions (banks). In addition, I pointed out that institutions specializing in nontraded loans could not be run efficiently as mutual funds. Par-value deposits like bonds are an optimal part of a financial package to most efficiently monitor management and ensure an efficient choice of assets. Hence, this argument also explains that bank deposits have been par-valued because it has been efficient to use them to fund nontraded loans.

The chapter also discussed the Suffolk System and the check clearinghouses, two multilateral arrangements to further economize on the provision of payment services. They introduced centralized collection, collective net settlement, centralized holding of reserves, more extensive interbank lending, and payment finality. All involved more sophisticated uses of private credit to reduce payment costs. Consequently, the cooperative organizations imposed numerous rules and regulations on members and engaged in extensive supervision as well. For example, there were capital requirements and frequent examinations of member banks. Equally important was the power to exclude, by vote, a member shown to be weak. The private cooperative arrangements are particularly interesting because they represent the middle ground between an entirely decentralized payment system and one dominated by public authority. Hence, they provide examples, for comparison with actual and proposed public policies, of cooperative arrangements driven by efficiency rather than political concerns.

In the last part of the chapter, I focused on the possible need for public policies to protect the payment system. Although it has always been possible to make payments safely with cash, users of payment services have been willing to accept some risk for the benefits that private credit in place of commodity money has afforded. However, I explored whether the private development of the payment system was deficient by evaluating monetary policy, central bank lending, and deposit insurance in light of the earlier analysis.

Two features of efficient private bank structure, namely, par-value deposits and fractional reserves, implied a useful role for monetary policy in protecting the payment system. The clearinghouses could protect the banking system against a widespread run by temporarily restricting the conversion of deposits into currency. But currency restrictions were disruptive and the possibility of their use increased the likelihood of widespread runs themselves. Monetary policy was useful in this regard because it could, by creating the needed currency, protect the banking system against such disruptions.

In contrast to monetary policy, central bank lending neither creates nor destroys high-powered money. It involves making loans to individual banks with funds acquired by selling government bonds. I pointed out that private credit markets would be willing and able to provide emergency credit assistance on the same fully collateralized terms as the Fed discount window. Pledging rules explain the use of Fed emergency credit assistance. The efficiency gains of fractional reserve banking could not be had unless depositors gave up perfected collateral interest. This is reflected in the fact that banks cannot legally pledge specific assets against privately borrowed funds. The Fed's advantage is that it is allowed to prefect a collateral interest. I briefly considered altering the pledging rules. But whatever rule is judged to be socially optimal, it is difficult to see why the Fed and private lenders should not both be subject to it, in which case unsubsidized fully collateralized discount window lending would make no difference.

The Federal Reserve also extends loans, most importantly, as daylight overdrafts, in the process of making payments. Such loans are not perfectly collateralized as is discount window credit. Daylight overdrafts are conceptually analogous to the credit generated by private clearinghouses in connection with the provision of finality. Hence, some portion of Fed daylight overdrafts may be efficient. Similarly, it was efficient for private clearinghouses to limit their membership to an exclusive core of banks, with other banks accessing the clearing system through agent member banks. This suggests that it is efficient for the Fed to restrict direct access to its national clearing system as well, both to protect Fed daylight overdrafts and the interbank credit market.

Deposit insurance was the last public payment system policy to be evaluated. I interpreted such insurance literally as a means of allowing bank depositors to pool the risk of individual bank failures, not as a means of protecting the banking system against aggregate shocks. Taking this narrow view, I argued that deposit insurance could be viewed as over-coming a deficiency in the payment system. But the deficiency arises because branching, which is one important means for banks to diversify nontraded loans, has been greatly inhibited by the political system. I also pointed out some weaknesses in the use of uninsured deposits and bank capital as a means of protecting the insurance fund. Current pledging rules and discount window lending policy make it easier for uninsured deposits to be withdrawn from a weak bank before it is declared insolvent. It is also difficult for public authority not to bail out uninsured depositors *ex post*. Similarly, without the power to reorganize or recapitalize a weak bank before its net worth goes to zero, capital cannot provide a reliable cushion.

In light of this point, I discussed the narrow bank proposal as a sub-stitute for deposit insurance. My feeling, though, is that narrow banking would be unnecessarily costly because it would destroy the efficient joint application of information-intensive lending to the production of payment services and loans. Moreover, narrow banking would do nothing to pro-vide a better diversification of loans. Most important, although it would protect the checkable deposit guarantee from abuse by bank managers, it would not protect any additional deposit guarantee such as might be dif-ficult to avoid in the event of a large bank failure. On the basis of the behavior of the pre-Fed clearinghouses, I argued that a tough exclusion principle could provide an attractive alternative to narrow banking. Banks could continue to fund nontraded loans with transactions deposits, but the insurance agency could expel a weak or mismanaged bank, or one whose capital fell below a minimum requirement. The agency could even refuse to insure a bank too large or insufficiently diversified to handle safely. If society wished to protect depositors whose bank was expelled, it could do so by requiring sufficiently high minimum capital requirements and tough participation standards to protect the insurer.

Notes

1. See Lucas (1980), McCallum (1983), and Townsend (1980) for recent theoretical work motivating and emphasizing the medium-of-exchange role of money.
2. Jevons (1875) contains excellent descriptive and analytical material on the evolution of the payment system.
3. King and Plosser (1986) focus on this point.

4. See Townsend (1980; 1986), and references contained therein, for theoretical analyses of these issues.

5. Humphrey (1984, 6) reports about 70 percent of all transactions as taking place with cash, though by value cash transactions account for only about 1.5 percent of the total. Fama (1980) and McCallum (1985) discuss the possibility of an accounting system of exchange without money. See also de Roover (1979) and Usher (1967) on the early evolution of banking.

6. Richards (1929) contains a good discussion of goldsmith bankers and the evolution of English paper money.

7. The fact that a warehouse could charge a storage fee, that is, pay a negative rate of interest, does not diminish the usefulness of the analogy.

8. Boyd and Prescott (1986), Smith and Warner (1979), and Watts and Zimmerman (1983) contain excellent discussions of these issues.

9. An important exception, of course, was the temporarily fluctuating currency price of deposits that resulted from the restriction on cash payments during the pre-Fed banking crises. See Friedman and Schwartz (1963). Private banknotes and non-par checks could circulate at a discount. However, when presented in person at the bank upon which they were drawn, they were paid at par.

10. Fama (1985) contains a nice discussion of this view of bank lending. See James (1987) and Goodhart (1987) for further discussion of this point.

11. See Gorton and Haubrich (1987) for a discussion and interpretation of the recent rise in loan sales.

12. Williams (1984) makes this point with regard to grain banking.

13. Since a check represents a personal promise to pay cash in the future, its acceptability requires a means of judging the reliability of the writer. Hence, checks are used when reliability is assured, such as for repeated purchases at the same firm, as for rent or for the purchases of groceries.

14. It is worth noting that the use of trade credit among nonbanks is analogous to the use of interbank balances among banks.

15. Lindow (1963) reports a ratio of total bank capital (equity, loan loss reserves, and subordinated debit) to risk assets (total assets less cash and U.S. Treasury securities) from 1863 to 1963. The ratio falls from 60 percent in 1880, to about 20 percent at the turn of the century, to under 10 percent by the 1960s.

16. Strictly speaking, this argument explains only why bank deposits are valued at par. It does not explain why they are valued in nominal units and not, for example, indexed to the price level. Perhaps it is because banks evolved as commodity money warehouses. In any case, this is a more general question, which is beyond the scope of this chapter.

17. Cannon (1911) and Spahr (1926) contain good institutional histories of check clearing.

18. Financial center banks, having numerous correspondent relationships with country banks, also provided check collection economies similar those provided by the Suffolk System for note redemptions.

19. For example, *The Constitution of the New York Clearing House Association* (1903), Sec. 20, p. 13) provided for expulsion of a member by majority vote.

20. Gorton and Mullineaux (1987) and Timberlake (1984) emphasize the private regulatory and supervisory nature of clearinghouses.

21. For alternative discussions of policy issues, see Eisenbeis (1987) and U.S. Congress (1987a; 1987b).

22. See Goodfriend (1987) for a discussion of the efficiency gains, feasibility, and mechanics of central banking under a gold standard.

23. Benston et al. (1986, 53–60) and Goodfriend and King (1988) make this point.

24. Goodfriend and King (1988) emphasize that last-resort lending is monetary policy. It is effective because the provision of high-powered money can prevent nominal interest rate increases and asset price declines from making the banking system insolvent.

25. For example, Continental Illinois Bank borrowed extensively at the Fed discount window from May 1984 to February 1985. It was in the window for over $4 billion during much of that time. See Benston et al. (1986, 120–24).

26. Mengle, Humphrey, and Summers (1987, 12) report total funds transfer daylight overdrafts of $76 billion per day. This is an enormous number when one considers that total reserve balances with Reserve Banks are around $35 billion. Daylight overdrafts are currently not priced. They are interest-free loans. Therefore, depository institutions have little incentive to economize on their use. To limit somewhat the use of intraday credit, the Fed monitors depository institutions according to "caps" and relatively informal guidelines, resorting to consultations with bank officials when necessary.

27. The Monetary Control Act of 1980 directed that Federal Reserve check float be priced at the Federal Funds rate. Hence, Fed check float has fallen from $7.4 billion in the first half of 1979 to under $1 billion today. See Dudley (1983), U.S. Congress (1983), and Young (1986).

28. Goodfriend and King (1988) evaluate the feasibility and desirability of discount window lending to illiquid but solvent banks.

29. See *American Jurisprudence* (1963, vol. 10, pp. 390–401) for the banking law on the pledging of bank assets. The ability of depository institutions to use repurchase agreements (RPs) as a funding source is a potential breach in the pledging prohibition for private lenders. Using RPs, legally characterized as a sale and repurchase of securities, effectively allows a depository institution to give private lenders a perfect collateral interest in the RP'd securities. The conflicting points of law on this matter, however, make it unclear at present whether insurance agencies such as FSLIC and FDIC, who resolve depository institution insolvencies, will respect a collateral interest for RP lenders. One would not expect to see private emergency credit assitance to banks based on RPs until the legal questions are clearly resolved.

30. The new Swiss Interbank Clearing System instituted in January 1988 has done so, at least for nonsecurity transactions.

31. For example, a national clearinghouse run by private banks was established in Canada around the turn of the century, well before the Canadian central bank was founded in 1935.

32. Goodfriend and Whelpley (1987) document the Fed's regulatory role in the evolution of the Federal Funds market.

33. Agency costs include the costs of structuring, monitoring, and bonding a set of contracts among agents with conflicting interests, plus the residual loss incurred because the cost of full enforcement of contracts exceeds the benefits. See Jensen and Meckling (1976, 306–310).

34. For a related discussion see Brickley and James (1987). Although nationwide branch banks would be diversified against local risks, as Edwards (1988) argues, hundreds of smaller banks would remain viable in a deregulated system. The large diversified banks, however, would be positioned to provide small bank depositors with private insurance, either directly or through loan syndications. It must be emphasized, however, that branching and deposit insurance only yield benefits associated with diversification and risk pooling. Neither is capable of protecting against aggregate shocks. As discussed, aggregate monetary shocks must be addressed with monetary policy. As Goodfriend and King (1988) emphasize, protection of the banking system against aggregate real shocks must be in terms of a tax and

transfer fiscal policy.

35. White (1981) provides evidence at the state level that deposit insurance was seen as a substitute for branching.

36. This suggestion is very close in spirit to that advocated in Benston and Kaufman (1988). See Stelzer (1981) for an interesting discussion of the antitrust implications of exclusion.

References

American Jurisprudence. 1963. Vol. 10. Rochester, N.Y.: Lawyers Cooperative Publishing Co.

Baxter, William F. 1983. "Bank Interchange of Transactional Paper: Legal and Economic Perspectives." *Journal of Law and Economics* 26 (October): 541–588.

Benston, George, J., Robert Eisenbeis, Paul Horvitz, Edward Kane, and George Kaufman. 1986. *Perspectives on Safe and Sound Banking.* Cambridge, Mass.: MIT Press.

Benston, George, J., and George Kaufman. 1988. "Risk and Solvency Regulation of Depository Institutions: Past Policies and Current Options." In *Restructuring Banking and Financial Services in America,* ed. William S. Haraf and Rose Kushmeider. Washington, D.C.: American Enterprise Institute.

Boyd, John H., and Edward C. Prescott. 1986. "Financial Intermediary Coalitions." *Journal of Economic Theory* 38 (April): 211–232.

Brickley, James A., and Christopher M. James. 1987. "The Takeover Market, Corporation Board Composition, and Ownership Structure: The Case of Banking." *The Journal of Law and Economics.* Vol. 30 (April): 161–180.

Cannon, James G. 1911. *Clearing Houses: Their History, Models and Administration.* London: Smith, Elder, and Co., 1901. Reprinted in *National Monetary Commission* (Washington, D.C.), vol. 6.

Constitution of the New York Clearing House Association. 1903.

Corrigan, E. Gerald. 1987. "Financial Market Structure: A Longer View." In *Annual Report,* Federal Reserve Bank of New York.

de Roover, Raymond. 1979. *The Rise and Decline of the Medici Bank. 1397–1494.* New York: Norton.

Dudley, William C. 1983. "The Tug-of-War over 'Float.'" *Morgan Guaranty Survey* (December): 11–14.

Edwards, Franklin R. 1988. "Consolidation, Concentration, and Competition Policy in Financial Markets: The Past and the Future." In *Restructuring Banking and Financial Services in America,* ed. William S. Haraf and Rose Kushmeider. Washington, D.C.: American Enterprise Institute.

Eisenbeis, Robert A. 1987. "Eroding Market Imperfections: Implications for Financial Intermediaries, the Payments System, and Regulatory Reform." In *Restructuring the Financial System,* 19–54. Federal Reserve Bank of Kansas City.

Fama, Eugene. 1980. "Banking in a Theory of Finance." *Journal of Monetary Economics* 6 (January): 39–57.

————. 1985. "What's Different About Banks?" *Journal of Monetary Economics* 15 (January): 29–39.

Fama, Eugene, and Michael C. Jensen. 1983. "Agency Problems and Residuial Claims." *Journal of Law and Economics* 26 (June): 327–349.

Flannery, Mark J. 1988. "Payments System Risk and Public Policy." In *Restructuring Banking and Financial Services in America*, ed. William S. Haraf and Rose Kushmeider. Washington, D.C.: American Enterprise Institute.

Friedman, Milton. 1959. *A Program for Monetary Stability*. New York: Fordham University Press.

Friedman, Milton, and Anna J. Schwartz. 1963. *A Monetary History of the United States, 1867–1960*. New York: National Bureau of Economic Research.

Garbade, Kenneth, and William L. Silber. 1979. "The Payment System and Domestic Exchange Rates: Technological Versus Institutional Change." *Journal of Monetary Economics* 5 (January): 1–22.

Goodfriend, Marvin. 1988. "Central Banking under the Gold Standard." In *Money, Cycles, and Exchange Rates: Essays in Honor of Allen H. Meltzer*, 85–124, ed. Karl Brunner and Bennett McCallum. Carnegie-Rochester Series on Public Policy, vol. 29.

Goodfriend, Marvin, and Robert G. King. 1988. "Financial Deregulation, Monetary Policy, and Central Banking." In *Restructuring Banking and Financial Services in America*, ed. William S. Haraf and Rose Kushmeider. Washington, D.C.: American Enterprise Institute.

Goodfriend, Marvin, and William Whelpley. 1987. "Federal Funds: Instrument of Federal Reserve Policy." In *Monetary Policy in Practice*, Marvin Goodfriend. Federal Reserve Bank of Richmond.

Goodhart, C.A.E. 1987. "Why Do Banks Need a Central Bank?" *Oxford Economic Papers* 39 (March): 75–89.

Gorton, Gary, and Donald J. Mullineaux. 1987. "The Joint Production of Confidence: Endogenous Regulation and Nineteenth-Century Commercial-Bank Clearing Houses." *Journal of Money, Credit, and Banking* 19 (November): 457–468.

Gorton, Gary B., and Joseph G. Haubrich. 1987. "The Paradox of Loan Sales." In *Merging Commercial and Investment Banking*, 123–144. Federal Reserve Bank of Chicago.

Humphrey, David B. 1984. *The U.S. Payment System: Costs, Pricing, Competition, and Risk*. Monograph 198–1/2. Salomon Brothers Center for the Study of Financial Institutions, Graduate School of Business Administration, New York University, New York, N.Y.

James, Christopher. 1987. "Some Evidence on the Uniqueness of Bank Loans." *Journal of Financial Economics* 19 (December): 217–235.

Jensen, Michael C., and William H. Meckling. 1976. "Theory of the Firm: Managerial Behavior, Agency Costs, and Ownership Structure." *Journal of Financial Economics* 3 (October): 305–360.

Jevons, William S. 1875. *Money and the Mechanism of Exchange*. New York: D. Appleton.

King, Robert G., and Charles I. Plosser, 1986. "Money as the Mechanism of Exchange." *Journal of Monetary Economics* 17 (January): 93–115.

Lindow, Wesley. 1963. "Bank Capital and Risk Assets." *The National Banking Review* (September): 29–46. Comptroller of the Currency, U.S. Treasury Department.

Litan, Robert E. 1986. "Taking the Dangers Out of Bank Deregulation." *Brookings Review* (Fall): 3–12.

Lucas, Robert E., Jr. 1980. "Equilibrium in a Pure Currency Economy." In *Models of Monetary Economics*, ed. John H. Kareken and Neil Wallace. Federal Reserve Bank of Minneapolis.

McCallum, Bennett. 1983. "The Role of Overlapping Generations Models in Monetary Economics." In *Money, Monetary Policy, and Financial Institutions*, 9–44, ed. Karl Brunner and Allan H. Meltzer. Carnegie-Rochester Series on Public Policy, vol. 18.

———. 1985. "Bank Deregulation, Accounting Systems and Exchange, and the Unit of Account: A Critical Review." In *The New Monetary Economics, Fiscal Issues, and Unemployment*, 13–45, ed. Karl Brunner and Allan H. Meltzer. Carnegie-Rochester Series on Public Policy, vol. 23.

Mengle, David L., David B. Humphrey, and Bruce J. Summers, 1987. "Intraday Credit: Risk, Value, and Pricing." *Economic Review* 73 (January–February): 3–14. Federal Reserve Bank of Richmond.

Merton, Robert C. 1977. "An Analytic Derivation of the Cost of Deposit Insurance and Loan Guarantees." *Journal of Banking and Finance* 1 (1): 3–11.

Mullineaux, Donald J. 1987. "Competitive Monies and the Suffolk Bank System: A Contractual Perspective." *Southern Economic Journal* 52 (April): 884–898.

Richards, R. D. 1929. *The Early History of Banking in England*. London: P. S. King and Sons.

Smith, Clifford W., Jr., and Jerold B. Warner. 1979. "On Financial Contracting: An Analysis of Bond Convenants." *Journal of Financial Economics* 7 (June): 117–161.

Spahr, Walter E. 1926. *The Clearing and Collection of Checks*. New York: Bawlers Publishing Co.

Stelzer, Irwin M. 1981. *Selected Antitrust Cases*. Homewood, Ill.: Richard D. Irwin.

Timberlake, Richard H. 1984. "The Central Banking Role of Clearinghouse Associations." *Journal of Money, Credit, and Banking* 16 (February): 1–15.

Townsend, Robert M. 1980. "Models of Money with Spatially Separated Agents." In *Models of Monetary Economics*, ed. John H. Kareken and Neil Wallace. Federal Reserve Bank of Minneapolis.

———. 1986. "Financial Structures as Communication Systems." In *Technological Innovation, Regulation, and the Monetary Economy*, ed. Colin Lawrence and Robert Shay. Cambridge, Mass.: Ballinger.

U.S. Congress. 1983. *The Role of the Federal Reserve in Check Clearing and the Nation's Payments System*. House of Representatives. Committee on Government Operations and Committee on Banking. Finance, and Urban Affairs. 98th Congress, 1st Session.

————. 1987a. "Risk in the Payments System," by Thomas F. Huertas. In *Structure and Regulation of Financial Firms and Holding Companies*, pt. 3, 361–389. House of Representatives. Committee on Government Operations. 99th Congress, 2d Session.

————. 1987b. "Payment System Risk," by Oliver Ireland. In *Structure and Regulation of Financial Firms and Holding Companies*, pt. 1, 500–508. House of Representatives. Committee on Government Operations. 99th Congress, 2d Session.

Usher, A. P. 1967. *The Early History of Deposit Banking in Mediterranean Europe.* New York: Russel and Russel.

Watts, Ross L., and Jerald L. Zimmerman. 1983. "Agency Problems, Auditing, and the Theory of the Firm: Some Evidence." *Journal of Law and Economics* 26 (October): 613–633.

Westerfield, Ray B. 1921. *Banking Principles and Practice*, vol. 3. New York: Ronald Press Co.

White, Eugene Nelson. 1981. "State-Sponsored Insurance of Bank Deposits in the United States, 1907–1929." *Journal of Economic History* 41 (September): 537–557.

Whitney, D. R. 1878. *The Suffolk Bank.* Cambridge, Mass.: Riverside Press.

Williams, Jeffrey C. 1984. "Fractional Reserve Banking in Grain." *Journal of Money, Credit, and Banking* 16 (November, pt. 1): 488–496.

Young, John E. 1986. "The Rise and Fall of Federal Reserve Float." *Economic Review* (February): 28–38. Federal Reserve Bank of Kansas City.

COMMENTARY
by Clifford W. Smith, Jr.

The approach by Goodfriend in his chapter is useful and productive. Instead of simply taking a historical perspective and describing the evolution of the institutions comprising the payment system, he employs contract theory to provide a unified discussion of the underlying economic forces driving that evolution. In that sense, the primary contribution of the chapter is not in the exposition of the facts but in their organization and analysis. In fact, I would argue that while many are likely to be familiar with the historical record with which Goodfriend deals, few are likely to have tied it together into such a coherent package.

The analytical techniques Goodfriend employs to analyze the payment system are not new. Contract theory has been employed to examine a number of contracts, markets, and institutions; for example, corporate bond contracts (Smith and Warner 1979), private lending agreements (Smith 1980), insurance contracts (Mayers and Smith 1981), executive

I would like to thank Charles Plosser for helpful comments and suggestions. This research was partially supported by the John M. Olin Foundation, the Lynde and Harry Bradley Foundation, and the Managerial Economics Research Center at the Simon School.

compensation contracts (Smith and Watts 1982), lease contracts (Smith and Wakeman 1985), franchise agreements (Brickley and Dark 1987), ownership structure in the thrift industry (Masulis 1987), and ownership structure in the insurance industry (Mayers and Smith 1986).

In this analysis, the first step is to identify the structure of relevant contracting costs. One can identify several costs associated with the contracting process; for example, there are negotiation, information, administration, and litigation costs. These costs are special cases of what Jensen and Meckling (1976) call agency costs.

Jensen and Meckling define an agency relationship as "a contract under which one or more persons (the principal(s), engage another person (the agent) to perform some service on their behalf which involves delegating some decision making authority to the agent." They define agency costs as the sum of three components: (1) monitoring expenditures by the principal, (2) bonding expenditures by the agent, and (3) the residual loss. Monitoring costs and bonding costs are simply the out-of-pocket expenditures by the principal and agent, respectively, to control or guarantee contract performance. The residual loss is the opportunity cost that arises because it is expensive to completely control the agent's actions.

The Jensen and Meckling agency problem is a special case of the more general contracting problem. As they note, costs arise whenever cooperative effort is required. Frequently, there is no clear-cut principal agent relationship. Consequently, there is no useful distinction between monitoring and bonding costs; and thus, total contracting costs are simply the sum of the out-of-pocket contracting costs and the opportunity cost of the contract.

Let me be forthright about my general comments—I have great sympathy with the application of contract theory to provide a positive analysis of these issues. Thus, my comments will focus on two basic areas: (1) There are several cases where I would offer alternative mechanisms to explain the observed institutions. (2) There are times when I believe that the chapter focuses too narrowly on the banking industry and not enough on what I would call the financial services industry.

To understand the markets in which banks tend to specialize and dominate, one must know the costs facing not only the banks but also the major competing institutions. For example, banks' costs would be lower if they held only marketable securities rather than also holding nonmarketable loans as assets. But the market for publicly traded securities is very competitive. Since banks have no comparative advantage in the public securities market, their holdings of these securities basically are dictated by regulatory and liquidity considerations. Because of specialization and regulation, banks do have a comparative advantage in nonmarketable securities; hence they devote significant amounts of resources to the origination and servicing of nonmarketable loans.

Within the private lending market, however, banks are not the only participants. Commercial banks have tended to restrict themselves to short-term demand loans or long-term floating rate loans. Private long-term fixed-rate loans generally have been supplied by life insurance companies, pension funds, or savings and loans rather than by banks. I believe that this specialization is primarily driven by interest rate risk exposure management considerations. Commercial banks have tended to offer short-term liabilities: demand deposits, time deposits, and short-term certificates of deposit. These claims reflect the bank's comparative advantage in supplying transactions services and liquidity. (Again, capital markets seem more efficient in supplying long-term fixed-rate savings instruments; because banks have no comparative advantage in this market, they are disintermediated.) Given this liability structure, making long-term fixed rate loans would expose the bank to the risk of interest rate increases. Life insurance companies and pension funds, however, have outstanding liabilities with longer effective maturities. Therefore, they have a comparative advantage in managing the interest rate risk exposure in making long-term fixed-rate loans (Mayers and Smith 1981).

Note that recent financial innovations reduce the requirements for this kind of specialization in lending activities. The development of the swaps and futures markets reduces the costs of managing a bank's interest rate exposure (Smith, Smithson, and Wakeman 1986). Thus, the bank now can make long-term fixed-rate loans and hedge the interest rate risk from its short funding by acquiring an interest rate swap.

Finally, by specializing in lending through private, less easily resold contracts, a bank more effectively bonds itself to keep a substantial fraction of its assets over their life. Since a potential concern of the bank's fixed liability holders is the riskiness of the underlying assets, this bonding helps control the potential conflict between the bank's depositors and stockholders.

I found interesting Goodfriend's discussion of borrowing at the Fed's discount window and the bank's ability to collateralize its borrowing.[1] In financial economics, there has been an extensive examination of the incentives to issue secured rather than unsecured debt (Smith and Warner 1979; Stulz and Johnson 1986). These incentives basically involve the ability of the corporation to segregate the cash flows from the assets that collateralize the loan from the cash flows of the corporation's other assets. An issue that Goodfriend does not explore is the potential monopsony power the extant regulation provides the Fed through the discount window. My impression is that looking only at the explicit interest charged borrowers by the bank understates the total cost. The Fed appears to impose substantial noninterest costs on banks which borrow at the discount window (Burger 1971). Thus, the benefits of collateralization are reduced from being forced to deal with a monopsonist.

Nevertheless, I believe that the problems that may arise from a bank's inability to collateralize non-Fed borrowing have been reduced by recent financial innovations. Setting up wholly-owned subsidiaries, loan sales, and providing letters of credit are alternative ways to segregate cash flows associated with specific bank assets (Mian and Smith 1988, James 1988). Thus, they are substitute mechanisms to achieve some of the gains from collateralization.

Goodfriend poses a provocative question with respect to bank accounts: Why are deposits valued at par in terms of currency? In other words, why weren't banks set up like money market mutual fund accounts, where the value of the account is continuously adjusted to reflect the value of the assets. I think that Goodfriend makes a constructive point here. You would have to restrict bank assets to those that are valued continually by the market. This vitually requires access to a deep active liquid secondary market for short-term instruments—a market that really has existed in the United States only for the last 30 years. However, I think there are additional considerations: (1) One would require a fairly sophisticated accounting system applied continuously to reduce incentives to time withdrawals and deposits to affect intrafund transfers. The changes in computer technology have made such a system economically viable only within the last 20 years. (2) By having one class of liability claimholder, the bank's claimholders are provided with limited incentives to monitor the managers. Recognizing this, managers of money market mutual funds bond themselves with respect to asset choice, voluntarily restricting themselves only to high-quality short-term instruments.

The converse of this second point is that if bank managers are going to be authorized significant discretion over the firm's assets, then the firm's liability claims must be structured to provide appropriate monitoring incentives. By promising payoffs to depositors that are unrelated to bank performance, the bank's equityholders (as the residual claimholders) have concentrated incentives to monitor managerial peformance.[2]

Of course, by providing deposit insurance, the incentive of insured depositors to monitor the performance of bank managers is essentially eliminated. However, I would not place too much emphasis on this point: (1) Small depositors probably do not have a comparative advantage in monitoring. (2) The market for large uninsured wholesale certificates of deposit seems to function fairly well in this regard (note the role of this market in bringing the liquidity problems of the Continental Bank to a head). (3) The incentives of the Federal Deposit Insurance Corporation (FDIC) to monitor an insured bank's financial performance is likely to be stronger than that of a set of small uninsured depositors. (4) By pooling those derived demands for monitoring, the FDIC can invest in more sophisticated monitoring procedures, personel, and capital.[3]

I believe that expanding the scope of the discussion to include the entire financial services industry is especially important if we are to evaluate one of the central policy questions in this area: Are banks different? This policy debate focuses on rejecting one of two competing hypotheses: (1) Banks are inherently different from other institutions and we therefore require specialized regulation like Glass/Steagall and federal deposit insurance to protect the system: or (2) Banks are not inherently different from other institutions and the observed differences are primarily a result of regulation. I believe that Goodfriend's analysis provides strong support for the second hypothesis.

To go further and analyze the effect of specific regulations on the system is, I believe, a very difficult problem. To understand fully how the political process affects the system, a rich understanding of the incentives and constraints facing the politicians is required. Some progress has been made by political economists in understanding voting equilibria and hence the incentives of elected officials (see Downs 1957). Although there is much that is not yet understood, it seems clear that this problem is more difficult than the analysis of corporate managers, where there are strong incentives for firm value maximization. Unfortunately, even less has been accomplished in understanding the incentives and constraints facing policymakers in regulatory agencies like the Treasury, the Federal Reserve, or the FDIC. Given their indirect accountability to the voting public, this problem appears even more difficult. Finally, to isolate empirically the effect of a regulation, ideally, one would be able to observe two markets, identical except for the regulation. This can sometimes be approximated by a time-series analysis of a single market or a comparison of different financial markets within a country. However potentially valuable lessons can also be learned by comparing different countries with different regulatory systems. For example, Goodfriend argues that federal deposit insurance has been a valuable addition to the system because it is a substitute for the diversification effects restricted by limitations on branching.[4] I would argue that the existence of the Canadian Deposit Insurance Corporation provides a strong case that restrictions on branching are not necessary to explain deposit insurance.

In summary, I believe that Goodfriend's chapter provides a valuable initial step in the development of a unified analysis of the evolution of the institutions comprising the payment system. I expect that subsequent work building on this analysis will enrich our understanding of these institutions and the role of regulation in their evolution.

Notes

1. Goodfriend wonders why banks are restricted from offering collateralized claims to private creditors but government creditors are not similarly restricted. I would note that the government selectively exempts itself from restriction that it regularly imposes on the private sector. For example: (1) Congress has exempted its staff from compliance with overtime wage laws, OSHA, and EEOC regulations; and (2) there are no seatbelts in army jeeps. This admittedly does not answer the question he raises; however, it does argue that the question should be viewed as a special case of a broader issue.

2. As somewhat of an aside, I would argue that this discussion of optimal monitoring incentives suggests a change from recently established policy. In the Continental Bank reorganization, I would have insisted that the old equityholders' claims be worthless; giving that group anything undermines the incentives of other bank's stockholders to monitor their managers.

3. I believe that direct monitoring by the FDIC, Federal Reserve, Controller of the Currency, and State Banking Authorities is an important, flexible compliment to cruder rules like capital requirements (see Smith, Smithson, and Wakeman 1988).

4. On logical grounds, I think that this is an incomplete argument. Diversification can only is eliminate independent risks. While some credit risks are geographically localized, much risk associated with the business cycle and hence is marketwide. Moreover, bank default risk associated with interest rate exposure cannot be lowered by geographic diversification, given the degree of capital market integration in the United States.

References

Brickley, James, and Frederick Dark. 1987. "The Choice of Organizational Form: The Case of Franchising." *Journal of Financial Economics* 18: 401–420.

Burger, Albert E. 1971. *The Money Supply Process*. Belmont, Calif.: Wadsworth.

Downs, Anthony. 1957. *An Economic Theory of Democracy*. New York: Harper and Row.

Goodfriend, Marvin. 1989. "Money, Credit, Banking, and Payments System Policy." In *The U.S. Payment System: Efficiency, Risk, and the Role of Federal Reserve*, ed. David B. Humphrey. Boston: Kluwer Academic Publishers.

James, Christopher. 1988. "The Use of Loan Sales and Standby Letters of Credit by Commercial Banks." *Journal of Monetary Economics*, 22, 395–422.

Jensen, Michael C. 1983. "Organization Theory and Methology." *Accounting Review* 58 (2): 319–339.

Jensen, Michael C., and William H. Meckling. 1976. "Theory of the Firm: Managerial Behavior, Agency Costs, and Ownership Structure." *Journal of Fin-*

ancial Economics 3 (4): 305–360.

Masulis, Ronald. 1987. "Changes in Ownership Structure: Conversions of Mutual Savings and Loans to Stock Charter." *Journal of Financial Economics* 18: 29–59.

Mayers, David, and Clifford W. Smith, Jr. 1981. "Contractual Provisions, Organizational Structure, and Conflict Control in Insurance Markets." *Journal of Business* 54 (3): 407–434.

———. 1986. "Ownership Structure and Control: The Mutualization of Stock Life Insurance Companies." *Journal of Financial Economics* 16: 73–98.

Mian, Shehzad, and Clifford W. Smith, Jr. 1988. "Accounts Receivable Management Policy: Theory and Evidence." Working Paper, University of Rochester.

Smith, Clifford W., Jr. 1980. "On the Theory of Financial Contracting: The Personal Loan Market." *Journal of Monetary Economics* 6: 333–357.

Smith, Clifford W., Jr., Charles Smithson, and Lee Wakeman. 1986. "The Market for Interest Rate Swaps." *Financial Management* 17: 34–44.

Smith, Clifford W., Jr., and Lee Wakeman. 1985. "Determinants of Firms' Hedging Policies." *Journal of Finance* 40 (3): 895–908.

Smith, Clifford W., Jr., and Jerold Warner. 1979. "On Financial Contracting: An Analysis of Bond Convenants." *Journal of Financial Economics* 7 (2): 117–161.

Smith, Clifford W., Jr., and Ross Watts. 1982. "Incentive and Tax Effects of U.S. Executive Compensation Plans." *Australian Journal of Management* 7:139–157.

Stulz, Rene M., and Herb Johnson. 1985. "An Analysis of Secured Debt." *Journal of Financial Economics* 14 (4): 501–522.

CONFERENCE SUMMARY: AN OVERVIEW OF PAYMENT SYSTEM ISSUES: WHERE DO WE GO FROM HERE?

Manuel H. Johnson

It is a pleasure for me to be participating in this conference, which affords us the opportunity to analyze payment system issues from an economic and public policy perspective. My interest in the payment system began while I was at the Treasury Department. It was during that time that the Treasury made a long-term commitment to convert as many government checks as possible to electronic payments. I was a strong advocate of that commitment despite a substantial reduction in the float benefit enjoyed by the Treasury as payments were converted from checks to electronics. While the benefit of float enjoyed by the government has been significantly reduced, this has been offset by reduced government operating costs and improved services to recipients of such payments.

My interest in payment issues intensified two years ago when I was appointed chairman of the Federal Reserve's newly organized Payments System Policy Committee. That Committee, which consists of two other members of the Board of Governors and two Reserve Bank presidents, is responsible for recommending policy positions to the Board on major payment system matters. Jimmie Monhollon of the Richmond Reserve

285

Bank served with us in an *ex officio* capacity during his term as the Federal Reserve's electronic payments product director, and Bob Eisenmenger now plays that role. Since its inception, the Committee has focused most of its attention on the issue of payment system risk. That issue will continue to dominate the Committee's agenda as we work to develop a long-term strategy for controlling risk on large-dollar payment systems.

Finding solutions to credit and liquidity risks associated with large-dollar systems is critical because of the continuing growth of these payments and the large exposures faced by participants in these systems. This issue has taken a major share of this symposium's time, which is understandable, given both the Federal Reserve's and the industry's attention to this matter, as well as the fact that the value of payments flowing over Fedwire and CHIPS accounts for 82 percent of the value of all U.S. payments. I will discuss the risk issue in some detail, but first I would like to consider the more central issue of making the payment system—broadly defined—more efficient. This issue is of no small importance, for as Bob Eisenmenger as indicated, the resources spent by this country on processing payments may be as high as $60 billion annually. To put that cost in perspective, it represents about 1 percent of GNP.

The Humphrey-Berger chapter highlights one of the fundamental problems with the nation's payment mechanism. The most popular payment instrument other than cash is the paper check, which continues to grow in popularity. Although significant progress has been achieved in making the check collection system more efficient, the check is still one of the more expensive instruments to use. Humphrey and Berger estimate that the average cost of a check is $0.79, which is more than twice the cost of an automated clearinghouse (ACH) item. Despite this sizable cost disadvantage, the number of check transactions is 50 times greater than ACII volume.

One cause of the overutilization of the check is the market's failure to allocate the cost of float to the check writer. This failure may be one of the primary reasons corporate trade payments are still predominately made by check. There is, however, another major reason that the market has failed to adopt a lower-cost payment method, especially in the area of consumer payments. Banks typically do not price their services to encourage the use of the most efficient payment method. The common practice of charging a flat monthly fee or waiving fees if balances are above a certain amount does not encourage ACH utilization. Similarly, the lack of price differentiation between ACH and check also fails to encourage ACH direct deposit. Until corporations negotiate settlement terms for trade payments and banks develop more realistic pricing strategies, the annual growth in check volume may continue to outpace the growth in ACH transactions.

Given the heavy public demand for checks, and as a major payment system participant with a public interest perspective, the Federal Reserve is faced with an increasing dilemma: What is the proper balance between efforts to improve the check system and efforts to improve electronic payments services?

Congressional action in the past has led the Federal Reserve to take steps to improve the check collection system. For example, efforts to reduce Federal Reserve float, as a result of the passage of the Monetary Control Act, have been quite successful. Over 20 percent of the checks processed by the Reserve Bank clear at least one day faster today than prior to 1981. Accelerating the collection of checks increases the attractiveness of the instrument to the recipient. On the other hand, it encourages the growth of electronic payments by reducing the float benefits enjoyed by the check writer. But such inducements to move from checks to electronics are, unfortunately, modest because the float caused by the Federal Reserve is small relative to the float generated by delays prior to deposit and in bank clearings.

Last year, as part of the Expedited Funds Availability Act, Congress gave the Federal Reserve broad authority to improve the check system, with the expectation that the Federal Reserve would use that authority to speed the check collection and return process. Earlier this month, the Board approved a new regulation and a series of new services to be offered by the Reserve Banks designed to improve the processing of checks that are returned unpaid. These improvements will, over time, reduce the cost of the check collection system and the risks merchants face in accepting checks.

Thus, for the foreseeable future, and without the reforms mentioned by Humphrey and Berger, the check will continue to be overutilized. The foreseeable challenge of the Federal Reserve and the banking industry is, therefore, to develop new processing techniques to move the check system toward electronics. Congress has directed the Federal Reserve to consider the use of interbank truncation of checks and other electronic means to improve the check collection system. Studies have concluded that truncating checks early in the processing stream will reduce costs by eliminating the movement of paper. The banking industry initiated a program to truncate checks at the bank of first deposit about 10 years ago, but unfortunately the types of checks eligible for truncation under that program are quite limited. The Federal Reserve Banks will be working with the banking industry to increase the volume of checks eligible for interbank truncation and to provide services to assist banks in clearing these checks electronically. Federal Reserve involvement hopefully will spur the development of this promising technique.

In comparison with the check, the ACH is a very efficient payment mechanism for a variety of consumer and corporate payments. The ACH is the most successful electronic payment network in terms of volume. I exclude automatic teller machines from this conclusion because they are primarily a new method for delivering an old payment instrument—cash. Yet we need to ask (1) whether the ACH is as efficient as it could be; and (2) whether more can be done by the Federal Reserve and others to encourage use of the ACH.

On the first point, I would agree that as long as the ACH mechanism is *not* all-electronic, the ACH will not operate at its optimal efficiency. At present, over 80 percent of ACH payments are submitted for processing on magnetic tape or delivered to the receiving bank on paper listings. This requires extensive manual handling at the banks, their processors, and at the Reserve Banks. Consequently, the ACH is more prone to human error and delays than if all payments were exchanged via telecommunications.

The Federal Reserve has been promoting a more completely electronic ACH by offering reliable, secure, and cost-effective electronic connections. In addition, we have set high fees for the manual aspects of ACH processing to cover the higher cost of these services and to create incentives for depository institutions to use direct electronic access to the Reserve Banks. These measures, however, have not been sufficient to cause a widespread conversion to electrionic ACH access.

Perhaps the time has come to establish a sunset date for institutions to convert to ACH electronic access. This approach was recently taken by the New York Automated Clearing House in its mandate to New York member institutions to convert from manual tape exchanges to data transmissions by 1990. This policy has generally been viewed as positive by the financial community and has met with little resistance from the New York member institutions.

Other than converting to an all-electronic ACH, is there more that the Federal Reserve and the financial community can do to encourage the use of the ACH? For example, should the Federal Reserve subsidize the ACH for the good of the payments mechanism? Prior to 1986, we did subsidize the ACH. This policy, however, had little effect on consumer and corporate demand for electronic payments because the Federal Reserve's cost of several cents per transaction is a small fraction of the total handling cost of an ACH transaction.

Bernell Stone has identified a number of improvements that can be made to make the ACH more attractive to banks and their corporate customers. However, in my view, those changes alone are unlikely to accelerate the growth of ACH payments. Until progress is made on shifting the cost of float to check writers or until banks develop new pricing strategies that reflect check costs, use of the ACH will in all likelihood continue to grow at its current pace.

Another significant challenge facing the Federal Reserve and the banking industry is reducing the risk associated with large-dollar payment networks. While there is risk of financial loss from using any payment instrument, the risk of a catastrophic loss that could destabilize the entire payment process is far greater on large-dollar networks. Exposures on Fedwire, of course, are fully absorbed by the Federal Reserve, but there remains the specter that an individual bank unable to settle its position on a private network could induce other banks to fail as well. Indeed, the Federal Reserve's concern about systemic risk in the late 1970s and early 1980s was the original catalyst for the development of the Federal Reserve's payment system risk reduction program. This background is discussed in the chapter by David Mengle.

That daylight overdraft program is now under intense review. The Payments System Policy Committee has recently reviewed a System staff report that analyzed a series of policy options as a first step in developing the next phase of the risk reduction program. At a later date we will hear the views of the Large-Dollar Payments System Advisory Group on these options, and the Policy Committee will then develop a specific proposal to be reviewed by the full Board and eventually published for comment.

It is fair to say that the Policy Committee's views are still evolving. Nonetheless, I would like to share with you the nature of the options facing the Committee and the Board. As is true of most complex issues, significant trade-offs will be required to achieve risk reduction without unduly hampering the payment system. On the one hand, we want to reduce both the Federal Reserve's own direct risk of loss from an institution that fails while in overdraft with us; such risk, after all, is borne by the taxpayer. There is considerable support for an approach that shifts more of the risk exposure to private-market participants, on the presumption that if risk responsibility can be clearly assigned, markets will not only allocate daylight credit more effectively but the level of aggregate exposure will also decline.

On the other hand, as payments and intraday exposures shift to private networks and intraday markets, the systemic risk rises, which remains one of our major concerns. Indeed, a prerequisite of any policy that shifts daylight exposure to the private market is the planned adoption by CHIPS (Clearing House Interbank Payments System) of policies to further internalize participant banks' risks, that is, to make banks responsible for the risk they create by some form of settlement finality and loss sharing. But, even after such steps are taken, there still remains the gnawing concern that a significant increase in the share of intraday credit in the private sector may expose the banking system to unacceptably high risk. This balancing of systemic concerns against the efficiency and likely reduction in exposure associated with assignment of risk responsibility to its creator is at the heart of the decision-making process on evolving payment system policy.

Development of a revised program is further complicated by several important constraints, which require the policymaker to face and choose among still additional trade-offs. Indeed, it is impossible to reduce risks without breeching some of these constraints, and thus our decisions will require some complicated weighing of costs and benefits. For example, we certainly do not want the next phase of the risk reduction program to slow payment flows, nor do we want to increase unduly the cost of transmitting payments. We also need to be sensitive to the competitive impact among providers of payment services. Moreover, we must be cautious that our daylight overdraft policy does not interfere with the conduct of monetary policy or increase the cost of the Treasury's operations unnecessarily. Finally, we must be sensitive to the possibility of driving risk offshore, with the same exposures to the U.S. financial system hidden from our view or beyond our control, and we must guard against a policy that inadvertently places U.S. banks at a competitive disadvantage vis-à-vis foreign bank suppliers of dollar payment services.

Thus, in making our policy decision we will be forced to balance competing goals. The techniques available to us for developing policy—the menus from which we will choose individual or a combination of policy steps are well known. We can, for example,

- Lower caps
- Prohibit daylight overdrafts
- Adopt explicit prices on our own intraday credit
- Collateralize intraday credit
- Impose higher clearing balances

The Committee has not decided what policy option or combination of options is the best course of action. Any policy or combination of policies that significantly increases the cost of using Federal Reserve intraday credit will have similar effects on payment users and suppliers, namely, the development of intraday private credit markets and higher user prices for large-dollar payment services. There is, I think, a growing consensus that such a development will more prudently and efficiently allocate the private benefits and private risks—and I hope reduce the public and total risks—of our nation's large-dollar payment networks. But while all policy approaches can end up with the same general impact, each of these options implies different trade-offs between direct and systemic risks, as well as different effects on the speed and cost of payments.

The choices will be difficult, but the time for choosing policies has arrived. And, I, for one, am optimistic that the private sector and the Federal Reserve have come to recognize our common problems and are considering similar ways of addressing them.

I have highlighted just a few of the many challenges facing both providers and users of payment services. Both the Federal Reserve and the banking industry share in the responsibility of meeting these challenges. Congress has charged the Federal Reserve with promoting a stable payments system. In addition, the mission of the Federal Reserve in providing payment services is to promote the integrity and efficiency of the nation's payment mechanism. The banking industry, acting as both a user and provider of payment services, has a large economic interest in reducing both risks and the resources allocated to payment processing. The Federal Reserve has worked very closely with the banking industry in developing the large-dollar risk reduction program that is now in place. If we continue to work together, I am confident that progress will be made on meeting additional challenges.

List of Conference Attendees and Their Affiliations

Peter W. Allsopp
Assistant Chief of the Banking
  Department
Bank of England

Steve Beckner
Market News Service

John H. Beebe
Senior Vice President and Director of
  Research
Federal Reserve Bank of San
  Francisco

Robert P. Black
President
Federal Reserve Bank of Richmond

Robert H. Boykin
President
Federal Reserve Bank of Dallas

J. Alfred Broaddus, Jr.
Senior Vice President and Director of
  Research
Federal Reserve Bank of Richmond

Charles J. Buchta
Executive Vice President
First Interstate Bank of California

Roland K. Bullard, II
Vice Chairman
CoreStates Financial Corporation

Ronald G. Burke
President and Chief Executive Officer
Bank Administration Institute

James T. Byrne
Senior Vice President
Morgan Guaranty Trust Company

Bradford N. Carden
Assistant Vice President
Federal Reserve Bank of Richmond

Robert T. Clair
Senior Economist
Federal Reserve Bank of Dallas

Donald R. Cohenour
Vice President and Comptroller
U.S. Central Credit Union

293

Philip E. Coldwell
Chairman
Coldwell Financial Consultants

William C. Conrad
Senior Vice President
Federal Reserve Bank of Chicago

Anthony G. Cornyn
Assistant Director
Board of Governors of the Federal
    Reserve System

Charlotte Crystal
Business Reporter
The Richmond News Leader

Donna G. Dancy
Vice President
Federal Reserve Bank of Richmond

William B. Davenport
Counsel
The First National Bank of Chicago

Wilhelm David
Bundesbankdirektor
Deutsche Bundesbank

Michael DeLoose
Vice President
Conference of State Bank Supervisors

William E. Douglas
Commissioner
Financial Management Service
Department of the Treasury

Patricia E. Dowden
Vice President
CoreStates Financial Corporation

Lawrence E. Echelmeyer, Jr.
Senior Vice President & Manager
First Interstate Bank of California

Richard C. Emigh
Senior Vice President
CoreStates Financial Corporation

Catherine England
Director of Regulatory Studies
CATO Institute

Edward C. Ettin
Deputy Director
Board of Governors of the Federal
    Reserve System

Douglas D. Evanoff
Senior Financial Economist
Federal Reserve Bank of Chicago

Roy L. Fauber
Senior Vice President
Federal Reserve Bank of Richmond

Robert M. Fitzgerald
President
Chicago Clearing House Association

Charles Freedman
Adviser to the Governor
Bank of Canada

Charles W. Furbee
Senior Vice President
Federal Reserve Bank of Chicago

Thomas E. Gainor
First Vice President
Federal Reserve Bank of Minneapolis

James F. Ganley
Senior Executive Vice President
Irving Trust Company

Matthew D. Gelfand
Economist
Board of Governors of the Federal
    Reserve System

R. Alton Gilbert
Assistant Vice President
Federal Reserve Bank of St. Louis

Thomas J. Greco
Assistant General Counsel
American Bankers Association

Roberta J. Green
Senior Vice President
Federal Reserve Bank of New York

Kenneth A. Guenther
Executive Vice President
Independent Bankers Association of
America

Motoo Haruta
Professor of Economics
Nihon University

Arnold A. Heggestad
William H. Dial Professor of Banking
University of Florida

Stephen C. Holahan
Senior Vice President
Connecticut National Bank

Thomas F. Horan
Director
SRI International

W. Lee Hoskins
President
Federal Reserve Bank of Cleveland

Walter A. Howell
Executive Vice President
The Riggs National Bank of
Washington, D.C.

George R. Juncker
Vice President
Federal Reserve Bank of New York

Robert J. Kaminski
Senior Vice President
Continental Illinois National Bank

Edward J. Kane
Everette Reese Professor of Banking
and Monetary Economics
Ohio State University

Marshall Kolin
Econometrician
U.S. Postal Service Headquarters

James R. Kudlinski
Chairman of the Board and Chief
Executive Officer
Frontier Federal Savings and Loan
Association

Richard W. Lang
Senior Vice President and Director of
Research
Federal Reserve Bank of Philadelphia

Jeffrey C. Marquardt
Economist
Board of Governors of the Federal
Reserve System

Martin Mayer
Author and Columnist
The American Banker

Elliott C. McEntee
Associate Director
Board of Governors of the Federal
Reserve System

Robert D. McTeer, Jr.
Senior Vice President
Federal Reserve Bank of Richmond

Jack M. Meckler
Senior Vice President
First Wachovia Corporate Services

Thomas C. Melzer
President
Federal Reserve Bank of St. Louis

Gerald F. Milano
Executive Director
California Bankers Clearing House
Association

W. B. Millner, III
Executive Vice President and Chief
Financial Officer
Signet Bank

Cathy E. Minehan
Senior Vice President
Federal Reserve Bank of New York

Mary Mitchell
Arlington, Virginia

George W. Mitchell
Retired Vice Chairman
Board of Governors of the Federal
    Reserve System

Jimmie R. Monhollon
First Vice President
Federal Reserve Bank of Richmond

Donald R. Monks
Executive Vice President
Irving Trust Company

Charles A. Moran
President
Government Securities Clearing
    Corporation

William R. Moroney
President and Chief Executive Officer
National Automated Clearing House
    Association

Thomas R. Morris
Staff Writer
Richmond Times Dispatch

Ayo Mseka
Editor
Corporate EFT Report

Neil B. Murphy
Professor of Finance and Marketing
Virginia Commonwealth University

J. William Murray
Senior Vice President
First National Bank of Maryland

Arthur V. Myers, Jr.
Senior Vice President
Federal Reserve Bank of Richmond

Michael W. Newton
Assistant Vice President
Federal Reserve Bank of Richmond

David O. Nordby
Executive Vice President
Continental Illinois Corporation

Richard R. Oliver
Vice President
Federal Reserve Bank of Atlanta

Yoshiharu Oritani
Associate Adviser
Bank of Japan

Kenneth L. Parkinson
Executive Editor
The Journal of Cash Management

Franco Passacantando
Associate Director of Research Studies
Bank of Italy

Carl E. Powell
First Vice President
Federal Reserve Bank of San
    Francisco

Randall J. Pozdena
Assistant Vice President
Federal Reserve Bank of San
    Francisco

Richard K. Rasdall, Jr.
Senior Vice President
Federal Reserve Bank of Kansas City

James D. Reese
Senior Vice President
Federal Reserve Bank of Richmond

Robert E. Reitz
Vice President
Norwest Bank Minnesota, N.A.

Thomas M. Richards
Manager
General Accounting Office

John S. Roberts
General Manager
Canadian Payments Association

John R. Rodelli
Vice President
Continental Illinois National Bank

Seymour R. Rosen
Senior Vice President
Citibank

Jack Rosenstock
Senior Vice President
Chase Manhattan Bank

Frederick J. Schroeder
Economist
Board of Governors of the Federal
    Reserve System

Michael Serlin
Assistant Commissioner
Financial Management Service
Department of the Treasury

O. Darwin Smith
Executive Vice President and Group
    Executive
NCNB Corporation

Richard L. Smoot
Executive Vice President
Provident National Bank

George M. Stetter
Director of Cash Management
Merrill Lynch and Company

Edward J. Stevens
Assistant Vice President
Federal Reserve Bank of Cleveland

William H. Stone, Jr.
First Vice President
Federal Reserve Bank of Philadelphia

Bruce J. Summers
Senior Vice President
Federal Reserve Bank of Richmond

Stephen C. Swaim
Group Director
Federal Reserve Audit Site
General Accounting Office

Albert D. Tinkelenberg
Senior Vice President
Federal Reserve Bank of Richmond

Walker F. Todd
Assistant General Counsel and
    Research Officer
Federal Reserve Bank of Cleveland

O. J. Tomson
Chairman and Chief Executive Officer
Citizens National Bank

Walter A. Varvel
Vice President
Federal Reserve Bank of Richmond

William H. Wallace
First Vice President
Federal Reserve Bank of Dallas

F. Jean Wells
Specialist in Money and Banking
Library of Congress

Ottomar Werthmöller
Member of the Board
Deutsche Bundesbank

David D. Whitehead
Research Officer and Senior Finance
    Economist
Federal Reserve Bank of Atlanta

Florence M. Young
Adviser
Board of Governors of the Federal
    Reserve System

Flavian E. Zeugin
First Vice President
Swiss Bank Corporation

Linda Fenner Zimmer
Payment Services Correspondent

Index